# Afro-Cuban Costumbrismo

UNIVERSITY PRESS OF FLORIDA

Florida A&M University, Tallahassee
Florida Atlantic University, Boca Raton
Florida Gulf Coast University, Ft. Myers
Florida International University, Miami
Florida State University, Tallahassee
New College of Florida, Sarasota
University of Central Florida, Orlando
University of Florida, Gainesville
University of North Florida, Jacksonville
University of South Florida, Tampa
University of West Florida, Pensacola

# Afro-Cuban Costumbrismo

## From Plantations to the Slums

· · · · · · · · ·

Rafael Ocasio

UNIVERSITY PRESS OF FLORIDA

Gainesville · Tallahassee · Tampa · Boca Raton
Pensacola · Orlando · Miami · Jacksonville · Ft. Myers · Sarasota

This book may be available in an electronic edition.

First cloth printing, 2012
First paperback printing, 2015

Library of Congress Cataloging-in-Publication Data
Ocasio, Rafael.
Afro-Cuban costumbrismo : from plantations to the slums / Rafael Ocasio.
p. cm.
Includes bibliographical references and index.
ISBN 978-0-8130-4164-3 (cloth: alk. paper)
ISBN 978-0-8130-6176-4 (pbk.)
1. Blacks in literature. 2. Blacks—Cuba—History. 3. Blacks—Cuba—Social conditions.
4. Slavery—Cuba. 5. Cuban literature. 6. Cuba—Religion—20th century. 7. Cuba—Social life
and customs. I. Title.
PQ7382.O26 2012
860.9'97291—dc23      2012009922

The University Press of Florida is the scholarly publishing agency for the State University
System of Florida, comprising Florida A&M University, Florida Atlantic University, Florida
Gulf Coast University, Florida International University, Florida State University, New College
of Florida, University of Central Florida, University of Florida, University of North Florida,
University of South Florida, and University of West Florida.

University Press of Florida
15 Northwest 15th Street
Gainesville, FL 32611-2079
http://www.upf.com

I dedicate this book to my sister, Edna Ocasio-Medina, whose
kindness to others continues to be my inspiration
to be the best man I can be.

# Contents

# Preface

## A Mulato Fino in the Twenty-First Century
## —A Personal Reflection

Aché awó, aché babá ikú, aché. Aché tó bógbo madé lo ilé Yansa. [Bless Mayor, dead father, bless me, all the dead in Yansa's house, in the cemetery. With the permission of my godfather, of my godmother.]

> Lydia Cabrera, *Anagó: Vocabulario lucumí (El yoruba que se habla en Cuba)*

Africa me dio la gran facultad para cantarle a mi oricha y a mi tambó bata. [Africa gave me the great skill to sing to my orisha and to my bata drum.]

> Celia Cruz, "Elegua quiere tambó"

Lydia Cabrera, one of the first Cuban folklorists, anthropologists, and compilers of Afro-Cuban oral traditions, early in her field research placed emphasis on transcribing the numerous Black religious rituals that had survived in Cuba. Through interviews with former slaves in the first part of the twentieth century, her groundbreaking work firmly established the important role of Afro-Cuban religious practices in the development of Cuban identity. As Cabrera extensively documented, Afro-Cuban religious traditions encompass a diversity of popular traits, such as music, food, and the peculiar use of the Spanish language, including the incorporation of African words in the so-called Cuban Spanish. Literature, as a creative expression, also has drawn inspiration from Afro-Cuban traditions in a process that reflects the changing attitudes of the times in terms of acceptance of these as representative of Cuban culture.

The highly ritual nature of Afro-Cuban belief systems has reverberated in my Caribbean background, and I have found them to be fascinating, perhaps because of their similarities to such practices in my native Puerto Rico. This natural attraction informed not only my choices of readings, but also my critical angles in my explanations of *lo caribeño*. This book sets out to attempt a risky enterprise to offer a definition of Black Cuban culture, approaching the subject from the cautious, neutral stance expressed by the Spanish grammatical construction of lo caribeño.

Not coincidentally, Cabrera's own quest to explore *lo cubano* took place during her period of exile in Miami. I too started to research these fascinating Black ceremonies during my residence in the United States. Perhaps Cabrera, like me, understood their resonance as an immigrant, a stranger in a foreign land and learner of new traditions. In my many years of living in the United States, I have come to realize that religious life among immigrants takes on an important dual role. On the one hand, it serves as a reminder, a sort of calendar of social events, as Roberto González Echevarría has stressed, of communal "fiestas," celebrations that are absent in the United States, a mainly Protestant country of few seasonal rituals. The memories of long-past celebrations in one's distant motherland provide a soothing cultural connection, a feeling of being present in, even when physically absent from, the geographical markers that make up one's country.

The other role of these flexible religious practices is adaptability to adversity. This condition may be a prime example of the strong Caribbean tendency to adapt to foreign situations and to re-create in a process that is often described as syncretism. As reflected in the popular Puerto Rican saying "A falta de pan, galleta" [In the absence of bread, crackers], Afro-Caribbean religious practices have adapted, and often reshaped themselves, to fit the new physical circumstances in the United States. These practices are readily adaptable to specific restrictions on their urban settings, whether you are in the Puerto Rican barrio in New York City; in Miami's Cuban enclave, the Saguesera; or in the Buford Highway area of Atlanta, Georgia, the unofficial, highly populated Latino barrio, an urban corridor blocks east of the fancy neighborhood of Lenox Road.

The modernized syncretic elements of Afro-Caribbean religious devotions are clearly displayed in the urban setting of an Atlanta barrio. If you walk into any of the local *botánicas*, you are greeted at the door by the mischievous Elegua, you go through rows of Santa Bárbara and Changó figurines, and you may come across the menacing figure of La Santa Muerte. A Mexican goddess-protector for those in professions involving a high risk of physical danger (such as law enforcement) and, recently, a patron to those who dare to cross into the United States through the wilderness of the Mexican border, La Santa Muerte has numerous followers among working-class Latinos, particularly Mexicans.

Another, less obvious characteristic of the Atlanta *botánica* is a stronger than usual, pungent, herbal smell, which to the untrained visitor would seem

appropriate in a botanical shop. Upon closer examination, one would soon notice the presence of plants and vegetable roots different from those in traditional
Caribbean practices. This, according to one *santera*, the Cuban woman owner of
my favorite *botánica* on Buford Highway and "high priestess" of various Afro-
Caribbean religious belief systems, is due to the needs of her multiethnic and
multiracial clientele. She often brags that most of her clients are not from the
Spanish Caribbean basin but are mainly Central Americans, particularly Mexicans, and African-Americans. Her comment seems to reflect concern about the
future of her own store, as other Mexican herbalist shops have already opened
nearby and thus have become her competition, but she is also mindful of her
ability to serve a multicultural clientele. To that effect, she also performs more
"modern" religious practices, such as Wicca, a fact that speaks to her flexibility to incorporate nontraditional rituals into an already multiethnic "urban"
Santería as practiced outside the Saguesera's "Cuban" enclave.

As in past years, many still come to this Caribbean *santera* with problems of
the heart and of the soul; however, her undocumented clients often have more
pressing physical ailments. Without health insurance, their only available treatment is what the *santera* can provide them with herbs that are familiar to them.
That function and her incorporation of practices of Mexican origin, such as
those of La Santa Muerte or Wicca observances, are examples that most closely
illustrate the often abstract concept of religious syncretism, of which Santería is
a prime example. To me this flexibility is proof of lo caribeño's strong ability to
survive by means of cultural hybridity.

This book is my exploration of the development of hybrid elements of Black
cultures in Cuban and, by extension, in Caribbean national identities. This is a
process that I have experienced firsthand. In an original project, I had intended
to explore diverse sociopolitical and sexual elements involved in the formation
of the mulatto, a byproduct of Spanish slave-trade colonist practices. Mulattoes
in literature have received much critical attention, particularly female mulattas,
as protagonists of nineteenth-century Cuban abolitionist novels, written beginning in the 1830s. Mulattoes appeared as part of a highly developed literary
movement known as Costumbrismo, in short essays written in the earliest part
of that century. Perhaps because the Costumbrista writer displayed a somewhat
negative attitude or often took an openly racist stand against the Black characters, these essays have not received full attention from literary critics.

Cuban Costumbristas documented national customs and provided socioeconomic background useful for their critical comments on the state of the
nation. Slavery, at the heart of Cuba's sugarcane financial boom, provided plenty
of Black-related themes, often taken as examples of the ways that representative

traditions have impacted the development of a Cuban identity. Because of stringent political censorship, however, themes related to slavery were severely limited in Cuban publications. For example, publication of abolitionist novels, a genre that took shape on the island before it did in the United States, was prohibited. Those articles offer the first glimpses of Black characters that later became important in larger literary projects, particularly in the abolitionist novel.

As I wrote the initial manuscript, something took me by surprise. Other Black characters came to the forefront, competing for my attention, just as they had provoked curiosity in the Cuban Costumbrista essay writers of the nineteenth century. Like the Costumbrista writer, I became mindful of my own preferences for certain Black figures. The lives of some characters reminded me of events of my own childhood as the child of a multiethnic Puerto Rican couple. In presumably fictional works, there were composites of historical figures. The White writers of these essays recognized the Blacks' manipulation (often to their advantage) of inherently racist systems, such as the highly structured Cuban society of the nineteenth century. Their actions still ring true today in a system determined by socially acceptable behaviors.

The drafting of this book, unlike any of my previous research projects and publications, may have started during my childhood. The son of a White man and a *mulata fina*, I grew up in Puerta de Tierra, an *extramuros* neighborhood of the historic walled city of Old San Juan. This neighborhood grew outside the city walls, very much like the slum areas outside Old Havana, where some of the nineteenth-century Black characters, particularly mulattoes, lived, worked, and survived the economic limitations that slavery imposed upon them. Puerta de Tierra was, and still is, predominantly Black, and like the Black *extramuros* neighborhoods in Havana, it was a cradle of African-based religious practices.

In spite of the rich Afro–Puerto Rican culture around me, I was raised as a *mulato fino*, a critical term that I use throughout this book. This racial label has long been used widely in Puerto Rico to describe light-skinned Blacks, those who can pass as Whites (such as I), who are incorporated into mainstream Puerto Rican culture. Like the nineteenth-century Cuban mulato fino, I was kept away from traditional Black cultural patterns and warned that they were *cosa de negros* [a Black thing]. Those lessons I learned from my mother, the ultimate mulata fina, who raised me to believe that I was White and who therefore insisted that I behave accordingly, following proper Puerto Rican manners in dress, speech, and hair grooming.

My mother's conformist behavior, like that of the mulata fina of the nineteenth century, was a way to work around a racist system that bound women to jobs related to their ethnicity. As with the experiences of mulattoes of the abolitionist novel, however, an alignment with the status quo often led to unexpected results.

As I wrote this book, I was well aware of my affection for the Cuban slave Juan Francisco Manzano, who became my favorite mulato fino. Although a Black slave, he was reared in privileged house-slave conditions, and he considered himself a learned man. Eventually he drafted the only existing autobiography written by a slave in the Spanish-speaking Caribbean. There was a price to pay; he became a foreigner to his own racial background, whose traits he despised. He adopted those of a refined Cuban gentleman of the nineteenth century. For those effects, he attempted to speak refined Spanish, he enjoyed dressing in fine clothes, and most importantly, he knew that he was not like other slaves (or freed Blacks), whose company he never sought.

I was educated in a primarily White private school. Like Manzano, I had little contact with the Black culture around me, including physical participation in the many music festivals and religious feasts (fiestas *de santos*) that had their roots in my marginal neighborhood. My mother could not keep me from hearing, however, the alluring *toques de tambores*, drum dances that were part of Santería ceremonies. Our religious practices at home, like those that Manzano reproduced in his memoirs, were confined to the strict Catholic rituals of the sixties and seventies.

Visually I was aware of a number of Black character types, some of which had literary counterparts in nineteenth-century Cuban Costumbrista literature. Black women bound to cultural traditions particularly populated my childhood. Today I recognize that, like the Cuban nineteenth-century female slaves or freed Black women, they worked within the economic boundaries of a racist sociopolitical system. Their dealings within an oppressive, racially divided society, which left them haggling to survive by any means necessary, was a common theme in the biased view of White Cuban Costumbrista writers. These characters inspired pity in the Costumbrista writers, who presented them in their subservient position. The Black women in my neighborhood were at the heart of my barrio, fighting for their survival.

The Black female types of my childhood were, as in many of the Cuban Costumbrista essays, vendors or providers of services. Doña Chea sold *maví*, a Puerto Rican type of root beer, and Doña Tomasa ironed my father's work shirts. My favorite of the Black women was Doña Sofía, who served *fiambrera*, a home-delivery food system that my mother sometimes used when she felt too ill to cook for us. Although my mother was a good cook of Creole Puerto Rican dishes, Doña Sofía's cooking had a different flavor, perhaps representative of her Afro-Puerto Rican heritage.

A well-known Black woman in my close-knit neighborhood was La Negra Vicenta, whose "darkest" skin was not only a reference to her dark ebony tone but also to the services she provided to the community. I never spoke her nickname. I called her Doña Vicenta, perhaps because to my childish ears all the information that I had about her indicated that she was a *santera*, and I was afraid of her. Back in the late sixties, in the Puerto Rican argot, the term *santera* referred to a woman practitioner of "Spiritist" practices, whether or not she had been initiated into Santería, as the Cuban Regla Ocha was known, and still is known, in Puerto Rico. Through thinly veiled conversations among some of my women neighbors, I heard about some of Doña Vicenta's services. For instance, she performed *santiguos*, body cleansings, a combination of praying and rubbing of special oils on the affected body area. She also prepared concoctions of herbal body splashes individually designed for many purposes—for example, to attract a suitable lover for a desperate female client. Today I know that herbalist women like La Negra Vicenta also provided gynecological services, but as a male child I never heard from women anything about this.

La Negra Vicenta's reputation was strong, and even my cautious mulata fina mother was drawn to her charms. As a small child I remember having been taken to her apartment for a session of *santiguo* for a bad case of stomachache, or *empache* in Puerto Rican slang. (I had eaten too much and could not digest the food.) To this day I remember the complex series of hand massages, combined with the performance on my body of the sign of the cross (*santigüar*, hence the name *santiguo*), and the sharp smell of the coconut oil that La Negra Vicenta used to anoint my stomach while massaging. As in today's economy, in my marginal neighborhood, La Negra Vicenta's health services often replaced costly medical care, particularly in such mild cases as my own.

As an adult I had no knowledge of Santería. I knew about some names of the mighty gods, the orishas, which I had learned from the classic salsa songs of the seventies. Arguably, Puerta de Tierra was the birthplace of Puerto Rican salsalike rhythms. My favorite singers were "El Cantante," the Puerto Rican Héctor Lavoe, and the Cuban La Lupe, also known as "La Gigigi," who were among the first salsa megastars said to have been initiated into Santería rituals in New York City. La Lupe, in particular, was well known for her lavish fiestas *de santos*, feasts of saints that Santería practitioners offer to their patron saints. She also sang *en lengua*, the ritual Yoruba of Santería ceremonies, in songs such as "Elube Changó." To my adolescent ears, however, she was singing in a make-believe African language, a *jeringonza*—a tongue-twister that was fairly common among salsa players. It was only during my first trip to Cuba that I realized that La Lupe's songs were her tribute to key orishas, such as Changó, and that she, indeed, sang in Yoruba.

Another salsa star of my childhood was Celia Cruz, whose songs also made numerous references to Santería practices. Although she publicly proclaimed not to be a practitioner, she claimed for herself a special devotion to la Virgen de la Caridad del Cobre and was often seen at la Ermita de la Caridad in Miami (Cruz 74, 117). Whether Cruz was telling the truth is not important here, but it is true that Caridad is often syncretized as Ochún, a powerful Santería entity whose rendition in songs by Cruz was a favorite among her fans. Cruz's syncretism included her wearing fabulous dresses, echoing African female garb, in bright yellow, Ochún's favorite color. A fancy orisha, Ochún is described in one of Celia's songs, "Elegua quiere tambor" [Elegua wants a drum beat], as wearing "seven skirts."

My formal entrance as a scholar into the world of Afro-Caribbean cultures took place in a most unusual way. In 1989 I traveled to Havana for the first time. Tired of the official revolutionary rhetoric and wanting to find "real" Cuban music, I stumbled upon Black marginal neighborhoods. There for the first time I had my fortune told, in a "shell reading." That was then the extent of my knowledge of Santería other than my basic knowledge of orishas, of which Ochún was my favorite. Hey, if she was Celia's favorite, she had to be cool, no?

Because the Cuban Revolution had encouraged representation of the rich cultural background of Santería in the media and in literature, I had expected to find in official cultural centers' intellectuals interested in my newly discovered subject. To my surprise, in 1989 few writers in Havana wanted to reveal that they practiced Santería. They dismissed my interest as appropriate for sociologists or anthropologists at best.

I continued visits to the Black *extramuros* neighborhoods of Havana, which reminded me of my own barrio of Puerta de Tierra. I was looking for a more vibrant Cuba, not that of the official Communist officers whose boasts about the wonders of a political system did not match a Havana already visibly in shambles. In those Black neighborhoods, away from the highly prescribed political cultural centers, I met the warm Caribbean culture that I am accustomed to as a Puerto Rican. Afro-Cubans welcomed me as an *hermano boricua*, a Puerto Rican brother—the nickname that I preferred to the somewhat stilted *compañero*, the Cuban translation of the Communist "comrade." In those Black neighborhoods I met religious practitioners who became my means of entrance into the close-knit Santería family, my family while in Cuba.

How can I summarize my activities in Havana with my Afro-Cuban friends? Through them I experienced a special kind of blessing. It was they who, following the Yoruba oral folk-tale tradition of the *pataki* folk tales, told me their favorite stories of the orishas, the mighty spiritual powers that rule in Santería's spiritual realm. These stories were told to me as examples for me to follow, or to avoid. The orishas, I learned, can sometimes display naughty behaviors. In a loving, nurturing tradition, the *pataki* speaks about how life can be messy, at times extremely messy. For instance, there is that inexplicable slavery, or even the more than fifty years of Communist dominance on the island. It also reveals that even the worst of crises will pass—yes, even that of the Castro brothers.

The settings of my visits were humble *solares*, open spaces between houses or patios inside apartment buildings, a Caribbean tradition of bringing the party out for everyone to enjoy. In those open patios I also enjoyed some of the best live Cuban music I have ever had the pleasure of hearing, even better music than that in the famous Tropicana nightclub in Havana. In the Caribbean tradition, I joined in playing some of the iconic Afro-Cuban musical instruments. Have you ever played a *güiro* or a *chequere*? This musical gourd instrument will transport you to the origins of Caribbean music, making you swing to the beat of contagious rhythms.

Those *solares* were also the background for religious festivities, known as *bembes*, preludes to complex rituals closed to the uninitiated. There I was reminded of my bicultural condition as a *blanquito*, a whitey, and as such I was often reminded to leave the premises whenever "secret" ceremonies were to take place. The allure of the forbidden, on the one hand, and the tensions implied in the interaction of opposite racial groups, on the other, would remind me of similar tensions that White Costumbrista writers of the nineteenth century openly expressed in writing on Black subjects in Cuba, often in heated, prejudiced images.

In short, while in Cuba I experienced a significant racial element in the formation of lo caribeño. In those Black *solares*, I was linked to my new Cuban friends by blood through the saddest, but perhaps the most significant, historical incident in the development of a Caribbean brotherhood. I was struck by parallels between the particular institutions resulting from cultural practices of Spanish slavery in Cuba and those in Puerto Rico, including, as I experienced as a child, the dominance of Black popular traditions in marginal urban centers, an inspiration for one of my passions today: salsa.

As I wrote this preface from the comfortable surroundings of my overwhelmingly White neighborhood in Decatur, Georgia, so far removed from my childhood barrio and from the Havana *extramuros* Black neighborhoods of the nineteenth century, I felt eerily close to my favorite mulatto character, almost two hundred years after his drafting his autobiography. My preoccupation to "look the part," to be *un caballero* [a gentleman], and engage in the mainstream behavior as it is often proclaimed in Puerto Rico, has been an important part of my life, particularly of my professional conduct in the United States.

Manzano's claim to Whiteness, based on a learned demeanor, has made me mindful of my own condition as a mulato fino. The caricature of the *negrito catedrático*, the wannabe Black professor, a popular character of the nineteenth-century Cuban *teatro bufo* (roughly the equivalent of the U.S. black-face theater), continues to haunt me as a reminder to find my own voice within the overwhelmingly White faculty of my teaching institution. Like the *negrito catédratico*, obsessed with perfecting a professorial image, I too struggle to find a middle point between my desire to project an image of professionalism acceptable within academia and to enjoy my marginal roots as a mulato fino.

So far, like Manzano, I do not have much to show for it. At least he wrote a poignant autobiography. The evidence of my personal search is a collection of Black religious folkloric pieces, with which I have turned my house into a "Latino museum," and this book, my tribute to all who, like those Black women of my childhood, attempt to navigate the often stormy waters of a racial power structure.

# Acknowledgments

I am very grateful to the staff of the library of the Centro de Estudios Avanzados de Puerto Rico y el Caribe: Francis J. Mójica, Jazmín Castillo, and Milagros Ramos.

I am indebted to the staff of Agnes Scott College's McCain Library, particularly to Casey Long and Debbie Adams.

My special appreciation goes to Agnes Scott College emerita professor Eloise Herbert for her patient readings of the multiple versions of this book.

# A Note on Translations

Unless otherwise indicated, all translations are my own. When I reproduce material from a published English translation of a text, I indicate that fact by preceding the page citation with the label "trans."

Wayne State University Press has granted permission to quote from the 1996 Schulman and Garfield edition of Juan Francisco Manzano's *The Autobiography of a Slave/Autobiografía de un esclavo.*

# Introduction

## Nineteenth-Century Costumbrista Writers
## on the Slave Trade and on Black Traditions in Cuba

Costumbrista essays, which are only the painting, objectively, whether to
condemn or to exalt a whole epoch or a whole class.

Azorín, "Comento a Larra"

Manuel Moreno Fraginals established the period of 1518–1873 as that of the
slave trade in Cuba ("Aportes" 13). April 1873 was the arrival date of the last
documented shipment of *piezas negras*—Black pieces, as slaves were known in
the dehumanizing slave-trade argot (Marrero 34). This was an illegal enterprise
since the slave trade had been abolished in 1820. Throughout the nineteenth
century, however, Africans arrived in Cuba in great numbers. Domingo del
Monte, a distinguished Cuban abolitionist, estimated that of some 350,000
slaves working in Cuba in 1832, mainly on sugarcane plantations, only eighty
thousand were born in Cuba (qtd. in Pérez de la Riva, *Para la historia* 118–19).

After its legal abolition, the slave trade was still a large source of income in
Cuba for the many individuals involved, including foreigners, usually Americans
or Europeans. The Spanish historian Arturo Arnalte traced the highly organized
system of illegal trade in his book *Los últimos esclavos de Cuba* (2001) [The last
slaves in Cuba]. He used documentation of an 1854 disembarkation of some seven
hundred African slaves, most of them children, with approval by both Spanish
and Cuban public officials, as well as by slave traders and by sugarcane plantation owners. Slavery would become a trademark of the colonial experience in
the Americas, in "the most gigantic process of coercive displacement of human
beings known to history" (Moreno Fraginals, "Aportes" 13).

Today, historians still debate about the numbers of slaves that went into
Cuba, but they agree that the history of Cuban slavery could be divided into

two large periods. The first began with the specific regulations that provided for the establishment of slavery in Cuba, and it extended until the early part of the nineteenth century, around 1820, a date related to British-Spanish treaties attempting to curtail the slave trade. The second period continued until the abolition of slavery in 1886. During the first three centuries some 390,000 slaves arrived, but in the nineteenth century numbers increased significantly to some 530,000 (Pérez de la Riva, *Para la historia*; Arredondo 29–30; Guanche 47). Cuban intellectuals during the nineteenth century, aware of the large numbers of Africans on the island, examined and commonly protested the negative influence of slaves and their descendents on the development of an emerging Cuban identity.

The history of slavery in the Spanish-speaking colonies in the New World was carefully documented from its inception. As indicated in an initial Spanish royal license, of 1498, which allowed the importation of African slaves, the ideal prospective slave was seen in terms of a positive characteristic: "that they were born among Christians in order to help to convert Indians" (qtd. in Bachiller y Morales, *Los negros* 23). In Cuba, slavery, which had started with an official license dated 1513 (Serviat 11), developed a culture of its own, determined in part by the large number of slaves that entered the island throughout the nineteenth century. The traits of the perfect slave became a common theme in the many succeeding regulations.

Representations of slavery in Cuba first appeared in colonial chronicles, in books tracing the history of slavery, and in city ordinances concerning restrictions of the activities of slaves and of freed Blacks. For slave owners there were also instructions, known as *manuales*—manuals about the physical treatment of and the maintenance of slaves. Within the Roman Catholic Church there would be many further texts on the issue of slavery (Závala 339–44). One example was *Explicación de la doctrina cristiana acomodada a la capacidad de los negros bozales* [Explanation of Christian doctrine adjusted to the capacity of Black bozales], a collection of instructional writings on the proper evangelization of the recently arrived slave, known as *bozal*, written in Cuba in 1797.

The impact of African-based cultural and religious traditions in the development of a national identity, or Cubanía, was the subject of numerous debates. Throughout the nineteenth century, discussions placed slavery as inherent in a colonial status that made the island the wealthiest of Spain's last possessions. Slavery was a booming business, which expanded into several economic enterprises, both national and international, all of which exerted pressure to preserve the status quo. Thus, a strong censorship, which mainly restricted public political discussions, imposed limitations on the content of various types of writings to be published on the island. It even halted the distribution of foreign texts dealing with slave-related issues. The censorship of debates on slavery openly responded to Cuban authorities' efforts to shield the island from abolitionist influences, mainly British and U.S. American. The restrictions also clearly imposed limits to a positive characterization of slave cultures, and to other related byproducts, such as the so-called mulatto expressions. Such cultural manifestations came about as a direct result of the social and political regulations imposed upon slaves and upon freed Blacks within the highly restrictive Cuban society.

No Black tradition was considered to be authentically Cuban. The concept of Cubanness was much debated within diverging political national trends throughout the nineteenth century, as Cubans discussed the island's future of remaining part of the Spanish empire or of annexation to the United States or of full independence from Spain (Cepero Bonilla 61–78). Cuban Black culture was often referred to as *criollo* [Creole], as slaves born in Cuba were called in nineteenth-century literature, in opposition to African natives, known as bozales, a term that also conveyed that the African was not a native speaker of Spanish. Their respective expressions of popular culture were restricted to the marginal scenes that they inhabited: the mighty *ingenios*, the sugarcane mill plantations, or the slums of the major Cuban harbor cities, such as Havana. In the cities, slaves and freed Blacks worked in a variety of manual tasks, jobs that caught the attention of national and international writers visiting Cuba throughout the nineteenth century.

Slaves and freed Creole Blacks as peons of a complex political machinery were immersed in a highly divisive society organized around castes of color. Subjected to a prejudiced view of their native Black cultures, Blacks remained isolated from the larger, mainstream Cuban society. In spite of social repression, they managed to retain a number of native customs and cultural traditions, and some of these became well known outside their marginal confines. Speaking of Cuban Black culture, Jorge and Isabel Castellanos stressed the Africans' "extraordinary conservatism, their intense attachment to their customs" (1:56), as a major component in the creation of Black cultural products. Some of these customs, associated with ethnic types, grew in importance and eventually became subjects of various types of writings, particularly during the nineteenth century.

From the earliest writings on slavery, which were first published as political treatises or as historical accounts, the maintenance of that cruel institution and its inhumane practices was closely observed as it became the core of a booming economy, central to a highly organized sugarcane plantation culture. Political events of worldwide importance, such as the Haitian Revolution of 1804, which transformed Cuba into the world's largest sugarcane producer, made slavery a central topic of political debates. The importation into Cuba of hundreds of thousands of slaves throughout the nineteenth century had maintained a rich African culture. It had been documented, despite the biased views of founding fathers, which can be seen in historical texts such as the *Chapter Minutes of the City Council of Havana*, available today in two volumes covering the years from 1550 to 1574. The cultures of the field slave and of the freed created two types of characters that attracted the attention of numerous foreign travelers, who often wrote about them after visits to the sugarmills and to large Cuban cities.

The sugarcane plantation produced the first type of distinctive Black Creole traditions. Renowned Cuban artists such as Eduardo Leplante, Esteban Chartrand and Víctor Patricio de Landaluze made visual documentation of the *ingenio* in many engravings of the industrialized sugarcane plantation. A rigid system created specific classifications of slave workers, such as field hands and house workers. It encouraged internal divisions and conflicts among bozal and Creole slaves, and created a division of slaves into faithful or rebellious types.

A second type of Black Creole popular culture was found in Cuban cities. These characters were associated with the many trades that slaves and freed Creoles performed on a daily basis. City Blacks appeared more often in the literature produced in the nineteenth century because of their numbers and their visual availability as street vendors of various kinds (for example, of fruits and produce), or as handymen, musicians, craftsmen, medicine women, and coach drivers, among others.

Today, a notable Cuban source of documentation of the strong African and Creole Black cultures of the nineteenth century can be found in *artículos de costumbres*, short essays of customs whose main function was to document national popular traditions. In this literary trend, Cuban and Latin American writers imitated Spanish models. In the 1830s Spanish writers had set parameters for the Costumbrista movement. Their examination of national types and of their impact on local customs proposed to reflect the rise to power of the middle class and the complex changes occurring in the Spanish political arena (Kirkpatrick 31; Suárez-Murias 375). Literary critics agreed that it was particularly that close association with the socioeconomic and the political scenarios in Spain that defined Costumbrismo as a sort of "testimony of the Spanish transition," in a documentation of "a change, of a revolution, of an evolution that has transformed the face of the whole country or of its picturesque corners, and to give vent to, surrendering to memory, the nostalgia for all that is gone and forgotten" (Montesinos 43). Of particular interest were their explorations of social types, as in Spanish writer Mariano de Larra's articles. They allowed the readers in the first part of the nineteenth century to witness the formation in Spain of "the new frontiers being established between social classes" (Romero Tobar 422).

Cuban and Latin American writers adapted Costumbrista aesthetic trends to their own needs in their comprehensive analyses of national sociopolitical conditions. Their societies, like the Spanish, were experiencing radical changes in structure and witnessing the creation of new social types. Some of them, such as the Black Creole culture in Cuba, led to debates about whether they were representative of national identity. Among Latin American countries, Cuba developed a strong body of Costumbrista literature, which produced numerous definitions of the goals of Costumbrismo. One important trend was their often severe views of the state of Cuban customs. Their positive or negative opinions of the island's current social state would reflect indirectly their political opinions about acceptable national behavioral patterns.

Costumbrista writers cautiously handpicked topics pertaining to slavery, and they avoided material about the sugarcane plantation. One of the most contested themes was the treatment of slaves in the *ingenio*, the sugarmill. Such articles were among the most censored essays on Black themes.

Cuban Costumbrista writers also seemed to maintain self-censorship on issues pertaining to the unjust treatment of slaves or to the imposition of illegal regulations upon freed Blacks. Even so, they described certain slave types, such as the faithful, hardworking field worker, or the old, "retired" field worker, whose duty during his last years on the plantation was to serve as a watchman.

There were, however, few White types associated with cruelty on the plantations, with punishments and with exhausting work schedules. One of the White characters briefly described was the absentee plantation owner, who often preferred to live in the large cities and to visit the plantation on holidays. His place was taken by the administrator, who also served as manager of a number of men workers with specific functions in the production of sugar. One of these was the *mayoral*, the slave overseer, well known for abuse and physical punishment of slaves. None of the overseer's brutal practices appeared in published Costumbrista articles.

Also absent were other, more brutal White characters. One was the *rancheador*, the hunter of runaway slaves, a trade whose parameters were well documented in Cuban regulations. Their presence was well known, fully documented in local newspapers' want ads bought by slave owners requesting the hunting of runaway slaves.

Large cities also offered work for slaves and for freed Blacks. Havana was the preferred locale for Cuban Costumbristas and for foreign visitors writing memoirs. About urban settings, two prominent themes were insistence that the crime rate in marginal neighborhoods was related to activities of certain Black criminal groups, and that other social evils, such as the national tendency to engage in superstitions, were a direct result of foreign Black religious influences.

The most common subjects of Costumbrista articles on Black culture were related to music. Some examples were slave dances on the plantations or in Black parades performed on city streets during the Carnival or in other religious celebrations. Documentation of ethnic elements of these customs took a secondary role, since the writers often viewed these performances as primitive or immoral in character. To today's readers these articles reveal tensions, evident in subtle admiration for Black cultural traditions, as components of an emerging mainstream Cuban culture.

Nonetheless, some aspects of African customs, such as certain public visual elements of religious belief systems, or of musical and food traditions, began to appear as themes of nineteenth-century Cuban Costumbrista literature. These depictions of African culture, which the Brazilian anthropologist Roger Bastide referred to as "peaks of culture" (25), often left Blacks marginalized within the restricted physical and social structures assigned to them as workers. Within Costumbrismo, slaves and freed Blacks did not achieve the stature of figures of historical or of literary relevance. They were placed in specific social backgrounds, some of which were at the center of pressing socioeconomic issues.

In general, other subjects of typical Cuban Costumbrista articles were diverse. They included almost any aspect of daily life that writers considered positive examples of local color. Many articles were also warnings against examples of bad national folklore. They were not necessarily racially based, but without exception bozal and Creole Black cultural practices received heavy criticism as examples of uncivilized African behavioral patterns. In reporting about a peculiar folk tradition or in criticizing what they perceived as un-Cuban, including, of course, Black customs, Costumbristas considered themselves to be defenders of proper Cuban popular culture, in areas such as gastronomy, fashion, and entertainment.

Despite an inherently biased point of view, some Costumbrista articles made slaves and Black Creoles protagonists of their own stories. This is today a most important contribution of this type of essay. Their documentation of the bozal slave and of Black Creole figures speaks also about the developing mulatto popular culture. In spite of the limits imposed on free expression, numerous essays managed to offer glimpses of the conditions of slave and Creole Black communities thriving in Cuba throughout the nineteenth century. In these articles, readers today find small portraits whose images and life stories, although prejudiced or exoticized, reveal the conditions at the time of the writings.

This documentation reflected further national debate about the cultural elements associated with an emerging Cubanía identity. Some of these Cuban traditions—certain dances and religious expressions—had origins within Black Creole life and, at the time of the publication of the articles, they were enjoyed and even performed by White members of mainstream society.

Research by Cuban anthropologists and folklorists of the early part of the twentieth century identified some of those cultural components as key markers of Black or mulatto identities. For example, the late Cuban folklorist and short-story writer Lydia Cabrera (1899–1991) explored the survival of African customs incorporated into the *pataki* oral tradition of Yoruba origin at whose thematic center lies a rich repository of components of the religious belief system known today popularly as Santería. Cabrera's research of various types of Afro-Cuban religions started in 1928 with interviews with practitioners, including old former slaves. Through her fieldwork, traditionally neglected Black religions came into recognition as part of a rich cultural legacy. It also included other areas, such as the survival of African languages associated with celebrations in Black Creole rituals, music and dance (*Anagó* 16; *La lengua* 10). Cabrera diligently researched the rituals, one of which was Santería, or Regla Ocha, a source of rich oral literature performed in the native Yoruba language.

Unlike the earliest Cuban anthropologists, Costumbristas had not been limited to oral testimonies of former slaves. They had watched and documented bozal and Black Creole traditions. As in most religious rites, these had remained underground, restricted by laws or by city regulations or by the participants' unwillingness to perform in public. Rather than focusing on religious practices, Costumbristas often described more public cultural performances, such as musical activities of Black celebrations, with songs that were often performed in African languages and dances that were to become modes of popular entertainment.

Later Costumbristas attempted to document Black customs, whether associated with rural life in the *barracón*, the slave quarters developed in Cuba after 1844, or in all-Black meeting halls, known as Cabildos, that promoted Creole musical and religious practices. Most Costumbristas concentrated on city scenes, as part of a well-developed literary staging that moved away from initial mere documentation of these customs as examples of local color. These more mature articles often displayed highly developed plots, with Black characters of more symbolic importance.

This book examines various ways in which Cuban Costumbristas reported the strong presence of African traditions as developed by bozal and Creole slaves and by freed Blacks as agents of a strong popular culture, highly visible throughout the nineteenth century. In their handling of Black themes, Cuban Costumbristas addressed four main subjects: the particularities of the sugar-cane plantation, rich in slave cultures (as performed in different formats of acculturation by both bozal and Creole slaves); the development of religious systems within rural and urban settings; the documentation of Black musical expressions; and the incorporation of certain Black social types as literary characters, as workers of specific trades assigned to slaves or to freed Blacks or as marginal outcasts living in slum areas of major Cuban cities.

The analysis of these four fields of study aims to underscore the impact of Black culture upon the development of a criollo identity. The term Creole was also used in nineteenth-century Cuba to differentiate native Cuban identity, Cubanía, from imposed Spanish culture. This book also intends to examine the particularities that the nineteenth-century Costumbristas observed as eye-witnesses of the making of a new racial hybridity known today as "mulatton-ess." Although mulattoness was a racial concept handled in various types of documents (such as in ecclesiastical documents and in civil regulations against mixed marriages), it was with Costumbrismo that the concept took on a literary presence. Although Blacks as depicted by Costumbristas had little literary significance, their presence in these politically infused texts covertly address the role of Black Creole manifestations upon developing Cubanía.

The Costumbrista writer was a White male intellectual, whose biases reflected not only an upper-level social condition, but also his privileged gender position. An underlying trait of Costumbrista essays is, however, the fact that these writers could not escape the allure of Black cultural byproducts, some of which, such as music and religions, became common themes. With the exception of one case, there is no surviving text of the time authored by a Black Cuban. Costumbrista essays are today the only surviving testimonials of emerging Black traditions as practiced throughout the nineteenth century.

In addition to information about different types of slaves or freed Blacks, this analysis of aspects of Black life as presented in Costumbrista essays points out significant absences of details about the few documented Black characters. The essayists' silences were intentional. They were a component of the underlying political message in most Cuban Costumbrismo.

This book's multidisciplinary approach permits the pursuit of two goals. The first is to trace the earliest references to bozal and Black Creole customs in Cuban literature presented in nineteenth-century Costumbrista articles. The emphasis is on the writers' interest in documenting specific character types connected to various slave and Black Creole cultural practices—of slave workers on the highly structured plantations or of slaves and freed Blacks allowed employment in cities. The various types of labor produced distinctive characters, such as the street vendor, the elegant coach driver, the musician and the woman practitioner of natural remedies.

The book's second goal is to present a view of the development of rich Creole Black musical and religious traditions in Cuba. Music and religion were often inseparable, as will be indicated in this survey of key historical references. Eyewitness accounts, mainly by Spaniards and by other European visitors to Cuba, allow the reader to trace the methods used for evangelization of the slaves, particularly the catechism allowed to slaves, and other factors in the creation of the so-called syncretic Creole religious practices. These religious ceremonies also produced Black types, such as the *ñáñigo*, an outcast Black male that, according to one biased Costumbrista, was well known for his performance in "black magic" celebrations.

Chapter 1 introduces the reader to the development of Costumbrista trends in Cuba, with emphasis on the earliest images in print of slavery practices on the island. As a literary movement of importance even well into the nineteenth century, Costumbrismo reflected unique facets of the island's colonial history, including selective images of slave workers—data that became public knowledge only after it was played down as innocuous.

Part I of chapter 1 traces the earliest developments of Costumbrismo in Cuba. There was only timid incorporation of slavery issues as a literary motif. Restrictions on publication of abolitionist material determined not only the content but also the tenor of Costumbrista essays. Writers dealt with censorship of descriptive data, limited mainly to physical traits and to activities of slaves and of freed Blacks. In their collections of specific Black characters, Costumbristas exhibited types of subjects determined by the essayists' particular sociopolitical stand or by their reaction to official censorship of themes related to slavery.

The writer Anselmo Suárez y Romero's daring depiction of positive images of slaves in the ultramodern sugarcane mills—complex economic entities at the center of what Antonio Benítez Rojo referred to as "creole sugarocracy" (59)—is the subject of part II. Suárez y Romero's critical position was exceptional among Costumbristas, because in these articles he dared to deal with the inhumane lives of slave field workers subjected to harsh working conditions. Some of the workers became protagonists of tragic stories. Although slaves constituted a rather large population, the stringent censorship in Cuba of publications dealing with issues of slavery kept such subjects rather under control. Suárez y Romero skillfully navigated around this pressure and managed to offer portraits of rather crude scenes of a wealthy Cuban plantation. In this, he supported the Spanish Costumbrista project to "give evidence of a society in state of transition, of the greatest transformation of the cultural revolution of the middle class" (Escobar 125).

The life of a slave from a first-person perspective is the subject of chapter 2. Study of these memoirs of the Creole slave Juan Francisco Manzano offers a contrast between the life of Suárez y Romero's rural sugarmill slaves and that of an urban slave in Havana, such as Manzano. In this exceptional text, the only surviving Black memoirs completed during the slavery period, Manzano documented his living circumstances as a house slave. He was a refined and self-educated Black Creole who could read and write, and he painted portraits and even became an accomplished poet. He proudly viewed himself as a mulato fino, whose learned behavior was akin to that of the White gentleman, whom he carefully imitated. In his writing he followed literary canons, particularly the Romantic and Costumbrista traditions that he knew well through his connection to well-known writers, who served as mentors. Those writers, particularly his literary mentor, Domingo del Monte, may have directly influenced the content of Manzano's memoirs.

In his biased analysis of Black Creole cultures, Manzano failed to explore slave traditions, and he chose not to offer a full picture of the horrors in mistreatment of slaves, particularly of the field workers on sugarcane plantations. He preferred instead to remain associated with mainstream culture within his self-description as a learned Black who spoke and wrote in standard Spanish, a fact that separated him from other, raw slaves. He proudly became a mulato fino—a refined mulatto, a type that Costumbrista writing often reflected in urban Black male and female characters. Although his close association with a White power structure might have caused his memoirs to lose efficacy as an abolitionist text, it is today an important document as an example of a Black's self-depiction in response to literary canons and to social limitations upon incorporation of Blacks into mainstream society.

Chapter 3 examines other urban Black dwellers, whether slaves or freed Blacks, as part of a rather large population, working in a substantial number of trades and living in marginal neighborhoods throughout Cuban cities. As recorded in the Minutes of Meetings of the City of Havana, dated 1550–65 and 1566–74, Black residents were limited to particular trades assigned even by gender. When some of these occupations became old-fashioned or outmoded by modern devices, some Costumbristas expressed strong interest in documenting them before their disappearance. This type of sentimental article was among the few expressions of a positive view of a Black tradition.

Documentation of Black customs and in particular of representative character types, is the focus of part I. It presents an analysis of Black women, public figures often depicted as essential components of a booming Creole Black urban culture. Because in a slave society Black women were "subordinate to all men and hence suffered sexual as well as economic oppression" (Bush 8), the negative characterization of certain Black female types demonstrates the subversive mechanisms that female slaves or freed Black women had at their disposal to confront the gender-based impositions of mainstream culture. Like Black males, Black women had to live and work in specific locations, such as certain urban neighborhoods, and their whereabouts, as street vendors or as medicine women, became favorite themes for Costumbristas.

Chapter 4 is an examination of the resolution among Costumbristas to bring Black characters to the forefront, particularly freed urban Black men. In contrast to a basic and rather monolithic representation of Black female types, these male figures had remarkable, different sociopolitical values as literary characters. The section titled "The Uppity Blacks and the Black Thugs in Urban Cuban Life" illustrates the Costumbrista's handling of two specific types of urban activities performed mainly by male Blacks. First, there was the Black *calesero*, the driver of the fashionable *calesas*—coaches whose large numbers crowded the streets of Cuban cities. The calesero represented the "uppity Black," the urban Black who attempted to integrate himself into nineteenth-century Cuban society. In contrast to this seemingly positive example of conformity to the cultural values of the dominant society, the second type is the *curro*, the Black thug, who dared to roam the streets of Havana as a cold-blooded criminal. The opposite of the calesero, the *curro* remained marginal to mainstream attempts (if, indeed, there were any) to indoctrinate him on acceptable social behavior.

Chapter 5 explores the complex development of Black religious beliefs, whether within the rural setting of the *barracón* [the closed-in slave quarters] or in all-Black urban institutions, such as *cabildos*. Costumbrista documentation of such events shows clearly that slaves and freed Blacks selected portions of their religious practices to be made public, as they paraded in costumes designed specifically for Catholic holidays. To a lesser extent they allowed certain types of popular manifestations, such as music and dance steps, to be associated with public expressions of syncretic religious celebrations, made well known by Costumbrista writers and graphic artists. The chapter highlights these two specific components, costumed parades and music, in the development of Black Creole rites and traces their impact on emerging popular traditions, which eventually transcended the color and social barriers so evident in the Cuban colonial system.

The first section examines rare firsthand testimonial accounts by runaway slave Esteban Montejo. Inspired by the Socialist Cuban Revolution of 1959, he responded to questions asked of him in interviews by sociologist Miguel Barnet about the various ethnic practices performed underground on a nineteenth-century Cuban sugarcane plantation. Those religious systems took shape in reaction to the Catholic Church's loose control or negligence in teaching doctrines and as examples of the Black slaves' desire to maintain native religious faith. There had been, however, exceptions to the Church's apparent apathy toward the slaves' evangelization. Even after the publication in 1797 of the first manual of catechism for recently arrived slaves, Blacks continued to incorporate elements of Catholic theology into developing Creole religious practices. Montejo's examples of the various types of bozal and Creole Black religious celebrations confirm cases documented in the manual of catechism of plentiful activity of syncretic religious practices among plantation slaves.

The importance of religious musical performances among members of various ethnic Cofradías and the adaptation of certain colorful figures are the focus of the second section. In spite of strong biases against their incorporation, icons of Black religious systems emerged as representative examples of a Creole national culture. Unable to have physical access to Black ceremonies, Costumbristas sought knowledge of Creole religions in public parades in the cities. Although their articles exhibited overwhelmingly negative and biased views, their portraits of these culturally inspired parades could not ignore the allure of Black exoticism. These demonstrations had continued a struggle to gain a place in viable manifestations of an emerging Cuban national Black culture.

Finally, this book seeks to engage multiple and diverse texts into a critical conversation illustrative of the complex issues of Cuban slavery at the peak of the sugarcane boom. Selected pieces demonstrate that these multifaceted sociopolitical components not only reflected the Cuban colonial status but also reacted to laws and regulations pertaining to slavery. This book tries to illustrate that the national development of a hybrid national identity, a mulattoness, was indeed an important component in the formation of Cubanía, a preamble to the national sentiments that propelled the wars of independence.

# Cuban Costumbrista Portraits of Slaves in Sugarmills

## Essays by Anselmo Suárez y Romero

We would never finish if we were to trace one by one all the old types of our society, contrasting them with those newly created by a century of changes. Man, ultimately, is always the same, although with different disguises in form: the courtier, who formerly flattered royalty, today serves and flatters the masses under the name of tribune; the devout has turned into humanitarian; the idler and the rake, into agitator and patriot; the historian into man of history; the heir of an entailed estate into pretender, and the working class into free citizens and into sovereign people. Time will pass, hours will mature, and all these types, today brand-new, will, like the others, pass into being old-fashioned and retrograde, and each of our grandchildren will reward us with bursts of laughter for the quips and derision with which we regale our grandparents today . . . Who will have the last laugh?

Ramón Mesonero Romanos, "El autor de Bucólica"

## Slavery in Cuban Costumbrismo

Costumbrismo promoted the writers' goal to highlight acceptable Cuban customs, as part of a national project that became a strong political movement throughout the nineteenth century. Roberto González Echevarría has defined the trend as one with "passionate interest in Cuba's natural world and in the idiosyncrasies of their homeland" (48). The first of such national self-portrait statements was published in 1792 in *Papel de Periódico de Cuba* [Periodical newspaper of Cuba]. It stated that the newspaper's purpose should be "To attack the habits and customs that are detrimental in common and, particularly, to correct the vices, painting them in their true colors, so that they are detested when viewed with horror, and to picture in contrast the highly prized attraction of virtues" (qtd. in *Diccionario de la literatura cubana* 711). This declaration set forth strong critical objectives for future Costumbrista articles, which for the most part exhibited rather rigid, ultraconservative opinions on acceptable national customs.

The Cuban scholar Salvador Bueno observed that the emergence in Cuba of newspapers and of other serial publications provided readers with plenty of Costumbrista articles designed specifically to document Cuban native folklore.[1] Bueno described these essays as "short works, almost always in prose, that in concise form and with satirical intention, or merely for amusement, described common practices, habits, customs, characteristic and representative types of a certain society" (*Costumbristas* ix–x). Their scope was predetermined to serve as "predominantly of social criticism and in the nature of reform" (*Costumbristas* x).

The initial articles published in *Papel de Periódico*, according to Roig de Leuchsenring, were geared more to "observations and their indictments and censure of the bad customs and vices of the Cuban population of their time" (*Sesquicentenario* 35). The themes of these early Costumbrista publications are mainly attacks against general ignorance, lack of knowledge by the people, lack of hospitals in Havana for the homeless, and lack of orphanages for boys and girls (*Sesquicentenario* 36). Other articles reflect the "character and customs of that epoch, its movement and social development, its needs, fashions, readings" (Roig de Leuchsenring, *Los periódicos* 49).

In his summary of Cuban publications such as *Papel de Periódico*, the Cuban writer José Lezama Lima explains that their goal was to discuss issues "essentially about [national] health (vaccination), about agriculture, about jobs and about curiosities (a Black who slept for six months)" (*El Regañón* 17). Such a limited scope, it can be inferred, explains the lack of articles dealing with Black issues. A stern political censorship banned certain subject matter, particularly news or reports about issues related to slavery.[2]

Other media available for Costumbrista publications, according to Lezama Lima, were *El Regañón de La Habana*, first published on September 30, 1800, and a year later *El Sustituto del Regañón*, which published positive commentaries described as being of "essentially good taste" (*El Regañón* 17). *El Regañón's* regulations about the type of articles to be published required that they be "interesting, that is, that they not be trivial or ill chosen" and that, in accordance with the editors' regulations, "they not use dry precepts" (qtd. in *El Regañón* 17).

Lezama Lima's collection of articles selected from those published in *El Regañón de La Habana* and *El Sustituto del Regañón* includes only two articles with Black content: one about aggressive Black coach drivers, known in Havana as caleseros, and another about the *mancaperros*, boys and male teenagers engaged in mischievous street-related activities, who were often Blacks. These two characters appeared often in Costumbrista articles dealing with life in cities, particularly in Havana.

The subject of slaves or freed Blacks was clearly inconsequential to contributors to the *Papel de Periódico*. Roig de Leuchsenring did not mention that Black issues were important subjects of articles. There were, however, two exceptional articles in which an anonymous writer commented on issues related to slavery. The first one addresses the use of stocks in punishment of slaves who misbehaved. The second one dares to depict White men associated with slavery practices. Both subjects were rarely treated in Costumbrista publications.

One untitled article, a letter by a citizen that attempted to illustrate the power of the plantation owner, was satirically signed "El Amigo de los Esclavos" [The slaves' friend]. It was published in *Papel Periódico* on May 5, 1791. The narrator mockingly called the sugar barons "exceedingly noble harvesters of sugar, gentlemen sugarmill owners, my favorite countrymen." The anonymous writer went on to offer a satirical view of their control of the Cuban economy of the time:

> You are the noblest and most select section of this republic, the neighbors most useful to the State and to the Fatherland of the whole Island, those who make the most precious grain that our fertile land produces, the ones who load the multitude of vessels that set sail for Europe from this spacious bay, those who with your industry, immense expenses and deadly sweats, cover with exquisite, sweet and tasty candies the tables of the Court, who maintain the commerce of Havana and move the commercial wheel of export and import. (Qtd. in Roig de Leuchsenring, *Los periódicos* 41)

This overexcited exaltation also led the writer to complain about the use of cells with *cepos* [stocks], a sort of prison, "where they put the Blacks to spend the night and to avoid in this way their flight" (qtd. in Roig de Leuchsenring, *Sesquicentenario* 40). The writer dismisses this practice with a seemingly negative reaction: "I have seen one suffocated [slave] brought out, only to live a very few hours and die without confession" (40–41). As a solution to the problem, the writer plainly recommends keeping the slave tied in the stocks, but set outside, "into the elements" (41).

Missing from this article, however, is a full description of the stocks as a terrible device of punishment. Historian Franklin W. Knight described it as "an enormous, fixed board with holes through which fitted the head, hands and feet of the delinquent slaves, either separately, or in any combination" (*Slave* 77). The author warned plantation owners that the practice caused a high rate of death among slaves, but this was not a denunciation of the horrific deaths caused by the punishment: "A harmful practice, which at dawn draws them out of those dark pens, breathless and sweaty, their pores exposed to the humid air, into the cold, and it causes them to develop colds, painful pulmonary conditions that lead to their death and to our financial loss" (42).[3]

The second article in *Papel de Periódico* daringly examines slave practices in a satirical portrait of another hated iconic figure on sugarmill plantations: the *mayoral* [overseer]. In an article published in 1791 under the title "Instrucciones que ha dejado un Mayoral de Azucarería a sus herederos" [Instructions left to his heirs by an overseer of slaves in sugar milling], a retired overseer recommends to his successor the best ways of handling his job. First, he stresses that he must look the part: "When you go out to deal with some master you will go very clean, armed with a good machete, a tight leather hat, red, trousers long and wide, of intense color, silver spurs, and nonchalantly a kerchief at the neck, a white shirt much crinkled but without a jacket or flounce" (qtd. in Pérez de la Riva, *El café* 125). This colorful attire corresponds to examples in engravings of the time.

Although the overseer was a strong, brutal man, he is advised to project an air of submission in front of his delicate boss, a conceited man who disdained doing the tasks he was trusting the overseer to do on his behalf: "Your manner is to be humble, for the moment you will promise to do a lot and more than all your predecessors" (125). The rest of the article stresses that the timid attitude would improve negotiation of salary and benefits: "You will ask for something, adding that others give you the same; but that for the privilege of serving 'the Gentleman' you will reduce the amount of payment" (125).

There was an ulterior motive for that generous offer, because it was common knowledge that overseers stole from their masters: "You can reduce it a bit; because you will take by the handful whatever the master denies you" (125). The theft is not possible, however, if the overseer does not befriend the Mayordomo, the plantation's accountant: "Close alliance with the Mayordomo, who will be your buddy, first so that he will clear your requests without objections, second so that he doesn't tell tales on you to the Master" (125). Other types of "tales" that an allied Mayordomo would have kept away from the master include the brutal punishment techniques that the overseer used on the slaves. That was not a subject of this article.

It would seem that strong official censorship managed to curtail Costumbrista writers' expression of their perceived role as commentators on a slavery-based society (González Echevarría 49). Perhaps the frequent references in historical accounts that portray the *mayoral* as a brave man curtailed the publication of negative portraits of this imposing figure.[4] Instead, the *mayoral* was often documented in positive terms. For example, historian J. M. de Andueza recorded in 1841 the daring actions of Don Antonio de Orihuela, an overseer who was considered to be a hero for controlling an 1812 slave revolt. De Andueza highly praised the "intrepid mayoral" to whose "sound judgment and presence of mind was due the good fortune of stifling in its beginning the fire of insurrection" (174). In a heightened, romanticized exclamation, de Andueza reproduced de Orihuela's call for action, presumably in addressing his crew of slaves, who were moved to stop the mob's attack on their plantation: "What will be better, guys, to join those frenzied fellows, or to shed blood for God and for the master?" (174). These words moved the men, whose reaction characterized them as loyal slaves, a preferred image that obliterated any indirect reference to rebellious slaves.

Cuban Costumbrista writers were fairly vocal, however, in their privileged role as social commentators. Cirilo Villaverde, well-known writer and public figure, in his prologue to the *Colección de artículos satíricos y de costumbres* [Collection of satirical articles and of customs] (1847), by fellow Cuban José M. de Cárdenas y Rodríguez (1812–1882), defined his critical function as "the one that has brought forth the accursed tendency to see the weak side where the rest of the peoples see only the strong side; he who burns with lively desire to improve his species by raising its moral standards; where he finds mania, absurdity, laziness or extravagance, there he lashes his whip" (qtd. in Cárdenas y Rodríguez 8). Another important Costumbrista writer, José Victoriano Betancourt, writing for *La Cartera Cubana* [The Cuban portfolio] in 1838, was clearer about the aesthetic quality of his own Costumbrista articles: "my intention is very humble: to paint, although with a coarse brush and muted colors some customs, either rustic or urban, at times with the desire to indicate a reform, sometimes to make the article more interesting" (qtd. in Roig de Leuchsenring, *Los escritores* 143). Both of these intellectuals wrote important Costumbrista essays dealing with Black subjects.

Costumbrismo had a strong readership in Cuba. At the highest peak in popularity of Costumbrista writing, two works were published in Cuba that were among the first of such collections in Latin America: *Los cubanos pintados por sí mismos* [Cuban self-portraits] (1852) and *Tipos y costumbres de la Isla de Cuba* [Types and customs of the island of Cuba] (1881). The inspiration for *Los cubanos pintados* was publications along the same line in Europe. For example, in France, there was *Les français peints par eux-mêmes* (1840–1842), and in Spain, there was *Los españoles pintados por sí mismos* (1843–1844). The Cuban collection's editor, who was also a Costumbrista writer, Blás San Millán, stated in his introduction the purpose of the volume:

> Cubans have wanted to portray themselves too and doubtless for the same reasons that have driven the French and the Spanish . . . for better or for worse to reveal their worth; their purpose is not to form caricatures, but portraits of exact, specific types, not individualities, but phenomena general among the population and [pictures] of their customs in each class. (Qtd. in Hernández Chiroldes 4)

The goal was to offer a portrait of representative social classes, which presumably would include trades associated with particular racial groups. For example, there appeared articles about the milkman in the cities, an occupation tied to men from the Canary Islands, as well as rural occupations, such as *el tabaquero* [tobacco grower] and *el peón de ganados* [ranch hand], also performed by Spanish men. *Los cubanos* did not include, however, even one article about Blacks in particular trades. That in spite of the fact that just as in the case of the milkman, freed Blacks and Creole mulattoes, both men and women, dominated a number of the manual-labor occupations in Cuban cities.

Costumbrista writers were in agreement with other social critics, such as historians, about the denunciation of social defects found in Cuban cities, which included White and Black elements. For example, Jacobo de la Pezuela, in his historical essay, a book entitled *Isla de Cuba* (1842) [The island of Cuba], described the gambling scene in Havana around 1833 (578). Blacks participated in these gambling enterprises, according to José de la Concha, who served as lieutenant general in Cuba. He described them in his *Memorias sobre el estado político, gobierno y administración de la Isla de Cuba* [Memoirs about the political state, government, and administration of the Island of Cuba] (1835): "Probably there were no fewer than 12,000 people who, without possessions or honest occupation made a living in the capital in the public gambling houses, both Whites and colored people, free and slaves. The idlers were innumerable . . ." (11–12).

The eventual incorporation of Blacks into formal Costumbrista articles reflected their increased importance in the highly structured, slavery-based Cuban society of the nineteenth century. Those innovations were the result, in part, of rapid changes brought into Cuba at the end of the eighteenth century. Historian de la Pezuela recorded the origins of Cuba's reformed, wealthy sugar industry as a consequence of the introduction of various types of processing in the latter part of the eighteenth century. He wrote that this new treatment produced preference for Cuban sugar in all markets and large profit margins for plantation owners. Their harvests brought them an "annual interest of twenty percent above the value of the capital investments" (333). Thus, there were born, according to de la Pezuela, "those fortunes so huge that today we see tolerance for unlimited spending for luxury despite reduced profits from products" (333).

At the heart of these fortunes was the *ingenio*, the sugarmill.[5] Throughout the nineteenth century, its machinery became more and more technical (Pérez de la Riva, *El barracón* 16). Planters abandoned use of the *trapiche*, primitive sugar extraction devices, and installed powerful steam machinery, beginning in 1820 (*El barracón* 16). The old *trapiche* had functioned with the labor of a small number of slaves. With the new extraction technology came the need for more Black workers. Newly arrived slaves populated in large numbers the fancy plantations of the nineteenth century. The images of slavery in wealthy nineteenth-century Cuba reflected the changing roles of slaves, some of whom coped with the sophisticated machinery of the sugarmills, a technology that included the train, which in 1837 allowed Cuba to reach modern status even before many European countries, including Spain (Pérez de la Riva, *La habitación* 12). That energetic, powerful, enterprising spirit would eventually become involved in the development of a Cuban nationalist spirit.

Black field hands appeared in Costumbrista articles depicted as particular types, often cast according to their tasks performed on the plantation, which were assigned according to their age. These images reflected the rigid social structure observed in Cuban slave society. Anthropologists and sociologists have documented Black populations in Cuba in the nineteenth century, dividing them into urban and rural groups (Heuman 139–43). Referring to these divisions, Franklin Knight commented that the ethnic groupings were akin to the sociological concept of castes: "The castes corresponded very roughly to the racial divisions in which membership was hereditary and defined by laws: the white population first, and then, in descending order of social rank, the free persons of color and the slaves" ("Slave Society" 112). Groups of slaves on plantations, particularly those working in sugarcane fields, were less frequently documented than the slaves or freed Blacks working in urban areas.

Speaking of the inherent division of Costumbrista articles based on type of character, Alberto Hernández Chiroldes, in his introduction to *Los cubanos pintados por sí mismos*, separates Costumbrismo into two types of works: (1) those that developed scenes or sceneries, and (2) those that explored specific types of characters. Scenic articles presented a plot line described and narrated by the author. The type-inspired articles explored qualifying characteristics or personal traits of individuals who represented a group (xiii). A further subdivision of the character types, according to Hernández Chiroldes, produced classification of (1) characters that described a trait, always negative, of a particular person; (2) characters that represented the most "singular and picturesque" habits of certain trades or professions; and (3) characters set within a specific situation or social condition (xiii). Unlike what might be expected, Black characters, particularly slaves on rural plantations, did not appear as types analyzed in *Los cubanos pintados*. In fact, there is in the list only one character associated with the powerful mills of the time, "El administrador del ingenio" [The administrator of the sugarmill], written by José María de Cárdenas y Rodríguez (1812–1882). The administrator was important because he was in charge of the management of the plantation, including decisions of punishment and rewards for the slaves, in lieu of an absentee owner, who preferred urban life to the isolation of the sugarcane plantation. Although the administrator was a repressive character because of the brutal physical treatment that he often imposed on the slaves, he was not called upon to implement the punishments. That was the duty of the overseer, a fact that was ignored in this article of customs dealing with a booming sugarcane plantation.

Salvador Bueno indicated another subdivision in Cuban articles of customs: those that center on portraits of life in the countryside versus those that deal with newly created customs of urban living (*Costumbristas* xiv). Articles about slavery, according to Bueno, introduced the reader to the indignities of that cruel institution (xiv). Descriptions of the working conditions of the slave were rather mild, perhaps because of self-censorship by the writer or because of censorship by newspapers and magazines that supported the institution of slavery.

The reason for the obvious lack of "Black articles of customs" could have been the strong censorship that Cuban abolitionist writers often spoke about (Bachiller y Morales, *Apuntes* 187–205; Knight, *Slave Society* 91). One writer affected by censorship, the Spaniard José María Andueza (1809?-?), wrote in 1837, "In Havana nothing can be printed without the official signature of the Censor and the signature by the Captain General (qtd. in Gómez del Valle y Ramírez 270, emphasis in the original). In his 1841 travelogue, *Isla de Cuba pintoresca: Recuerdos, apuntes, impresiones de dos épocas* [The picturesque island of Cuba: memories, sketches, impressions of two epochs], Andueza also denounced the heavy political censorship that Governor Tacón exerted upon local newspapers. The limits on free expression were described in terms of a censorship that served as another type of slavery:

Two political newspapers, if they can be so called, when their editors show no concern for politics, the reading of any one of its issues offers the saddest idea of the state of the press in that country: writers enslaved, oppressed by discretionary censorship in violation of laws and of the advances of the human spirit, cannot issue the most innocent political opinion. (104)

Publications in violation of official Spanish laws were not tolerated. For example, Eduardo Facciolo was executed because of publications by the newspaper of which he was editor, *La voz del pueblo cubano* [The voice of the Cuban people], an underground newspaper published 1851–1855, during a period of civil discontent against Spanish rule. The writers Ramón de Palma and Ildefonso Estrada y Zenea (1826–1912) were also implicated in the Facciolo incident; their legal case was dismissed (Riverend Brusone, *La Habana* 383). Censorship included publications from abroad; for example, the newspaper *La Verdad* [The truth] was printed in the United States and sent illegally into Cuba (382).

Cuban censorship of material about slavery was more acute than that imposed upon publications in Spain on the same subject. One notable case was the refusal to distribute in Cuba the novels by the Cuban Gertrudis Gómez de Avellaneda, who was living in Spain and had a strong reputation as a romanticist. Her novels *Dos mujeres* (1841) and *Sab* (1841) failed to clear censorship in Cuba, the former for its liberal view of marriage and the latter because of its abolitionist elements (Gómez del Valle y Ramírez 300). According to the censor responsible for keeping the books off the island, he did so because "he was informed that the first (*Sab*) contains doctrines subversive to the Island's system of slavery and contrary to the morality and good customs; the second (*Two women*) for being riddled with doctrines prejudicial to Our Holy Religion and an attack on conjugal society and a canonization of adultery" (qtd. in Pichardo Viñals, Documentos 26).

Cuban Costumbrista writers who addressed specific issues concerning slavery or the plentiful Black cultural byproducts may have intended to fulfill somewhat different functions within the restrictions imposed in the slave-driven, colonial society of Cuba. At the earliest stage of the development of the Cuban national identity, neither the Black slaves nor the Creole slaves were considered participants in the emerging national project of Cubanía. Slaves were subjects, however, of discussions about their treatment—an issue that appeared often in various sources, such as in local civil regulations, in city ordinances, or in laws granted by the Spanish crown.

A review of available publications of articles that appeared in Cuba as Costumbrista essays reveals that in spite of their large numbers, few slaves appeared as main characters or as subjects of literary significance. Critics have pointed out that Blacks were always presented in a negative light "for censure and ridicule" (Castellanos 4:90). Although some Blacks appeared in Costumbrista articles as minor literary characters, according to Castellanos and Castellanos, they were inconsequential in the national picture: "From the political and propagandist point of view they were neutral" (4:89). Like the real figures who inspired the articles, they were limited to specific settings related to institutions of slavery, such as slaves as workers at sugarmills, or freed Blacks as inhabitants of marginal urban neighborhoods. Some of these figures, the Castellanoses pointed out, symbolized the worst traits among Blacks. They represented social types specific to Cuban Black culture, such as *el curro del Manglar* (loosely translated as "the cocky Black man"), the criminal Black, the wily rascal, the ignorant fool, the lazy, opportunistic mulatta, the flamboyant mulatta, the absurd professor and the *ñáñigo* (4:90).[6]

This open bias produced not only negative images, but also inaccurate documentation of Black customs, especially those related to cultural practices associated with various religious groups in urban settings (Castellanos 4:92–93). Although it may seem that the Blacks were particular targets of the Cuban Costumbristas' scorn, this type of social profile also existed among their Spanish counterparts, who often presented negative portraits of marginal ethnic and socioeconomic groups (Varela 9). Such marginality of Black characters was within the scope of Costumbrismo, which intended to provide "a relatively transparent platform for the representation of 'Cuban' ideas and experience" (Lane 28). The Cuban Costumbrista writer was interested in offering portraits of Cuban mainstream society, a political view that often necessitated repression of slavery-related themes if the piece was to be published.

Within the minor space allocated for slaves or freed Blacks in Costumbrista articles, there was, however, a subplot that showed them restricted to terrible living conditions. Amid the biased portraits of physical descriptions and racist references, what strikes the reader today is that the Black's presence in most Costumbrista articles was intended as a lesson to be learned. Indirectly, this was a controversial comment on the development of a contested Cuban identity. The struggle to achieve national maturity, as reflected in colonial restrictions imposed by the Spanish crown, became indirectly a reflection on slavery and on the legal restrictions imposed upon freed Blacks. Even biased articles reflected the convoluted sociopolitical Cuban scene, and, most specifically, the field of action allowed for slaves and for freed Blacks and their interplay with racist power structures.

## Humanizing Slaves in a Cuban *Ingenio*: Black Laborers in Costumbrista Articles by Anselmo Suárez y Romero

> Oh Muse of grief! Give me thy crying
> Deepest, sharpest, and most sorrowful;
> May my voice be a dismal moan,

May my song be a heart-rending, ay!
If in my worship of you my faith and ardent zeal
Deserve reward,
Give me sad tears, without consolation,
To weep for immense despair.
And you, sacred indignation, you who inspire
Fierce impulses in fierce breasts,
That to the terrible rages
Of the noble heart come tightly bound,
Come, ignite my soul,
Breathe into it your severe tempests,
That facing the evil of all evils
Peace is dishonor, tranquility fades.

Concepción Arenal, "La esclavitud de los negros" in *El cancionero del esclavo*

In 1866, La Sociedad Abolicionista Española [The Spanish Abolitionist Society], based in Madrid, hosted a poetry contest on the theme of the abolition of slavery.[7] There were seventy-six entries. This substantial response perhaps illustrated national opposition to slavery, despite pressure by Cuban plantation owners, who demanded maintenance of slavery as their primary requirement for supporting Spanish control over Cuba. The introduction to the winning poems, published as *El cancionero del esclavo* [The slave's songbook], indicated the scope of the project, along with a provision to avoid legal conflicts. Far away from Cuban shores, the subject of abolition was presented carefully to compassionate readers, praising the poems as humanitarian and not as abolitionist:

> some are about charity in general, rather than about the abolition of slavery, which, being an act of such high virtue, cannot be confused with it; [ . . . ] others contain thoughts that, although sublime and generous, could be interpreted as contrary to the legal order with which this essentially humanitarian and peace-loving society has the duty of complying; others, in brief, either digressed too much, their authors carried away by the liveliness of their imagination, or they gave concrete form to only one aspect of the theme proposed by the Society. (10–11)

Slavery in Cuba had become a subject of international discussion in publications that appeared outside the island. Cuban abolitionists, led by the plantation owner and poet Domingo del Monte (1804–1853), formed a group that frequently met to discuss politics and to read their unpublished literary manuscripts. They often received international visitors, who were eager to hear about the thriving Cuban slavery, in particular the mighty sugarcane plantations. Through these foreign abolitionists, the world would come to know about major violations to regulations pertaining to the humane treatment of slaves, including abuses in physical punishments.[8] These visitors kept Cuban Costumbristas abreast of international efforts to promote abolitionism. One important visitor, Dr. Richard Madden, who was in Cuba as a British abolitionist commissioner overseeing violations to the suspension of the slave trade, became an important link between local abolitionists and Costumbrista writers, such as del Monte, and the international movement.

Costumbrista's exploration of the treatment of slaves was so severely censored that many aspects remained virtually unexplored. The many regulations about slavery and frequent items in daily publications, such as announcements of slave sales, kept the public aware, however, of certain details of the Cuban slave market, including horrific practices, such as those of the slave hunter. As restrictions on the slave trade affected the number of slaves available for sale, the activities of hunters of runaway slaves became more widely known by newspaper ads. The inhumane practices were effectively kept away from Costumbrista literature of the time. The newspapers' snippet views of the plantations were counterbalanced by more positive images of slavery, such as popular engravings that presented an almost exotic view of the sugarcane plantations, ignoring the gloomy working settings of these facilities.

The Costumbrista Anselmo Suárez y Romero's articles were unusual at the time of their publication because of their attempts to depict the slaves' grim chores and the often fatal workplace accidents in sugarmills. Critic González Echevarría considers his Costumbrista writings "the closest to being an ethnographer" (53). Slaves' lives on plantations were rarely examined except in trial documents when slaves faced criminal charges, usually after their capture as runaways. Foreign visitors, particularly British abolitionists, attempted to unmask the complex ways in which Cuban plantation owners provided slaves for their mills, even after the British-Spanish treaty of 1820 imposed a halt on the slave trade. Most of the travelers' accounts lacked the personal involvement that Suárez y Romero displayed in his articles. Similarities between data handled by Suárez y Romero, including legal references to slavery, and reports offered by international visitors, published abroad after their visits to Cuba, indicate, however, his in-depth legal and socioeconomic knowledge of Cuban slavery.

Although a number of Suárez y Romero's many articles remained unpublished, his book *Colección de artículos* [Collection of articles] contains seven articles that publicly explored specific aspects of the lives of slaves and of their particular tasks on a plantation. The articles have titles with descriptive references to traditions associated with life on a plantation: "Ingenios" [Sugarmills], "Bohíos" [Huts], "Los domingos en los ingenios" [Sundays in the sugarmills],

"El guardiero" [The guardsman], "La casa de trapiche" [The cane-press build-ing], "El corte de caña" [The cane harvest], and "Los bohíos al oscurecer" [Huts at dusk]. A collection by Salvador Bueno of works by Costumbrista writers includes one more, "El cementerio del ingenio" [The cemetery at the sugarmill]. Suárez y Romero offered a portrait of a rich slave culture thriving on sugarcane plantations. Although thematically Suárez y Romero restricted his articles to censure of the miserable circumstances of slavery practices, he celebrated coun-try Black life values as examples of the slaves' struggles to maintain their tradi-tions in spite of objectification of them as slaves. Cautiously, Suárez y Romero indicated that the Blacks' protection of tribal traditions was a system of rebel-lion that, in fact, was to be preserved as part of the developing Cuban identity.

Anselmo Suárez y Romero was born in Havana on April 21, 1818, into a fam-ily active in local politics. His father, José Ildefonso Suárez, friend of and con-sultant to the Spanish governor of Cuba, Miguel Tacón, became involved in 1838 in a "certain accusation," a political crisis that forced Suárez to move to the countryside (Cabrera Saqui 7). There he lived briefly until he left the island for Spain, where he died in Seville in 1843. Why he left Cuba without his family re-mains unexplained (Roig de Leuchsenring, *Los escritores* 169). The critic Bueno labeled Suárez y Romero a member of a fallen "Patrician family" (*Bosquejo* 24).

Suárez y Romero received a bachelor's degree from the Real y Pontificia Uni-versidad in Havana. In 1838 he and his impoverished family (his mother and his six siblings) moved to Puentes Grandes, and at the end of that year to a plantation named Surinam in Güines, in the province of Havana. He had had to interrupt his law studies at the University of Havana. He took on the education of his younger brother, Lucas, who, according to Suárez y Romero, two years later "woke up completely mindless" (qtd. in Cabrera Saqui 8). His brother's disablement and the surroundings of the plantation, particularly the beauty of the Cuban countryside, had an impact on Suárez y Romero that he carefully documented: "I was giving him classes in the sugarmill, far away from all noise, caressed by the breezes, with the magnificence of our fields before us, listening to the murmur of trees and looking toward the pure blue sky" (qtd. in Cabrera Saqui 8).

This perfect stage was in contrast to dangerous epidemics, mainly cholera, that frequently plagued the plantations. There was constant fear of that evident in his personal letters.

On the plantation Suárez y Romero managed to write Costumbrista articles, essays of literary and sociopolitical criticism, and a longer Costumbrista article, "Biografía de Carlota Valdés" [Biography of Carlota Valdés]. He recorded his experiences in overseeing the functions of the sugarmill at the request of Domingo del Monte, a well-known poet and abolitionist, whose literary gatherings between 1831 until his exile in 1844 brought together in Havana a number of writers and intellectuals who supported abolition (Bueno, *Domingo del Monte* 10; Fernández de Castro 37–42).[9]

Del Monte's contribution to the Cuban Costumbrista movement was summarized in fellow writer José Jacinto Milanés's praise of his literary patron: "I was seeking a way of writing Costumbrista articles about our country, resolved, because of your advice, to paint our Cuban things and to put aside [Spanish] peninsular things" (qtd. in Bueno, *Domingo del Monte* 11). His association with del Monte was pivotal in his early career literary career. In a letter dated June 25, 1842, to del Monte, Suárez y Romero attributed to him the beginning of "my love of writing" (*Centón* 76).

Commissioned by del Monte, between 1838 and 1839 Suárez y Romero wrote the manuscript of *Francisco*, an abolitionist novel. It was not published until 1880, in an edition printed in New York. Del Monte also collected proabolition texts, such as the autobiography of a former slave who became a poet, Juan Francisco Manzano, edited by Suárez y Romero, and *Petrona y Rosalía*, an abolitionist novel by Félix Tanco y Bosmeniel. Del Monte entrusted the manuscripts to the British abolitionist Richard Madden (Díaz iv).[10]

Del Monte was also an important connection between up-and-coming writers and prospective publishers in Spain. For example, in an 1838 letter to the editor of *Correo Nacional de Madrid*, del Monte complained that censorship of Ramón de Palma had forced the young writer "to speak only of love" because "what the shackled Havana press produces is reduced to the narrow limit" (del Monte, *Ensayos* 206). As in much of his correspondence, del Monte signed this letter as Gonzalo Fernández de Oviedo, a reference to the Spanish chronicler Gonzalo Fernández de Oviedo y Valdés (1478–1557), whose *Historia general y natural de las Indias* (1547) [General and natural history of the Indies] devotes considerable attention to Cuba's natural and political history.

The 1830s had been marked by slave revolts in Cuba (Fernández Robaina 15; Cepero Bonilla 54–55), in a tumultuous period that by 1870 had produced the deaths of more than a thousand slave owners, overseers and administrators (Moreno Fraginals, "Aportes" 41). By 1838, Cuba was at its peak of economic power, as one of the world's richest sugar producers (Knight, *Slave* 3). That position required importation of large numbers of slaves: "In two generations the black element of the population had risen to be the majority in the society" (Knight, *Slave* 22). These facts necessitated the presence of Madden in Havana, who was investigating violations of Cuban-Spanish international treaties concerning the slave trade.[11]

Madden's interest in collecting abolitionist literary material from Cuban writers speaks of the importance of these types of texts as part of his strategy to present his legal case against the Spanish government. His interaction with Cuban activists also increased the interest of local writers in testimonial accounts by foreign visitors, such as Madden, who spoke directly against violations of the human rights of slaves by Cuban slave owners and against the local authorities' support of illegal shipments of slaves into Cuba.

Suárez y Romero displayed interest in evading the censorship of publications in Cuba. A true intellectual, he could speak and translate Latin, Italian, French and Portuguese, with "admirable accuracy" (Roig de Leuchsenring, *Los escritores* 171). His knowledge of foreign languages, particularly French and Portuguese, would have kept him aware of numerous writings in France and Portugal on controversial issues pertaining to slavery. These languages were also useful for communicating with the many foreign travelers who came to Cuba attracted by the modern machinery of the sugarmills, mainly 1840–1870 (Ely 508). The presence of foreign travelers visiting Cuba became a literary motif of Costumbrista writers.

In 1840 Suárez y Romero returned to Havana, where eventually he became a well-known professor, offering courses at various institutions of higher learning in Havana. He became a mentor of future important political and literary figures. For example, he taught José Martí at the Colegio San Pablo (*Diccionario de la literatura cubana* 989). In spite of these teaching posts, financially he had a rather precarious life because of his large family and their struggling family business.

In 1866 he finished a law degree, with a thesis that posed the question of whether the means of sustenance could increase at the same rate as the population. The choice of this subject may have reflected his firsthand observations of commercial business at the Surinam sugarmill, a subject widely discussed among sugarcane barons (Moreno Fraginals, *Sugarmill* 144). Suárez y Romero hated to work at the plantation—a fact fully documented in his letters to his mentor, del Monte, and to his friend and fellow writer, José Zacarías González del Valle.

Suárez y Romero never practiced law. Perhaps he felt overwhelmed by the increasing political tensions in Cuba. Such apprehension was evident in a letter from the Cuban patriot José Martí, who, writing from Mexico on October 16, referred to a letter that he had sent to Suárez y Romero during Martí's undated imprisonment in Cuba: "I believe that I wrote to you once from prison and you did not understand an anguish of mine; this is a small, forgotten debt, which I shall repay you with the lively affection that I have for your worth and noble character" (qtd. in Cabrera Saqui 13). Suárez y Romero did admit that he had not answered Martí, but denied that he had been afraid to get involved in Martí's political platform: "It was not from fear of being compromised, since he was imprisoned for political causes, a circumstance that never has intimidated me from visiting other friends in like cases. But for not answering his letter I had reasons that perhaps were unfounded, and I find it impossible to reveal them here" (qtd. in Cabrera Saqui 13). Whether his hesitation was due to fear of getting involved in public political controversies has not been documented; however, his Costumbrista articles seem to indicate his willingness to embark on the controversial subject of the horrors in slavery practices.

Suárez y Romero may not have participated actively in the Cuban political scene, but he dared to publish his *Colección de artículos* [Collection of articles] in 1859 with the support of del Monte and the well-known Costumbrista writer Cirilo Villaverde. This was a change from the original title, "Estudios de costumbres campestres" [Studies in rural customs], as he had indicated in a letter to del Monte, dated October 21, 1839 (Bueno, *Del Monte* 100). He was hoping then that the articles would be published in spite of censorship: "since if it does not pass them, my friends will read them, and in the future I shall write no more while there are obstacles" (100). Suárez y Romero's original concept was to publish the book as a compilation of letters, in the fashion of an "album," a favorite literary concept of the time.[12]

In a letter to del Monte, dated June 25, 1842, Suárez y Romero sent his mentor one of his articles, which he referred to as a "letter." He asked del Monte a favor. "Please be so kind as to correct scrupulously whatever defect you may find, knowing that I shall not become angry if you just tell me that it isn't worth a red cent" (qtd. in del Monte, *Centón* 76). There is no recorded documentation of the reasons for the twenty-year delay in the publication of the collection.

It is clear that Suárez y Romero continued to write "letters," in spite of the censorship exercised on his articles: "The rest of the letters will be in the style of the one that I wrote in 1838 in Puentes-Grandes" (*Centón* 76).[13] José Zacarías González del Valle, in a letter dated June 25, 1839, to Suárez y Romero, acknowledged having received one of these "letters of customs" (134). González del Valle shared del Monte's positive criticism of that article of customs, saying, "I read your letter about the sugar plantations, which I judge to be most beautiful and perfect in the descriptions; today I carried it to Domingo [del Monte] and he praised it highly; especially to his liking are the poetic colorings, purity and sonority of the sentence where you describe the green-gray plains of the plantation, forming a horizon, plains stripped of abundant trees, where one or another palm remains to deplore with perennial murmur of its stalks its vanished companions" (135). This preoccupation with the loss of the landscape was a recurrent theme in Suárez y Romero's articles.

Suárez y Romero hesitated to present his articles to the public. According to his introduction to the collection, for eight years he had intended to make his work public. At the urging of some unidentified "close friends for whom I have high regard," he agreed to publish his book (*Colección de artículos* n.p.). In an unusually brief introduction, of barely two paragraphs, he attempted to explain why he had chosen not to write "several pages to explain the circumstances that have driven me to write on the matters treated here" (n.p.). Believing that it would be better "to allow the readers complete freedom to judge," he ended his argument with an indirect defense of his patriotism and his love for Cuba: "Permit me to say only that if with this book I do not expect to enlighten my fatherland, I believe at least that it does not contain anything that can pervert the heart; and also to make clear that I would regret profoundly any attribution to me of intentions that I am far from harboring" (n.p.).

Suárez y Romero's indirect apology to the political authorities—Spanish and local representatives of the colonial empire—was not exceptional. Other writers dealing with taboo subjects such as slavery often wrote apologetic defenses, which highlighted their love for the fatherland. According to the critic Raúl Cepero Bonilla, it was not until the War of Independence of 1868 that Cuban intellectuals openly opposed Spanish rule in Cuba, including "a resolute position in facing the phenomenon of slavery" (23).

Suárez y Romero's collection of multithematic articles was most likely his own selection, deemed to be politically innocuous in order to evade censorship. Other Costumbrista writers cautioned him about the way he should address subjects related to slavery. He wrote of that in his letters to del Monte and González del Valle. The published result was Suárez y Romero's choice to depict the landscape, fauna, and flora of the countryside surrounding an unidentified sugarcane plantation, presumably the Ingenio Surinam, which he knew so well. He stressed elements of life on the plantation, including a well-developed view of slavery, in articles that have been described as "very formal . . . because of his concern for both the white and black populations of the island" (Suárez-Murias 376). His images of the rural landscape are strong, for which he has been labeled "the singer of Cuban nature" (Roig de Leuchsenring, *Los escritores* 169).

In Suárez y Romero's interest for the landscape, he spoke about the encroachment of sugarcane upon the formerly green plains, a major problem throughout the nineteenth century (Moreno Fraginals, *The Sugarmill* 20, 77; Marrero 20). The historian Ramón de la Sagra in his *Historia económica-política y estadística de la isla de Cuba* [Economic-political and statistical history of the island of

Cuba] (1831) wrote about the destruction of flora and its consequences to the environment:

> People will see the temperature go up and the rains become less frequent . . . there will be disappearance of the abundant, beneficial dew, which makes up for the lack of water during the droughts . . . and in times of great heat they will not experience the refreshing breeze from the woods or the soothing fragrance of wild flowers. In short, wherever trees are annihilated, a scene of loneliness and of death will replace the smiling spectacle of a young, wild nature, that offered to reward with usury the efforts of well managed industry. (Qtd. in Cantero 62)[14]

None of Suárez y Romero's critics have fully recognized the limits imposed upon the writer's expression in order to avoid censorship or to conform to good aesthetics (Castellanos 2:60). Manuel de la Cruz, among the earliest of Suárez y Romero's critics, strongly reproved his tendency toward excessive praise of nature: "Anselmo Suárez y Romero, a gaudy stylist, meticulous, flowery, who had rehearsed in descriptive genre picturing types and sketching landscapes of Cuban nature, types and landscapes in which naturalness is sacrificed to the enchantments and music of style" (*Obras* 58). Another similar criticism pointed out his highly romanticized descriptions of Cuban nature: "sometimes sinning because of too much affectation" (Mitjans, *Historia* 215).

José Lezama Lima, a more modern critic and poet, explained Suárez y Romero's attachment to nature as an attribute of a romantic poet. "Romantic poetry expresses our countryside, the terrible anxieties that are arising in the evolution of the nation's configuration. Solitude, exile and death batter our poets" ("El romanticismo" 249). This excessive fascination with the landscape was in line with an exhilaration appropriate for the romantic spirit, of which Cuban poetry had outstanding exponents among Latin American writers.

In "Devaneos y recuerdos del campo" [Idle pursuits and memories of the countryside] (1846), Suárez y Romero fully developed a concept repeated in most of his "sugarcane plantation" articles: a slave owner, visiting his plantation during a holiday, describes the layout of the *ingenio*. The autobiographical echoes are notable. In a letter to del Monte, dated October 21, 1839, Suárez y Romero lamented that a cousin and a brother had become seriously ill, so that he had to "manage the plantation during the interim," a task that he satirically described as "a job that with my ideas, I will give away to anybody" (del Monte, *Centón* 100). His experiences at the plantation were very negative. He described himself to his friend Gómez del Valle as "lonely and exiled" (8). His dislike for administrative tasks may also explain his preference to ignore the harsh labor at the mill in favor of reflections about the natural surroundings.

Through an unidentified narrator, the reader of "Devaneos" is led into the plantation and its surrounding countryside. The marvelous landscape, in a classical *locus amoenus*, or the perfect place for contemplation, reflects examples of natural animism:

> The breeze perfumed by the flowers' fragrance sweetly caresses our temples like a mother's kisses and its invisible breath makes the harp of the Cuban fields, the green stalk of the Indian palm, moan like a sigh, like a complaint, like a sob, like the Oh's torn from the soul when, not able to contain the love that embraces us, we weep tears of fire. (295)

This phenomenon, and other natural wonders, such as listening to the animals and insects in a "night of magic moon" (296), inspired the narrator to "meditate, and imagining that in the same place a sigh was breathed by others or a happy song was sung, there passes through my soul that vague, sweet or heart-rendering sadness of memories" (297). The countryside offered Suárez y Romero not only a respite from the busy life of Havana, but also the means for his entrance into a reflective state of mind.

The conclusion of "Devaneos" is not, however, melancholy praise of the Cuban landscape, as one might expect. The narrator's daydreaming, surrounded by the "august silence of the night," is suddenly interrupted by a sound from the plantation's bell tower, followed by the yells of the overseer, who is calling the slaves to gather in order to stop a fire that has broken out in the sugarcane fields. The action line is extremely short. The foreman's shouts and the bell's sounds make the slaves "speedily get up and a few moments afterward they are seen running in noisy excitement toward the supposed site of the fire" (297). The narrator, an anonymous eyewitness of these events, remains aloof from the emergency. Finally, he cries out, "I don't know why, I don't know why a tear flows from my eyes" (297). The weeping is left unexplained, and there is no direct acknowledgment of the slaves' roles in saving the sugarcane field from the fire, a common occurrence on plantations. Fires were often set on purpose by the slaves as a way to protest the hard work.

Suárez y Romero's fascination with the Cuban landscape is evident in several of his other articles, although it may have been a pretext for introducing the figure of the Black slave. The articles place the narrator, himself an eyewitness, at specific geographical points within the expansive Cuban landscape. This is, for example, the case in "La colina" [The hill] (1849), from which he often observes the sunset and, in the distance, his own house, "the white walls of a house surrounded by mangos where in another time I was blessed" (298). This is one of only a few times that the master's house, known as *la casa grande*, appears in his articles. These houses were architectural jewels, and their landscapes were often quite elaborate (Pérez de la Riva, *La habitación* 56–63). Even the mention in passing of the mango trees seems to imply the lush landscape of the house, because those trees were imported into Cuba to become part of the plantations' well-groomed landscapes (Pérez de la Riva, *La habitación* 55). This subject is barely treated in his articles; its absence leaves to the reader's imagination the lavish life of the master in contrast to the harsh reality of the slave.

In the lush vegetation of the hill, one tree in particular, the ceiba, was personified; it welcomed the climber with "arms outstretched" (300). Although the ceiba tree had religious significance for some African groups in Cuba, that fact is not evident in the narrator's praise (Cabrera, *El monte* 149). Instead, he makes an oblique reference to the first mass celebrated in Cuba under a ceiba: "that sacred tree that was the first under whose shade your sacrifices for the sake of the human race were here remembered" (300). This episode, which had become part of the symbolic construction of the Cuban nation, was repeated almost verbatim in Miguel Rodríguez Ferrer's *Naturaleza y civilización de la grandiosa isla de Cuba* [Nature and civilization of the great island of Cuba] (1876).

Suárez y Romero's sketches of nature minimized or ignored the presence of the slaves in spite of the fact that they, because of their work in the fields, were proximate to nature. Examples include "Palmares" [Palm tree grove] (1852), in which Suárez y Romero praised the beauty of the palm grove, which he declares his favorite tree: "There is no tree more beautiful than the palm . . . there is no paintbrush that can paint them, no poet that can sing of them worthily on his lyre" (304). The narrator's wish is that, as a true native, born on Cuban soil, he be called to sing the palm grove's praise, like others before him:

> I know that you receive worship in the heart of all sensitive creatures, I know that you are admired and loved by even the foreigner born in distant climates, by the very African who with his sweat waters the fertile land of Cuba; but, oh, those of us who first saw light at your side, those of us who as children have played among you, those of us who have grown up at the same time that new knots were appearing on your trunks, we must look upon you with even more enthusiasm. (305)

As in the case of the ceiba, there is no reference to the *palma real* [royal palm] as a tree with a connection to Creole Black religious devotion.

The most striking element in this positive characterization of the "Africans," or slaves born in Africa, is the narrator's inclusion of them among "creatures of sensitivity." He excludes slaves, however, as active admirers of the palm tree, choosing rather to present foreign visitors' frequent praise of its beauty in the Cuban landscape, an image repeated in other articles.

Suárez y Romero knew that for his articles to be published, they had to focus on "the green plains of the sugarcane plantations where the palms weep because of the absence of the cedars and the mahogany trees that the axe will cut down" (1839 letter to del Monte, *Centón* 71). Another article, "El sol en el palmar" [The sun in the palm grove] (1854), stresses the beauty of the Cuban landscape, displayed for an "erudite and sensitive foreigner"—a woman who was visiting the narrator's properties came to admire it (316). The role of international visitors as characters is important. They provided Costumbrista writers with "a naïve amazement [ . . . ] in order to justify himself to the reader of the theme of his article" (Varela 7). While the narrator placed himself as "mediator between the gaze of the foreign observer and his own culture," he craftily allowed the visitor's opinion, not his own, to provide the concluding remarks (González Echevarría 54). As in previous articles, the narrator attempts to impress his visitor on a promenade into the countryside, away from the plantation and the harsh noises of the slave workers. Repeating some of his customary romantic language, he proudly shows his guest his favorite spot for listening to "the laments, the complaints, the caresses, the sobs, the exclamations of the breeze among the elegant crowns of the palm grove" (316). This moment of sentiment provokes the usual sentimental tears from both characters. The silence is broken by the foreign woman, who speaks in "one of those conversations in which intelligence both functions and wanders, in which there is no touch of anything frivolous, and which shows that a woman can also be concerned about the most transcendental matters" (317).

One of the woman's questions is about Cuba's racial ratio, perhaps in response to her observations of the slaves at work. The narrator does not answer her questions, nor does he take his visitor to the spot where he often spies on the slaves' activities. The ending is symbolic of the narrator's concept of the Cuban landscape, an extension of his understanding of the Cuban national spirit, an emerging Cubanness that denied the slave a significant presence, in favor of "the splendid fields of my country, the palm grove lighted by the sun's first gleam, and the ineffable sounds of the wind among the stalks" (318).

The poor conditions of the slave quarters did not appear as part of Suárez y Romero's articles on landscape. In a 1839 letter to del Monte, Suárez y Romero described his life on the plantation in rather sad terms: "Isolated on the plantation, seeing day and night only enormous factories, monotonous and insipid, the grounds, the cane fields, and then to complete the sadness of the picture, without seeing any spectacle other than that of miserable men working endlessly for others" (del Monte, *Centón* 38). This dark description of the *ingenios* was in sharp contrast to other elaborate portraits written at the time.[15]

In traditional Costumbrista writing, Blacks, particularly slaves, were left out as representatives of rural traditions, in spite of the fact that they too were farmers, and local peasants sought out their products (Barnet 23; trans. 26). Instead, the peasants became the preferred protagonists of Costumbristas, who placed them as a central entity or depository of an autochthonous rural Cuban culture. Suárez y Romero fancily labeled the peasant a "labrador" (294) in "Devaneos y recuerdos del campo," a farmer who appears as a mere background shadow in his articles.[16] In "La colina" [The hill], there is another passing glimpse of him as a shadow character: "a farmer who leads toward the houses the team of elegant oxen" (301). The narrator emphasizes the elegance of the oxen, in contrast to the plain *labrador*, who remains underdescribed. Suárez y Romero did not place the *labrador* either as part of the plantation working crew or as buyer of the slaves' produce.

Also not stated by Suárez y Romero are the historical data that traced the rivalry between slaves and farmers. One comment from a Lieutenant General José de la Concha described in 1853 this social tension:

> The guagiros [*sic*] or farmers of Cuba have always been the first and principal repressive force in Blacks' uprisings: from them come the farm overseers, in charge of the control of slaves and, consequently, responsible for imposition and execution of punishments. (24)

Another historian, J. M. de Andueza, in his *Isla de Cuba pintoresca* [Picturesque island of Cuba] (1841), described the brave actions of a farm manager, Antonio Orihuela, who, aided by "spirited farmers," successfully stopped a slave rebellion in 1812 (174).

Often the peasants lost their lands to the growing sugarmills, which turned fields of coffee and tobacco into sugarcane plantations (Guerra y Sánchez, Industria 62). Suárez y Romero clearly preferred slaves to his farmer neighbors. As shadow characters, his peasants remained nameless, whereas some of the slaves eventually had names and personal story lines. His indifference toward the Cuban peasant, who would eventually be known as a *guajiro*, was unusual among Costumbrista writers. Suárez y Romero did write at least one other article inspired by *guajiro* culture. A letter from José Z. González del Valle, dated January 3, 1840, to Suárez y Romero, acknowledged his receipt of a "letter," entitled "Guajiros" (174), which, unfortunately, González del Valle had not had time to read. That letter was published as "Guajiros" [Peasants] in 1840 (Bueno, *Costumbristas* 297–300). Suárez y Romero also had planned a project to gather "country verses and songs" (González del Valle 127). *Décimas*, the traditional poetic form of the Cuban *guajiro*, would become associated with "native" customs of the Cuban countryside.[17]

Juan Francisco Valerio (1829?-1878), in his collection of satirical articles of customs entitled *Cuadros sociales* [Social portraits] (1876), also displayed a negative view of the peasant. His article "En el campo" [In the countryside], criticized the *guajiro*'s habit of purchasing slave-grown produce: "But their commerce is not what you see, but in the hen that the Black of a farmer brings to sell and in order not to carry it back, he lets it go for tobacco or for a little rum and as with the hen [there is trade] of sugarloaf, of a bunch of tobacco, a big bag of coffee, of a third of a smoked pig" (159–60). In their contact with Blacks, particularly with slaves, with whom they traded agricultural goods, *guajiros* often took an adversarial position.

Not all writers displayed a strong negative sentiment against peasants. Manuel Mariano de Acosta and Antonio Pérez de Guzmán in 1830 made the following statements about the role of peasants, including their perceived rivalry with rural slaves:

Young White agriculturalists understand farm work perfectly in all its ramifications. With equal intelligence they handle harvests and living within their means, taming and teaching oxen and horses; they manage the plow, the hoe and the sharp scythe as well as they load and drive a cart. In general, they are lively, strong, spirited and well disposed [ . . . ]. Blacks are strong in labor, rustic, remarkable in great heat; but they are never equal to any White youth in aptitude, mastery and universality of operations, which the latter execute with skillful expedition and speed. (412–13)

The runaway slave Esteban Montejo in Miguel Barnet's *Biografía de un cimarrón* [*Biography of a Runaway Slave*] recognized that *guajiros* took advantage of slaves because, restricted to the plantation, Blacks were naïve and lacked finesse in the arts of haggling and selling their produce: "Truth is that the blacks were honest. Since they didn't know much yet, being honest just came naturally. They sold their things very cheap" (23; trans. 26). Montejo's opinion of the *guajiro*'s loyalty to the plantation owner explained the slave's hatred of the peasant, who, as Lieutenant General de la Concha had expressed, had close ties with the plantation owners: "*Guajiros* in those days lived better than people imagine. Almost every day they got a bonus from the masters. They were friendly to each other and did their dirty work together" (46–47; trans. 49).

Suárez y Romero preferred snapshots of slaves to stories of the *guajiro*. He severely limited, however, his recording of slave lives to specific physical activities on the sugarcane plantation. Writing to del Monte, in a 1839 letter, Suárez y Romero indicated that "I have experienced such a liking to observe the excesses of those [White overseers] and the suffering of the second [slaves], such pleasure in studying the customs conceived in slavery, rare and infinitely varied customs" (*Centón* 38). It is, however, evident that he explored only certain exhausting tasks, usually the maintenance of the sugarcane fields (caring for and cutting sugarcane) and a few of the steps in the extraction of sugarcane juice. He also went into the slaves' living quarters (*bohíos*), straw huts that served as primitive dwellings. In these choices Suárez y Romero was not different from the foreign travelers, particularly the British abolitionists, who often cried out against the slaves' exhausting work schedules. Cuban historian Manuel Moreno Fraginals explained that at the peak of production by the sugarmill in the 1840s, exploitation of slave labor was calculated to the extreme degree bearable within a previously estimated period of a slave's useful life ("Aportes" 28). Moreno Fraginals quoted two British abolitionist informants, J. Higgins and James Kennedy. The latter was one of the wisest observers on whom English diplomats depended. Kennedy's denunciations spoke about eighteen-hour working schedules for the slaves: "I have been an eye-witness of it . . . during the harvest time they seem reduced to madness, exhausted, totally depleted" (28–29).

Perhaps following the style of foreign visitors and seeking to complement their data, Suárez y Romero set out to describe the physical layout of the sugarcane plantations. His inspiration may have been the numerous manuals published throughout the nineteenth century as instructional material for the proper operation of sugarmills. His articles recorded the machinery associated with sugar production: the press, the huge *calderas* [boilers], and the buildings such as *casas de purga* [purge houses] for specific functions in the extraction of sugar from the *guarapo* [sugar cane juice]. That advanced machinery had displaced the slave as a subject of Costumbrista articles.

Suárez y Romero was taken aback by the hardship of slaves' duties on the plantation. In an 1839 letter to del Monte he spoke directly about this, referring to the slaves as "unfortunate men working ceaselessly for others" (*Centón* 38). In fact, he never characterized them as slaves. He repeated that the Blacks were "a race of wretched men under the power of a more fortunate race, that, inhumanly takes advantage of their efforts and their sweat" (38).

There was real interest in Cuba for information about the sugarcane mills. For example, in the graphic arts, the Spaniard Víctor Landaluze (1830–1889), between 1855 and 1857 provided a series of engravings for a travelogue collection entitled *Los ingenios: Colección de vistas de los principales ingenios de azúcar de la Isla de Cuba*; [Sugarmills: A collection of views of the main sugarmills on the island of Cuba] (Laplante). In that book Landaluze traced the history of and the current state of the most innovative sugarcane plantations of the time. His attention was mostly focused on the advanced machinery for the production of sugar, not the presence of the slave workers. The slaves appeared barely noticeable as miniature figures next to the imposing mechanical devices that allowed Cuba to become the world's largest sugar producer.

In common with Landaluze, Suárez y Romero drew themes extensively from many of the wonders of a booming technology, imported mainly from the United States and from Great Britain. One notable difference in Suárez y Romero's depiction of this sophisticated mill was his inclusion of slaves as handlers of the machinery and not the White technicians (often foreigners) who supervised the slaves' operations. In "La casa del trapiche" [The cane-press building], Suárez y Romero's central theme was the steam-operated extractor of cane juice; he praised modern machinery: "the voracious steam machine, like a mythical monster, rapidly swallowed all the cane thrown by the workers into the long, shiny cylinders" (262). Unlike Landaluze's engravings, in which miniature figures of the slaves seemed to attempt to disappear among the huge operational components of the various mechanical devices, in Suárez y Romero's articles the slaves appeared as masters of the machines that they were forced to operate, in a cycle that included little beyond heavy manual labor. In this handling, which Suárez y Romero bravely depicted, slaves would suffer accidents, which often led to their deaths.

Suárez y Romero intentionally wrote these essays from a historical perspective so characteristic of Costumbrismo. He spoke about the movement in his letter to del Monte, dated July 1839, describing the purpose of his plantation essays, which he labeled "letters of customs." The intended effect of the letters was stated in terms analogous to a sick body: "that may touch the wounds requiring cure as well as possible" (Centón 71). His interest in providing an accurate historical portrait of the sugarmill is particularly evident in "La casa del trapiche," written in 1853 at the peak of Cuba's international domination as a producer of sugar. He attributed to the steam-operated mill Cuba's grand entrance into the modern world and also the country's increased need for slaves: "Not many years ago in my country all the sugarmills were run by oxen; harvests on the plantations scarcely exceeded a thousand cases; the land acreage of one of these farms was not great; the numbers of black slaves were few, compared with those of many sugarcane plantations today. Today the intent is to make and have on a high scale. The deafening and civilizing steam moves the hammers of the mills, and the foot once placed on the infinite paths of progress, has to walk along it without stopping" (266–67). That progress, Suárez y Romero continued, involved destruction of his beloved countryside, which had started to collapse because of the marvels of modern technology, such as the arrival of the train, which was the mode of transportation between the mills and the shipping harbors. The train was at the center of modernity; it placed Cuba among the most advanced nations in the West (Zanetti and García). This view of a Cuba modernized at the expense of a ruined countryside was also the subject of work by other Cubans and foreign travelers.

Suárez y Romero offered, however, rather passive descriptions of the slaves' work. His portraits blended efficient slave workers with modern machinery, as illustrated in "La casa del trapiche." Blacks labor at the center of a busy sugarmill, observed (perhaps supervised) by an unidentified White male narrator: "I used to look at the Blacks going up and down from the loads of cane to the sugar mill. I would look toward the boiler room, [ . . . ], I looked at the thick beams and the robust posts that formed those buildings of colossal dimensions, I looked at the machine's wheels turning, so many pieces moving in admirable harmony, the extremely bright fire that fed it" (266). That heavy physical work prompts him to end this article with an invitation to reflection, a literary device common in his articles. Tired of observing the "hard tasks of the Blacks" (269), at one o'clock in the morning, with the arrival of a new shift of slaves, he decides to retire to his living quarters.

This exit is often repeated in other articles, almost a symbolic withdrawal from the tragic real scenery that the narrator did not cover. Suárez y Romero expressed a deep sense of defeat in his letter to del Monte on October 21, 1839: "So it seems that I am destined to see evils in my fatherland and not be able to remedy them" (*Centón* 100).

Even withdrawal into less disturbing scenery continues to remind the narrator of the evils of slavery. As he attempts to find solace in the lush nature surrounding the sugarmill, the pleasures of such an experience are interrupted by the insidious reach of slave activities at the sugarmill: "There in the distance one could see the river's pool bathed in light. I listened again to the screeching of the wagons of refuse from the sugarcane, and I do not know whether from joy or from sadness, tears ran down my cheeks" (269). Although there is no direct explanation of his seemingly excessive sentimentality, the closing lines suggest the real reason for his tears: "From my bed I heard later the noise of the sugarmill and the Blacks singing. Sensitive creatures know what one experiences then" (269). The reference to "sensitive creatures" remains unqualified, although it seems plausible that it refers to the slaves, some of whom are singing in order to make the work less oppressive. This was one of Suárez y Romero's most revealing statements of abolitionist sentiment; however, it was framed as part of his overwhelming emotions that only Cuban nature and slave songs seemed to soothe.

One significant feature of Suárez y Romero's articles was his division of slaves into two basic groups, following the national trend of the time: the bozales, or African-born, and the criollos, meaning Creoles, or those born in Cuba. For Suárez y Romero, who had set out to collect the sugarmill's "strange customs," the criollos' imperfect knowledge of African cultures, including native languages, made them less credible as a trustworthy source and, therefore, less important as literary characters (Suárez y Romero's letter to del Monte, *Centón* 38). The bozal slaves' monolingual limitation disqualified them, however, as prospective protagonists of any of the essays; they remained isolated from the Spanish-speaking slaves, the Creoles, who became Suárez y Romero's most thoroughly explored literary characters.

That preference led him to consider them better workers and more loyal servants to their masters. This prejudice was not specific to Suárez y Romero; other Costumbrista writers, and even Black writers—for example, the runaway slave Esteban Montejo—had similar biases against bozales. The choice of character type severely restricted his writing about African-based cultural productions, limiting his observations specifically to the Creoles' music, drumming and songs. There were no references, for example, to the slaves' religious practices, perhaps because those rituals were performed away from the prying eyes of a curious master or, as Montejo stressed in his memoir, those activities were confined to the closely knit bozal community.

Also absent from Suárez y Romero's articles was commentary on the lax religious education of slaves, although it was mandated by Spanish ordinances. As foreign visitors to the plantations repeatedly documented, violation of the requirements to provide for evangelization of the slaves was countenanced by even the Catholic Church.

An unusual feature of Suárez y Romero's view of slave life is evident in his choice to have his narrator write somewhat from the perspective of a slave owner. He avoided the use of the word "slave," preferring instead "my Blacks," as in "Los bohíos al oscurecer" [Huts at dusk] (278, 284). With that perspective, the narrator traveled from an unidentified city to his plantation to supervise the slaves' work during harvest season. Perhaps the city was Havana, if one assumed that the inspiration for the article was the plantation that Suárez y Romero supervised in Güines, located near the capital, in the province of Havana. The city represented modernity, against which the narrator advocated life in the countryside, including that of the rural areas around the sugarmill. The action was set during the harvesting of the cane and the subsequent activities leading to the production of sugar—the busiest season of the year.

The "working slave" articles contain descriptions of the slaves' tasks and their grueling work schedules and, at times, exchanges between the slaves and a kind narrator. In those conversations are glimpses of intimate details about the slaves' lives; they are mainly stories about their family members, giving the reader a more personal view of the Creole slaves.

The narrator's view of the hard-working Creole slaves was, however, highly sentimental. His return to the countryside brought forth lost, cherished memories of innocent childhood times, including his interaction with certain types of slaves. It seems as though he was caught between his upper-class position as a landowner who was financially dependent on slavery (an institution that he seemed unable to condemn openly) and his recognition of the hard lives of his loyal slave workers. This characteristic of a sense of having "unfinished business" could also be part of Suárez y Romero's desire to write in the mode of a serial novel. Indirectly, González del Valle, his friend and editor of his novel *Francisco*, referred to this sentiment in his letter to Suárez y Romero, dated September 4, 1839: "Do you know that your letters about the countryside give me very much pleasure? That reading your account interests me like that of a novel" (146).

Rather than developing a plot, Suárez y Romero's articles focused on an extensive documentation of slaves' confinement in quarters called *bohíos*, which were primitive, indigenous huts. His descriptions of the *bohíos*, including the musical life that took place around them, are often quoted by Cuban historians as examples of the rich cultural life that slaves maintained in spite of the rigors of labor on the plantation.

Although short articles, the details about slave life, particularly physical descriptions of the *bohíos*, were abundant. They included details of the exteriors of the primitive huts and of their rundown surroundings—the *conuco*, a patch of land provided for cultivation. Close to the plantation's working structures but at a safe distance from the main house, the huts formed an area that Suárez y Romero referred to as "slum of the sugarmill" ("Los domingos en el ingenio" [Sundays in the sugarmills] 249).

Suárez y Romero's preference to set the hut as a significant literary stage was evident in his article "Bohíos" (1840). Here, as in other articles, the narrator sets out to perform one of his exploratory promenades, in the afternoon as usual, but it is different from his other excursions into the countryside. This one takes him into the slave quarters. The reasons for this trip are obscure: "I don't know why I like so much to walk among the bohíos, despite their sad, humble appearance, nor why I prefer that walk to the movement and the noise of the buildings housing boilers and cane press" (244). His view of these quarters did not give him the joy he felt when he saw the lush Cuban countryside; nor did it bring him happy memories, but a moment for personal reflection. It was clear that he went through the slaves' shanties to document information that could be categorized into two distinctive themes: (1) details about the construction of the *bohíos* and the slaves' ways of dealing with the roughness of the living conditions in the huts and (2) images of specific types of workers, their names and their impact on his life.

As if gathering cultural data, the narrator describes the shack as "a rectangle although imperfectly laid out, with a saddle-roof, the one most used in all the country houses" (246). He continued to explain the life that took place in spite of the limitations of these dwellings. Each hut was the sole responsibility of the slave inhabitants. Without much help from the master, each slave built a wooden frame with a roof made of straw, a natural material readily (and freely) available near the plantation. The ribs of the narrator's beloved palm trees provided most of the straw. Slaves could work on their hut constructions only during holidays. The narrator did not mention which holidays, although he indicated that slaves had hardly any free time, only to eat and to sleep, and that Sunday was their day off. Consequently, the final structure was poor, as he described it in indirect social criticism: "One can imagine how the work will come out when, in addition to their haste to finish it, and to the poor, scanty materials, one adds the coarse character of the slaves" (246).

Details about the interiors of the huts formed most of the data of the article, information that more closely defined the "rustic character of the slaves." There was little to be said about the structures of the hut: "The layout of the rooms is the same in all huts" (246). All the huts had two spaces, a living room and a back room. A living room served as a social space and as a dining room, and it was often where inhabitants slept. A back room had multiple uses: "to keep the drawer for clothes, to hang sacks with heaven knows how many things inside them, to put the baskets in which they rock their little ones, and to allow sleeping space for the godchildren and for relatives, since the owners of the bohío stay in the living room" (247). In the back of the hut they kept the chickens, inside rather than outdoors, because of frequent robberies, in spite of the vigilance of both the overseer and the chickens' owners. This arrangement, the narrator stated, had created a rather unpleasant environment: "everything so dirty that it is disgusting" (247). Outside the hut were *barbacoas* [storage spaces] for the vegetables raised in a *conuco* [garden plot], and a *chiquero* [pigpen]. The plainness of the *bohío* was regulated. There was a prohibition against use of religious objects in front of the *bohío* or inside of it, which might differentiate one from the others in terms of hierarchy or religious association (Moreno Fraginals, "Aportes" 27). In short, the quarters' simple layout, as historian Moreno Fraginals pointed out, was part of a plan to give the overseer easy access to the slaves for security ("Aportes" 26).

The conclusion of "Bohíos" has the narrator considering the "rustic character" of the slaves' huts, which was, after all, his main interest. Absent from the piece is any indication of family life, as the narrator's description of the huts takes place when all of their occupants are out at work. There was, therefore, no comment on the personal effects that such an environment had upon the slave inhabitants. The whole piece has a tone of social discontent, evident in the gloomy descriptions of the huts. The ending paragraph, however, focuses on an undefined, excessive, sentimental quest:

> Seen from a certain distance, rather than homes of human beings, they look like heaps of dry straw. The ashen-grey color of the straw, the narrow, uneven and twisted streets, the weeds (malvas, bledos and escobamargas) with which they are riddled, the threshing tools that among the vegetation cross each other in every direction, so clean and flat and glossy that they shine in the sunlight, and, finally, the air of poverty and of melancholy that everything exhales there, lead one to think deeply and to be sad for a long time, especially at certain hours of the day! (248)

This withdrawal from obvious signs of outrage at the sight of an example of oppressive practice is a technique repeated in Suárez y Romero's articles. Although this was a way of avoiding open expression of abolitionism, the overwhelming sentimentality of the piece, reflected in the customary romantic fit of crying, illustrates an animated feeling of distress.

In Suárez y Romero's view, the *bohío* was, however, an important means of expressing abolitionist sentiment. "Los bohíos al oscurecer" [Huts at dusk] introduced the reader to the dirty surroundings of these dwellings and, more daringly, brought to the forefront an inhabitant, set as a portrait of a character type. The character is an old woman slave, retired from farm work because of her advanced age and because she was now in charge of the care of newborn Creole slaves. The description of the old woman, framed within the confines of her primitive dwelling, is highly emotional:

> The hut was open, and on the doorjamb an old Black woman was sitting. She wore a nightshirt and a kerchief of red cotton covered her braids. She bent her head to her breast, and from my point of view, some words were audible, confused, that she was speaking to herself. Her stature was tall, her constitution must have been very robust; but now her arms and her emaciated breast indicated that if in other days she had cut down and loaded cane beside the strongest Black men, that time had passed, her old age and its aches and pains permitting her nothing except to live always

in the limited environment of her hut and to care for the child, whom in a basket hanging from the twisted wooden posts, her daughter had left with her when she left for the field. (286–87)

The old woman, who remains nameless, was blind—a fact that impressed the narrator and heightened the character's tender, motherly care of the child:

> Each time the child cried, the old woman said something to him; she got up, rocked the basket for a while, and again placed herself in the doorjamb. The hesitation of her steps told me finally that she was a blind slave that, now useless for all work, was allowed to live in her hut. Her isolation during the hours when the Blacks were in the fields, the cries of the child who stirred in a blanket, the darkness of the hut, the old lady's words carried to my ears by gusts of wind, her harsh manners, her nearly male features, left a profound impression on me. (286–87)

The almost religious implications of a barely veiled Virgin Mary perhaps brought to readers another common maternal image of the Black woman, who served as nanny and often as wet nurse, that became a favorite image of abolitionist novels.

The sad portrait of an old slave woman introduces the intended humane message of the piece. In a personal disclosure similar to others in previous articles, the narrator speaks directly to his reader in order to clarify what he meant by "profound impression." He was speaking to those who, like him, more than once had observed a blind slave woman sitting by a hut. The image may have prompted them to "drop a coin into her hands, and for a long time, you may have remembered her features even among the gifts of your happy life" (287). Like the owner of the plantation, the reader probably had known such an old woman, during his own happy, privileged childhood: "you sat down next to her in innocent abandon, and with her you probably chatted, asking her many things with ingenuous interest" (287). Now this motherlike image, "the image of the Black woman," would remain imprinted in the reader's memory, as was the author's memory of the old woman, now crying, who had told her personal stories to the generous boy, now a master. Although these events are not narrated directly, they summarize the humble life of a strong woman, now an abused worker:

> she shed a tear before you as she told you about those times when she had played on the grounds in the moonlight, with your mother or your father when they were all children; when during the early mornings and during the nights, she occupied a place in the line; when with a string of glass beads and earrings of fake gold, her braided hair well combed, her feet

in shoes that day, and dressed in zaraza cloth, she danced to the savage beats of the drum until her limbs were soaked in shiny sweat; and when, upon returning from the church one Sunday, she presented to her masters her newborn daughter, already baptized, whose offspring is the one now deeply asleep in a perpetual night, with no world other than that hut, she rocks in the basket suspended from the two twisted posts. (287–88)

Suárez y Romero's articles carefully introduced specific types of slave workers, all of which were well known by the general public, since their services were often advertised for sale or requested for purchase in city newspapers. The selection of characters in Suárez y Romero's articles was small, however, perhaps because his preferred slave types were too innocuous to arouse accusations of abolitionist sentiment.

In Suárez y Romero's articles, with the exception of "El cementerio del ingenio" [The cemetery at the sugarmill], slaves appeared without names, a fact that makes this piece more personal, almost like a daring attack against the anonymity of the newspaper advertisements about slaves. Published as part of the collection *Ofrenda al Bazar de la Real Casa de Beneficencia* [Offering at the market of the royal house of Charity] (1864), the plot of "El cementerio del ingenio" was simple, like those of other sketches. While visiting the plantation during Easter vacation, the narrator leaves some friends at the big house and sets out on an afternoon walk. Wandering around the property, he finds himself staring at the walls of the slave cemetery. Unlike other articles, in this one, his tears are provoked by his thought of "an infinite number of persons from my family, an infinite number of friends, an infinite number of beings whom I had loved and respected without having had any contact at all with them" (338). His "family members," were, of course, slaves who served him throughout his lifetime, as a child and as an adult. They were a considerable number; some five hundred slaves were buried in "that small piece of soil so often watered by the sweat from their brows" (338).

The narrator's overwhelming remembrance of his slaves, began with these words: "I, who had been one of your owners, should grieve for the memory of you" (338). Memory brought to life those slaves who had had an impact on his childhood. Listed in order of importance, and almost as in a religious experience, their images came to him in a vision: "The first one that came to me as when I used to see him when I was a child" (338).

That honor fell to Pedro, from the Macuá nation, who was the slaves' cook: "With his body now bent and his hair completely white he would go out into the dawn to collect the necessary wood and then return to shell the corn, to peel the vegetable roots, to stir up the fire and to stir the coarse food with his stick, standing next to the caldron, enduring the streams of steam and of smoke that rose to the straw roof" (338). The narrator and his siblings enjoyed Pedro's company, and they spent countless hours with him, in spite of his "old age, his ailments and his dulled wits" (338). His death, and that of all other slaves, went unnoticed. The narrator remembered that upon his return to the plantation for an Easter vacation, he found out that his good friend had been buried unceremoniously. His final place, and that of others, was a wild, uncultivated strip of land adjacent to the pasture. There had been no religious service: "the cadaver . . . wrapped in his blanket, and carried by two Blacks who opened the door, dug the grave, dropped their co-worker into it, and then returned to the factories to continue their labor" (338).

An unusual feature of "El cementerio" was that some of the slaves had more extensive parts in the plot than others. Their roles went beyond mere description of their tasks. One of these slaves was "El mina Rogelio," an African-born slave, "tall in stature and athletic in build" (339). Well respected by Blacks and by Whites because of his serious work ethic, he had never been punished, and he had accumulated a considerable number of goods. Although he was highly sought out by the women slaves of his plantation, he "had given his heart to an African woman of the same tribe as he, belonging to the slave crew of a coffee plantation a league away" (339). Against regulations, in an impossible love, Rogelio maintains secret relations with his lover (whose name remains unknown to the reader) until he is discovered and slaves from her plantation attack him. "Defending himself like a lion," Rogelio kills two of his assailants while others flee. His death is fully described as the brave deed of a romantic hero: "badly wounded, he manages to leave the coffee plantation, he crosses the other farms, he wades across the river and he arrives on the grounds of the sugarcane plantation. Nearly dying, he enters the woods; he thinks that perhaps he would never again see the woman that he adores, and reaching a mamey tree, he ends his life" (340). There is no indication of his lover's fate.

Another slave with a rather lengthy role was Gertrudis. As a counterpart to the tragic story of Rogelio, the plot of Gertrudis presents her as a sensitive soul, a quality that Suárez y Romero's previous articles had also attributed to slaves. As a type, Gertrudis was the beautiful Black woman, "whose beauty made many of the plantation's slaves' hearts beat faster" (340). She was born on the plantation to multiethnic parents, a Carabalí father and a Mandinga mother. References to African ethnicities were often at the center of debates among plantation owners about the best or worst type of personality to endure the physical and mental impositions of slavery (Guanche 48–60). Like Rogelio, Gertrudis was an unusual character, not only because of her mixed heritage, reflected in her beauty, but also because of her demure manner, described in romantic terms:

> With laughter perennially on her lips and always singing, Gertrudis walked along the path of her existence as if it were sown with flowers, and she was one of the innumerable examples presented to us by that sex capable, because of the delicate sensitivity of their soul, of dreaming of happiness in any situation of life. How much wit and friendly joy there was in the laughter and in the songs of Gertrudis! They were like those rays of the sun that penetrate the deep obscurities of caverns, like those brooks that meander through the forests and like those magnificent wings of birds that perch on the steep mountain crags. (340)

A dedicated daughter, Gertrudis rejects the offer of the narrator's mother to move her with the owner's family to their city home, a tradition that the lady of the house bestows on one of the best Creole female slaves upon her reaching twenty years of age. As in a beauty contest, Gertrudis wins that honor, "with scarce attention to anything other than her beauty" (340). Gertrudis declines that easier life and chooses to work in the sugarmill in order to remain with her parents, with her siblings and with her other relatives.

Gertrudis's death was a statement about the harshness of the physical labor in the sugarmill (Hall, *Social Control* 14, 17–18). While feeding cane into the mill, Gertrudis falls asleep and one of her hands gets caught by the press. Although the overseer and other slaves try to stop the machinery, their efforts are futile: "it was enough to cause all the arm and part of Gertrudis's body to become horribly destroyed" (341). About the scene of the wake, the narrator dramatically says, "I shall never forget it" (341). He speaks of his family, who had joined the slaves in mourning the death of the beloved Gertrudis: "we used to go frequently to mingle our tears with theirs [the slaves']" (341). The importance of Gertrudis's death is obvious when contrasted with the narrator's comment in passing in the article "El cementerio," in which he indicates that often slaves were buried without ceremony.

Another type of character of special importance was the rebellious slave, prone to escape, and therefore known as a *cimarrón*, or runaway. This was perhaps because the *cimarrón*'s constant desire to escape was taken as a reason to impose severe punishments, a fact that was fully documented by slave laws (Deschamps Chapeaux, *Cimarrones* 2). This character appeared a few times in Suárez y Romero's articles, in spite of the fact that more plantation slaves escaped than city slaves (Deschamps Chapeaux 2). Daringly, in "El cementerio" the narrator portrays a male slave character, Teodoro, who spends most of his time in shackles because of his constant attempts to escape. His death by suicide is narrated succinctly: "One day, Teodoro, from a jobo tree among whose branches he had hidden, heard the dogs barking. He threw around his neck a rope with a noose, and when the dogs sank their teeth into his feet he was already hanged" (338). As if censoring himself, Suárez y Romero did not document the frequency of slave deaths by suicide.

Another terrible figure associated with the *cimarrón*, the *rancheador* [slave hunter] is also conspicuously absent from Suárez y Romero's articles. The mere mention of his presence is totally erased, even though there were repeated references to the hunting dogs, his favorite tool in capturing runaway slaves. The *rancheador* does not appear as a protagonist in any Costumbrista articles, perhaps because of the likelihood of deletion by censors.

One *cimarrón* character in a Suárez y Romero article is an unnamed male slave in "El corte de caña" [The cane harvest], who is released from his shackles after a White female visitor to the plantation pleads on his behalf. Because of the similarities of the two stories, it is plausible that these two slave characters were the same, a technique that Costumbrista writers often used. Although the psychological profile of the *cimarrón* would not be explored in Costumbrista articles, it would become a subject of importance to Costumbrista novelists. Perhaps while writing, they knew that their novels were to be published outside of Cuba, so they did not censor their presentation of the *cimarrón* as Suárez y Romero obviously did in his articles.

In contrast to the runaway slave, there was in Suárez y Romero's articles the faithful and trustworthy slave. This figure was involved in several tasks, most of them domestic jobs in the big house. One of them was the family's calesero [coachman], who appeared to be represented in a good light in Suárez y Romero's "El cementerio." Carlos, described as "a Black Creole born on the plantation," after losing his sight asks the master's permission to move back to the plantation to live with his family (339). His remaining days and his death are described: "He wove baskets in idle time, and during the grinding he collected cane in the stack, making quotas just as others did. But the changes in food and in labor soon led to his death" (339). The calesero, with colorful, impeccable uniforms of high hats and black leather boots, became a favorite character of Costumbrista essays set in cities. Their coaches, also known as *volantas*, were also favorite subjects of graphic artists.

Opposite of the suave calesero in terms of acculturation, the unindoctrinated slave, or the Negro bozal, who remained uncontaminated by Cuban culture and Spanish language, was the most common shadow character in Suárez y Romero's articles. Although he (all of the examples in Suárez y Romero's writings are men) might have been an outstanding worker, he remained faithful to his native African background. One notable example is Fernando in "El cementerio," the only bozal slave with a proper name in any of Suárez y Romero's articles: "Fernando always bore a cloud of sadness on his face; his songs were always, uniquely, African; he never danced except to the drumbeat, and with his carabelas [Africans of the same nation], he never spoke any tongue but the language of his tribe" (341, emphasis in the original). Fernando's self-marginalization is clear in this description, a trait that is stressed in others of Suárez y Romero's articles, and there is not even a mention of his ethnic origin. This is an odd omission, since slave owners bought workers of preferred ethnic groups, as Suárez y Romero indicated in other articles.

"El cementerio" must have stood out for the reader of that time as an article of customs that was highly sympathetic to the working slaves in a Cuban sugarmill. Although there is no discernable abolitionist sentiment in it, there is a humane cry for better treatment of these loyal workers and dear friends. Again, as if attempting to find a way to counterbalance such dangerous feelings of befriending slaves, the ending counteracts any angry feelings against slave owners. Upon the narrator's return to "la casa de vivienda" [the master's house], where some female friends and his sisters entertained themselves playing the piano, the narrator explains his happy disposition: "I was laughing with joy, but this joy did not have the bitter aftertaste that usually accompanies happiness that comes only from the earth" (342). The highly romantic feeling of happiness precluded any possibility that the piece could be considered abolitionist. It was a happy ending, different from that of other articles that left the reader feeling uneasy about revelations of the experience of slavery.

As part of his attempt to present neutral images of slavery, Suárez y Romero displayed a preference for older slave characters, whom he remembered in their current condition, or as workers under his management, or as young playmates in his privileged childhood. Old age as a symbol of a decaying institution is present throughout the articles. Frequently, slaves came to beg the narrator for retirement. One old slave's request of a benevolent narrator was paraphrased in standard Spanish: "I have several sons to work in my place; let me go to rest and keep warm, until I die, beside the fire of my hut" ("La casa de trapiche" [The cane-press house] 264). Significantly, the narrator did not record the answer to this request. In "El cementerio," collectively, the narrator summarizes the tasks performed by the retired old slaves: "they served as guardsmen at the boundaries, they took care of the henhouses, they stirred the sugar in the driers, they removed the dirt from the sugar blocks, they washed in the tanks, they walked from sunrise to sunset behind the working ox" (342).

The *guardiero* was clearly Suárez y Romero's favorite slave type. His article

"El guardiero" [The guardsman] was unusual in that it was the only one in which a slave was a main character in a plot drawn solely from his own life experiences. In Suárez y Romero's articles, the *guardieros* serve as guardsmen in various capacities. In this article, one serves as a gatekeeper of a *tranquera*, as the gates of the wooden privacy fences were known in Cuba. These activities were undemanding; they allowed the guard free time to engage in other tasks in order to survive financially (Ortiz, *Los negros esclavos* 269–70).

Suárez y Romero's description of the *guardiero* followed to the letter the legal dispositions about the living quarters of slaves in rural plantations—an indication of his in-depth knowledge of legal issues pertaining to slavery practices in sugarmills. On November 14, 1842, Governor Gerónimo Valdés proclaimed the first legally binding stipulation of the presence of a *guardiero*, who served as an appointed watchman: "At the hour for retiring to sleep (which on long nights will be at eight and on short nights at nine), the roll of the slaves will be taken so that only the guardieros will remain outside their rooms. Of them one must be designated to keep watch that all keep silent and to inform immediately the master or the overseer about any movement of the coworkers themselves, of any people who arrive from outside and of any other happening whatsoever" (qtd. in Pérez de la Riva, *El barracón* 20). According to the testimony of runaway slave Esteban Montejo, however, White men working at the sugarmill had the task of spying on slaves. Montejo had respect for old male slaves, some of whom were repositories of ancient religious practices already ignored by most of the young generations of slaves.

In "El guardiero," in spite of the numerous details about the protagonist, Suárez y Romero denies his protagonist a name. The structure of the story is different, in that it brings in a complex plot. As in other articles, a narrator strolls around the plantation, which brings him into contact with key slave workers. As illustrated in previous articles, the slaves were confined to workplaces, to the sugar press and boiler rooms, and they were forced to live in poor, depressing conditions in humble huts within the limits of the plantation and within easy reach of the overseer.

One group of slaves that makes a brief appearance here is the slave *criollitos*, as children born in slavery were known in Cuba. They appeared as a regular group of children, whose shouts and jumps into the air distract the narrator, presumably from the ugliness of the adult slaves' work. Description of them is minimal, serving merely to contrast their childlike joie de vivre with the grim reality of their surroundings. They often become the master's children's playmates, a fact that the narrator of other essays remembers with nostalgia for a happy childhood. In this sketch, the narrator's angelic sister befriends and plays along with the *criollitos* as he had played as a child.

Slave children were of interest to foreign visitors. For example, the French traveler Ernest L'Epine in his 1833 travelogue *Un Parisien dans les Antilles* [A Parisian in the Antilles] made the following observation after his trip to a Cuban plantation: "About twenty little children of all shades of color, from coffee with cream to English shoe polish, passing through chocolate and the color of bread with honey, are rolling around on the floor" (qtd. in Pérez de la Riva, *El barracón* 33). His testimony included a description of their caretaker, a slave woman, who was observed as she fed the children: "in front of the door an old woman feeds eight little children crouching at her feet, the little ones wait anxiously, mouths open, eyes fixed for arrival of a turn to receive a bite of rice or of cornmeal that the 'fattener' kneads in the palm of her hand and puts into their mouths with her fingers. Hens lying in wait peck the crumbs. A girl armed with a stick scares them; without that they would come to eat up, even on the lips of the guests, their part of the banquet" (33). This was an unappealing scene of a social practice still current in Africa.

In a rather dull opening, the narrator decides to continue his stroll alone into the slaves' quarters. It is then that he stumbles upon the *guardiero* and, as in other articles, he remains hidden. In a voyeuristic position, he sets out to observe the slave's whereabouts around his hut. These observations stressed images of darkness, very much like the scene in L'Epine's testimony about the slave nanny, in contrast to the previous idyllic scenes of Suárez y Romero's narrator's childhood innocence. The scene combines elements of sociological curiosity, such as his detailed description of the humble hut that the *guardiero* inhabited. Suárez y Romero made the *guardiero* the focus of the action, not merely part of the background.

The *guardiero*'s story stressed the sadness of "retirement" after a long life of slavery. He now has been relegated to spending his days taking care of "some hungry hens" and doing upkeep chores around his dilapidated hut. His description is given in basic terms, but it produces a poignant portrait that addresses the feeling of decay that overwhelmingly informs the whole piece: "before I was born, he used to knock down, robust like an athlete, trees like cedars and ácanas where today green fields of cane stretch" (253). He is now a tragic, defeated figure, "leaning on a tall stick of rattan, bent with the weight of years and of tasks that destroy the mind more than do the years" (256). Unlike other old slaves in previous articles, there is no indication that this *guardiero* has had an impact on the narrator's life or that he had been part of the narrator's privileged childhood as the son of the plantation owner. This choice may have been, however, another technique to make the character appear less personal and less like an abolitionist figure.

In spite of the narrator's sentimental detachment from the *guardiero*, a gloomy feeling develops in his detailed descriptions of the slave's shabby hut, almost as an extension of this old man's miserable life. The only revelation of his life story is the fact that he has been an outstanding worker at the mill. There are no examples of the *guardiero*'s well-performed tasks, for which, the narrator seems to hint, his sole payment is an allowance to live in the poor *bohío*. The narrator focuses on the *guardiero*'s current state of being, which is a dull existence. In short, nothing much has changed for a trustworthy retired slave. He continues an existence of economic want, tending his tiny *conuco* garden plot, raising chickens, and selling handmade baskets.

One episode is of great sentimental value. The *guardiero*'s trustworthy (and, it seems, his lone) companion was a dog, which helped to keep wild animals away from his few chickens. The description of how that dog had come into his possession is cruel—symptomatic of life under slavery. The slave encounters an overseer killing newborn puppies: "he was smashing them with barbaric coldness against a stone fence" (260). The *guardiero* humbly asks permission to keep the last surviving dog. Although, "[the overseer] still wanted to kill it as he had its brothers," he grants the *guardiero*'s wish (260). This is the only example of the overseers' cruelty in any of Suárez y Romero's articles, other than references in passing to sounds of whipping used to encourage the slaves' physical labor. Antislavery activists amply documented overseers' cruel behavior, but in Suárez y Romero's works, references to it are absent. The fact that the narrator chooses to tell of the overseer's violent behavior toward defenseless dogs may have been intended as a comment on this man's well-known ability to inflict pain in brutal punishment techniques performed on slaves.

After this drawing of a mild view of the *guardiero*'s gloomy life, the end of the story changes to include highly symbolic content. The music of an African instrument, the marimba, "to whose dark sound he [the guardiero] was accustomed to sing in the afternoons," becomes the focus of a rather sentimental scene (260). The narrator has come to hear the old man play and sing, and it affects him profoundly: "I waited with a curiosity mixed with sadness that I cannot explain, for his rough fingers to strum the thick strings" (260–61). His brief description of the music and singing is different from others in previous articles: he does not label this production as "primitive" or "barbaric." The closing of the scene places the *guardiero*'s music in harmony with the natural sounds that are, for the narrator, a constant source of meditation: "At the same time that he was singing and playing, there were sounds from yagüey leaves, from the river, from the palm trees and the cane, making so many harmonies together into an exceeding sad concert that it would be useless to seek in other places" (261).

Even if one considers the essentially voyeuristic nature of many Costumbrista articles, the contemporary reader of Suárez y Romero's essays must have been struck by the narrator's constant insistence on making himself an active spectator in areas that slaves inhabit. Often he conceals himself in order to observe unobtrusively certain Blacks' activities, supposing that otherwise they will not perform their regular routines freely or will stage a fake version acceptable to a White eyewitness: "I hid myself behind a tree, because, if there is a White person in front of them, the Blacks become embarrassed and they don't sing or dance; from there I could observe them as I chose" ("Ingenios" 40). As he remarked to del Monte, through his management of the Surinam plantation, he had been constantly exposed to the sad activities performed by Blacks, "from waking up to going to bed, one has before him only pitiable scenes" (*Centón* 38). That inside knowledge made Suárez y Romero different from other abolitionist writers who only knew about these brutal conditions through first-person "letters," such as Suárez y Romero's articles.

Suárez y Romero's narrator attempted, however, to present his concern for the slaves' well-being as a matter of personal pride. After all, his numerous claims that as a child he had interacted with and befriended slaves gave him another type of ownership. That control was not physical, but it entitled him to engage in spying visits to the workers' private living quarters, available to him as the plantation's master.

Suárez y Romero's literary friends had high expectations for these rural articles of customs, which González del Valle labeled "Black compositions" (57). His trust in Suárez y Romero's fidelity in reproducing scenes at a plantation was total, particularly since, as he expressed in a letter to Suárez y Romero, he himself had never been to one: "Reading your picture, which I judge to be exact (since although to this day I do not know what a plantation or an overseer is), by true and infallible inductions, I have come to know it" (65). González del Valle (1820–1851), who was also a reputable abolitionist and a member of the del Monte literary group, trusted that Suárez y Romero's writing could provide Madden "an exact idea of the state of opinions about slaves and the slave trade among young people who think about their country" (57).

Madden seemed to have agreed with González del Valle. In a letter to del Monte, dated July 13, 1840, Madden expressed his admiration for Suárez y Romero's *Francisco*, which had as a subtitle *Ingenio o las delicias del campo* [Plantation or country delights]. Acknowledging having received and read the manuscript, Madden wrote how impressed he was with Suárez y Romero's depiction of the plantation: "there is minuteness of description and closeness of observation and rightness of feeling that I have not often seen surpassed" (qtd. in del Monte, *Centón* 83).

Racist stands are slow to die. González del Valle acknowledged to Suárez y Romero having received his letter via a slave messenger, referred to as a "negrito" (86). This was in sharp contrast to Suárez y Romero's humane position in presenting slaves as literary characters or in his references to them as Blacks in his letters to friends.

There were complex reasons behind Suárez y Romero's documentation of those specific cultural markers of Cuban slavery that he wrote about. Edward Kamau Brathwaite, referring to possible reasons behind seemingly positive accounts about slavery, has observed, "On the eve of emancipation, at a crise de conscience, when the European planters in the West Indies were becoming aware of a plural society developing around them, and conscious of the need, if they were to retain their hegemony, to destroy, subvert, or psychologically control the black majority, a few books began to appear which described slaves in terms of their own culture" (78). In the heated Cuban political scene of the nineteenth century, the slow incorporation of slavery-related issues was a major factor in the expulsion from the island of prominent abolitionists. For example, historian José Saco, known as the author of the first contemporary work on Cuban and Latin American slavery (Mellafe 10), was ordered to leave Cuba in 1834. The historian Raúl Cepero Bonilla has argued, however, that none of the Cuban intellectuals showed a clear-cut rejection of slavery before the War of Independence in 1868. He cited as an example the self-defense by the Costumbrista writer José de la Luz y Caballero, who, when accused by the Cuban governor O'Donnell of having had a role in the slave revolution of 1844, publicly complained that such an accusation "wounded his feelings of honor and of loyalty" (qtd. in Cepero Bonilla 25). This critical stance was important. It anticipated the modern Cuban revolutionary historian Walterio Carbonell's statement that the lack of a national spirit prior to 1868 implied that the literary works prior to that date supported the "economic interests of the pro-slavery class to which they belonged" (35).

It is not surprising that Suárez y Romero attempted to protect himself from the wrath of other plantation owners. The psychological undertone of his pieces falls within the realm of "narratives of supremacy and superiority," which, as Henry Paget has pointed out, create an oppositional "racial other." The racial other was defined in terms of the ways in which members of the group differed from Europeans, "with differences carrying negative markings and evaluations" (163). This feeling of racial superiority is evident in Suárez y Romero's only piece that examines the life of a sugar baron, "El corte de caña" [Sugar cane harvesting] (1859). Whether he intended it to be a satirical view of the upper-level life of the master is not clear; however, its vague depiction of life in the master's house is unsympathetic. The focus of the article is not on that busy season in the fields but on a description of a narrator's entertaining visiting friends, presumably from the city. The group is treated to a complete tour of the facilities: "We walked through the groves, we ate fruit in the shade of the trees, we sat on the banks of the river, we went to the buildings housing the sugarpress, the boilers and the drying. We saw the labor required for production of sugar, and we often walked along the lanes of the garden" (270). These activities, unlike those in his previous articles, do not produce in him (or in any of his guests) the customary tears.

The object of this occasion is to entertain his idle guests, in contrast to the strenuous work taking place outside the house: "To the chords of the sonorous piano we danced some dances, and also, mixed with the distant noise of the Blacks' shouts, the sweet voices of several young ladies sang their melancholy Cuban songs or those elegant compositions by great artists that can never be heard without the soul's surrender to entranced dreams" (270). In short, this was the lavish life of the plantation owner, a symbol of modernity, which with the sophisticated sugar-producing machinery, included a house with bathrooms with running water and gas lights (Pérez de la Riva, *Barracón* 17). His description of the scenes in the big house has a sardonic tone: "Dinner was lively. Our compatriots' pale faces were tinted by a pink like the shades of dawn. There was conversation about dances, about the theatre, about outings. Ice chilled the water, the crystal glasses rang as they struck the china dishes, and the amber champagne bubbled in them" (271).

An impromptu decision takes the group of friends to the fields. They are attracted by the "squeaking of the carts that, laden with cane, were entering in line into the front grounds" (271). Although the narrator appears to approve of this stroll, his tone is critical of his friends' frivolous attitudes: "Everyone walks in a hurry, nobody wants to turn back, as if the harvest of the cane were a magnificent picture in which they expect to please sight and heart" (272). With much effort, "finally we drew near the slaves," who had been hard at work while the distinguished guests enjoyed a restful feast. Some young ladies were tired by the walk from the big house: "Some young ladies, tired, sat down on the straw without caring that they might be ruining their silk dresses" (273).

There are direct statements that contrast pleasant scenes at the master's house with the slaves' hectic work schedule, such as: "from dawn until dark, except for the time that they are given for eating, they are busy cutting cane that the mill's hammers are to devour, and that are to fill the landowner's money boxes" (273). Scenes descriptive of the slaves' actual physical work of cutting the cane were realistic, again in contrast with the fairly romantic view of the scene at the master's house.

Of particular interest is the narrator's fixation on women slaves who were cutting cane. They appear as strong and hardworking as the men in the fields: "Men and women cut cane, and at times some of the women have started clearing rows brandishing the blade of the powerful machete with a Herculean arm, a wider patch than that of the Black man working beside them" (273).[18] His preference to highlight female slaves was another calculated choice. It was because in the early part of the nineteenth century the number of male slaves exceeded females four to one (Pérez de la Riva, "Para la historia" 122). Although it may appear that Suárez y Romero could have been avoiding descriptions of graphic scenes, his selection of female characters would have had a greater impact on his reader.

The abolitionist sentiment that female slaves should not be subjected to the horrors of sugar production was, however, cleverly defused. As the group of visitors gathers to leave, a slave begins singing. Here the narrator's words indirectly suggest abolitionist views. He prompts the reader, "Hear him, nonetheless, and even if it takes effort to understand him, fix your attention on the words of his savage song" (274). The words were presumably in bozal, or Spanish with strong traces of an African language, for which the narrator served as interpreter.[19] In his song, the unnamed old slave thanks the "blancos" [Whites] who have come to watch the slaves' brutal work. In an effort to please the owner, he sings that the Blacks are well fed and clothed, seldom punished by whipping, and that they are medically well cared for; however, he also sings that "they could not resist the harvest evenings, that sleep overcame them, that while half-asleep they loaded the cane, that half-asleep they put it into the press" (275). In response to this complaint, although it is not stated that the visitors understand the text of the song, they throw money at the cane cutters, all of whom bow and ask for the Whites' blessings. As mentioned earlier, one of them, a rebellious runaway in cuffs, is released from his chains after one of the young ladies intercedes on his behalf.

This scene is an example of the slave's ability to mock the highly structured slave system in the format that Jorge and Isabel Castellanos described as a *puya*. *Puyas*, or songs, were intended to "condemn, with decision and wit, the sad situation of their life as slaves" (1:194). In Suárez y Romero's slave's *puya*, there were several components. First, it seemed to address the lack of connection between the *mayoral* [the plantation's overseer] and the landowner, who, absent from the plantation, depended on the overseer's reports about the slaves' conditions. In Suárez y Romero's articles the *mayoral* appears as a minor figure, but always a menacing one because of his whip, which gets mentioned either directly as part of his attire or indirectly in constant references to the sounds of whippings.

Those references may have expressed Suárez y Romero's strong dislike for this character.

The ambiguous figure as an absent plantation owner provided the narrator a source of authority in a role that was vague; it is not clear whether he himself was the owner of the plantation that he so proudly and benevolently displayed to his readers. His kind remarks about the faithful, hardworking slaves placed strategically implies a sympathetic characterization of these workers, who over-whelmingly outnumbered the handful of White inhabitants on the plantation.

Second, the exchange between the old slave and the White visitors is one of the few times in these articles that a slave dares to address a White observer, perhaps a master, although even that fact is not fully stated within the text. The indirect conversation falls within a rhetorical style described by Michael Craton: "The stratagems involved exaggerated deference and disguised satire as well as outright cunning, duplicity and mendacity" (231). The ending expresses indirectly the old man's request through the narrator, who appeals directly to the slave owners' "melancholy of your souls" (276).

The concluding paragraph stands out because it is a direct plea to sugarcane plantation owners who, like him, might view from their front gardens the facili-ties of their sugarmills, or they might be coming back from a promenade after supervising the slaves. Those activities were not joyous ones, perhaps because at the center was slavery, an institution that provided for the luxurious life of the Cuban landowners:

> How many times have you perhaps experienced what I have on returning by the front grounds at midnight, while resting in your room, while see-ing the comforts that you enjoy, upon reflecting that your soul and your heart can rise to lofty thoughts and to grand emotions! On how many occasions you probably have listened all night to the crunch of pieces of [sugar] cane in the press and the songs of the African barbarian! And on how many occasions, when you got up the following day, you have prob-ably looked toward the sun that has just risen, you have probably mixed with sounds of the happy hymn the doleful vibrations of the elegy. (277)

Suárez y Romero's documentation of the horrors of slavery is far greater than his depiction of slaves as characters of significant literary value. His slave charac-ters are plentiful, but few are protagonists. Rarely do they speak up or tell their own life stories. That absence makes the previously discussed scene even more meaningful. The slaves are mainly workers whose only objective, as the narrator frequently stresses, is to keep themselves away from physical harm. Seemingly speaking as a proud slave owner in "Los bohíos al oscurecer" [Huts at twilight], the narrator coldly states that in that year's harvesting "no Black who puts in the [sugar] cane has been caught by the arm and destroyed by the press in horrible agonies before the supervisor, running to stop the machine, could stop its motion, leaving the deplorable event in the spirits of all inhabitants of the plantation, for a long time, a memory of profound sadness" (279).

In Suárez y Romero's articles, the depiction of slaves is based on the type of work that they performed. The tasks on a plantation are many and harsh, shared equally by men and women. Slaves appear as types, such as the old blind woman in "Los bohíos al oscurecer" [Huts at dawn]. He seems to have had a sentimental preference for two types of slaves—older workers who are tragic figures, at the end of their lives, and exhausted by the heavy, physical work and younger women, who, like the slaves in "El corte de caña" [The cane harvest], are strong, efficient workers. The male characters are fewer and less prominent figures, in spite of the fact that male slaves overwhelmingly outnumbered women slaves. His selection of characters who are either old and retired slaves or young women workers may suggest a cautious effort to inspire compassion in the reader without overt expression of abolitionist sentiment.

The light political tone of these Costumbrista articles and their rather vague presentation of the slaves as protagonists of their own stories of grim lives may suggest that Suárez y Romero had hoped to publish them in Cuban newspapers. Literary friend Gómez del Valle even suggested that Suárez y Romero's "pieces on the countryside" should go to a particular journal (*Noticioso*), because the censor there knew Suárez y Romero and "there will be fewer reservations" (166). Suárez y Romero's articles were rather neutral agents of political change. Like all published Costumbrista writers, Suárez y Romero avoided the selection of protagonist figures associated with cruelty on plantations—the *mayoral* (the plantation overseer) and the *rancheador* (slave hunter), radical examples of the hidden horrors of slavery practices. They did appear in articles as mere shadow characters of very little consequence to the plot. An indirectly abolitionist statement was that they were solely responsible for some of the suicides that often took place on the plantations (Hall, *Social* 20–23).[20] Even this reality was muffled; subservient slaves who remained committed to their work, in spite of the harshness of their chores, would stay away from the perceived well-deserved wrath of overseers.

Suárez y Romero daringly placed his rural essays amid particular coordinates of a booming sugarcane plantation. Critic Alberto Ramos Santana, speaking about Costumbrista articles in Spain, stated that Spanish writers often drew up only vague details of known locations because the reader came to associate a character with that place (259). For Suárez y Romero, writing his Costumbrista articles from a sugarmill, his depiction of this locale went beyond the development of a rarely explored and controversial literary scene. The "keys of interpretation," as Ramos Santana suggested, were related to specific marginal locations in Suárez y Romero's articles, such as the slave cemetery and the living quarters, opposing the romanticized versions by Cuban artists, whose portraits of Cuban sugar factories presented a rather cleaned-up view of those plantations. Although foreign visitors would offer more extensive descriptions of some of these horrible work centers, they were limited to areas that visitors were allowed to enter, and to interaction permitted between slaves and visitors.

While Suárez y Romero was writing some of these articles, he was also busy at work on his abolitionist novel *Francisco*, drafted between 1838 and 1839. A more aggressive manuscript, as the subtitle "El ingenio y las delicias del campo" seems to indicate, it draws from Suárez y Romero's in-depth knowledge of rural life amid the physical coordinates of a sugarcane plantation. His bravado, absent from his Costumbrista articles, was inspired by his hopes to have the novel published abroad.

The political consequences of his abolitionist stand was for Suárez y Romero a major source of concern. His friend José Zacarías González del Valle attempted to put him at ease about Suárez y Romero's notion about the reasons behind Domingo del Monte's suggestions that Suárez y Romero delete passages that could be considered "subversive": "Do not think that Domingo [del Monte] told you [to edit] because he believes as you say that 'nothing must not be written for our good and that of the slaves.' None of that at all: he and I and all who are delighted by your work, do so because it reminds us of a principle of *justice* deeply and idiotically outraged, we do so because we hold in high esteem its circulation among those in whom improvement of conduct can be reached by reading it; and we will do it even smashing against the raging waves of our self-interest beyond the fatherland itself, because it is very petty and insignificant in the scales where the divine rights of humanity are weighed" (93, emphasis in the original). The reasons for those deletions, although they ultimately were done because of fear of accusations of national treason, were expressed in terms of the effectiveness of the political rhetoric in literary form. Presumably referring to those dialogues expressed by the subservient slave characters in *Francisco* (unlike in his Costumbrista articles, there is no sympathetic White character in the novel), González del Valle agreed with del Monte that they should be excised: "Even if Domingo indicated to you that you should suppress the *subversive* element, it is not because, perverting his good principles he believes it prejudicial, but because he saw that the novelist must not put harangues in the mouth of his characters, and especially not when they are implausible; that morality or the greatest politics that may dominate in your work will stand out all on its own, without pointing it out, or proclaiming it at every step" (93–94, emphasis in the original).

Suárez y Romero skillfully worked around the self-imposed literary coordinates of a social-minded Costumbrismo, as González del Valle himself urged him to observe in *Francisco*: "this novel of yours serves to go along correcting our customs, it is to come forth true, Cuban, and so provided with indisputable actions that one needs only see the portrait and abominate it" (94). Keeping in mind these political and literary restrictions and the prescribed silencing of any abolitionist views imposed upon Suárez y Romero, a notable decision in his Costumbrista articles was that, although they were silent and mere secondary characters, slaves appeared as important figures. They were central to the highly regimented sugarcane plantation, a socioeconomic system that few dared to explore in literary form.

Noticeably absent, and in line with Costumbrista production, there was no indication of cultural pride in slave cultural productions. Suárez y Romero's characterizations of the slave workers were clearly positive, however, thus revealing a slight antislavery motif. This in a literary arena of abundant biased portraits of Black types, although mainly as shadow characters, of minor importance at best, would be Suárez y Romero's most notable contribution to the development of the concept of Cubanness inclusive of the marginalized Black experience.

Later, unusual, extreme punishments were described by notable Costumbrista writers in lengthier abolitionist novels, such as Anselmo Suárez y Romero's *Francisco* and Cirilo Villaverde's *Cecilia Valdés*. The authors intended their publications to appear abroad, away from stringent Cuban censorship. The Costumbristas' often fierce vision of contemporary Cuban society is considered to be a precursor of the realist novel (Ucelay Da Cal 66). Abolitionist novelists such as Suárez y Romero and Villaverde had started their careers as Costumbrista essayists, an indication of its impact on the development of the nineteenth-century novel (Suárez-Murias 375).

Personal correspondence among abolitionist writers commenting on their encounters with local censorship indicate the strong influence of the sugarcane plantation owners, the main buyers of African slaves throughout the nineteenth century. Their power was documented in historical accounts of sugarcane plantation owners' transformation of Cuban social patterns by their imposition of slavery as a legal practice. This powerful influence on local laws became a focus of attention for abolitionist activists. There were, however, clear limits to free expression in publications, due in part to the plantation owners' control over Cuban and, arguably, over Spanish policies.

# 2

· · · · · · ·

# Juan Francisco Manzano's
## *Autobiografía de un esclavo*

### Self-Characterization of an Urban Mulato Fino Slave

The Black slave seldom ponders matters of planning, and about doctrines he understands nothing. He considers slavery almost a natural state of being. Most of his species are born slaves in their own country and they adapt to being slaves elsewhere; but their resignation to this position is not incompatible with the instinctive hatred that they feel for a race superior to theirs. Many times this passion is stirred up by their material needs, by abandonment, by their owners' excessive severity; and this and only this had provoked some insurrections that since the early days of the slavery trade broke out in Cuba as well as in the rest of the colonies.

Miguel Tacón in Jacobo de la Pezuela, *Ensayo histórico de la Isla de Cuba*

I realize that, no matter how much I try to speak the truth, I will never take my place as a perfect or even honorable man. But at least, in the prudent judgment of impartial men, one will see to what extremes the prejudice of the majority touches the unfortunate being who has become the victim of some weakness.

Juan Francisco Manzano, *Autobiografía de un esclavo*

Miguel Tacón, Spanish governor of Cuba (1834–1838), in his 1838 report of his activities on the island boldly expressed his personal opinion about the slave population there at the time of his administration. His statement was unusual not because it continued to uphold the same negative portraits about slaves produced in print in Cuba during the nineteenth century, but because at the time he was facing an active period of slave uprisings. The slaves' resistance contradicted not only his report's view of his opinion of Blacks' low intelligence, but also of their presumably natural disposition to slavery. In spite of the havoc that slave uprisings had caused, Governor Tacón supported this distorted characterization of the slave, a view that was also the official stand forced upon Costumbrista writers by official censorship.

Governor Tacón's image of the "good slave"—the meek and humble servant at the disposition of White masters—had already been shattered, however, by news of bloody slave revolts, particularly those after Haitian independence was acquired in 1804. His unsympathetic view of Cuban slaves was precipitated by his reaction to the slave rebellions that plagued Cuba throughout much of the century (Fernández Robaina 11–13). He referred to some of those uprisings in his description of the events of June 17, 1835, on the coffee plantation in the village of Aguacate, and of June 29 at the Magdalena sugarmill in the province of Matanzas; but he denied that slaves had much physical or intellectual power. He warned the Spanish government about a highly organized movement; however, he stated that "they presented no evidence of ramification, although it was clear that there was a spreading of dangerous principles among colored people, a propagation whose origin was located in one of the most important European countries" (582). Governor Tacón's veiled reference to Great Britain as the motivating power behind the slave revolts allowed him to deny the possibility that slaves could be gathering on their own accord.

Governor Tacón also ignored *palenques*, well-organized communities of runaway slaves in existence in Cuba in the nineteenth century (La Rosa Corzo, *Los palenques* 24; Fernández Robaina 8–10). The runaway slave had become a well-known public figure, mainly through published announcements in newspapers of their crimes and convictions, which often resulted in their executions. As indicated in proclamations about urban runaway slaves, many were seasoned slaves, accustomed to slavery and experienced in various trades. In short, they were the trustworthy type that Governor Tacón hailed as the perfect kind of servant. Thus, his implied "good slave," that image forced upon Costumbrista writers as a positive example of slavery, was, in reality, a deception cleverly orchestrated within the legal confines of the Cuban sociopolitical colonial status. The general consensus about the image of Blacks, as Antonio Benítez Rojo stated, was that "the Afro-Caribbean was a lazy being, unenterprising, irresponsible, and likely to acquire all sorts of social defects; a collective being incapable of governing himself and of properly constituting a state; in sum, a second-class citizen who had to be kept at a distance and who would have to be content with very little" (66).

Juan Francisco Manzano (1797–1853), an urban slave of a Creole family with literary connections in Havana, produced memoirs that contradicted Governor Tacón's low opinion of slaves and the attitude among Cuban slave owners in general. The text is today an extraordinary documentation of the experiences of a Cuban slave. In fact, it is the only surviving account of its kind written by a Cuban slave. Within a context of sociopolitical importance for understanding urban slavery practices, Manzano's memoirs refute Governor Tacón's biased opinion of Cuban slaves' inability to express abstract thoughts. That refutation is particularly evident in Manzano's in-depth evaluation of the effects of slavery on his own development.

In spite of the call for social justice that prompted Manzano to write his highly personal memoirs, he made a noticeable effort to please the intended White, and male, readers. Manzano wrote from an ethnically biased perspective as a "mulato fino." His self-description emphasized his upbringing in an upper-level household, leading to behavioral patterns akin to those of a White gentleman, including most prominently proper use of the Spanish language and abandonment of African-rooted customs. In the words of Randall Kennedy, Manzano shared the traits of a "White Negro," or the biracial individual "whose physical appearance allows him to present himself as 'White'" (1). Manzano's demeanor as a mulato fino not only made him behave like a White man but also to write as a Cuban intellectual would have. His close association with members of the Domingo del Monte group, including his close friendship with del Monte himself, had a strong impact on his memoirs.

Manzano was also an urban slave, a fact that provided him access to some of the glitzy activities available in Havana, and promoted his refined image as a mulato fino. He fully explored details of these in a vivid self-portrait. A main section of his memoirs reveals with particulars his childhood in Havana and his raising by a kind, wealthy mistress as a pampered house slave, a condition that Ann M. Pascatello labeled a "favored slave" (127). Upon the death of the motherly first mistress, his second mistress mistreated him badly. After years of hesitation, Manzano decided to escape from a plantation where he had been sent as punishment. The second part of his autobiography presumably detailed his adventures as a runaway slave and his subsequent capture, but writer Ramón de Palma, whom del Monte had entrusted with editing it, claimed to have lost that manuscript around 1839 (Friol, *Suite* 30). There is no indication why Manzano did not rewrite the missing part.

Another important trait in Manzano's self-rendering as a cultured mulato fino was his affinity for poetry. His poems appeared frequently in anthologies, magazines and newspapers in Cuba, gaining him national attention (Friol, *Suite* 91). Prior to drafting his autobiography, Manzano had published in Cuba two collections of poetry. His *Poesías líricas* (*Cantos a Lesbia*) [Lyric poems (songs to Lesbia)] (1821), according to Richard L. Jackson, was the first published book of poetry written by a Black in Cuba, "a considerable achievement, whatever its literary value, when we realize that the author had begun to teach himself to read and write just three years before" (26). His second was *Flores pasajeras* (1830) [Fading flowers].[1]

For instance, Manzano's wife, Delia, a free mulatta, was also a poet. In a letter to his literary patron, Domingo del Monte, dated September 29, 1835, Manzano reported that Delia, at that time seven months pregnant, was suffering because of the delay in her husband's gaining his freedom. To help her endure the stress that almost brought her three times to miscarriage, she wrote poetry: "the verses that she was composing were tender and loving, and now they are melancholy, I perceive the cause, no matter how much she strives to hide it from me, she is a poet and the soul of a poet is seen in her lines" (qtd. in Franco, *Autobiografía* 85).[2] As in his own case, Manzano emphasized that poetry writing was indeed a mark of a White-bound sensitivity, a trait that he denied existed in full-blooded Black slaves. Because of this strong attachment to poetry as a higher example of a White soul, it is odd that Manzano chose not to write his autobiography in a poetic format, preferring to explore a prose genre that, except for use in his letter writing, was new to him.

In 1835 Manzano was encouraged to write the first part of his autobiography by the abolitionist Domingo del Monte (Friol, *Suite* 29). Del Monte brought together important abolitionist and Costumbrista writers in literary gatherings (*tertulias*) where they could read in their totality literary manuscripts that had been censored or those whose authors feared their being examined by local censors (Williams 21). Del Monte's Costumbrista aesthetic as applied to the Cuban sociopolitical conditions of his day may have strongly influenced Manzano's memoirs, as it influenced the work of other writers. Manzano's participation in those *tertulias* and his friendship with Costumbrista writers resulted in his exposure to rich classical literary trends and informed his treatment of White values sympathetic to the oppressive status quo (Willis 203).

Del Monte's influence on the Cuban national scene was often a subject of commentary. For example, Costumbrista writer José Jacinto Milanés, writing to del Monte, described the latter's influence on his own literary production, with emphasis on Cuban customs representative of a rising national identity: "I was seeking a way to write articles of customs about our country, resolved, because of your advice, to depict our Cuban customs and to put aside the (Spanish) peninsular customs" (qtd. in del Monte, *Domingo* 11). Del Monte's correspondence with well-known Costumbrista writers, such as Gaspar Betancourt y Cisneros (1803–1866), reflects the writers' excitement upon receiving his reviews of their works. Betancourt y Cisneros wrote to del Monte after receiving positive comments: "I am very proud of your critique of my wannabe articles" (qtd. in

Figarola-Caneda 58). Betancourt y Cisneros also spoke about the heavy censorship of his article, specifically about having been told by a censor that he was "not permitted to write one word about white colonization" (qtd. in Figarola-Caneda 93)—a reference to indentured European workers, most of them Spaniards, brought to Cuba as cheap laborers.

The critic Salvador Bueno described the influence of del Monte on early nineteenth-century Costumbrista literature: "he curbs certain individualist influences of Romanticism in vogue and directs attention toward local Creole themes, toward collective problems" (*Domingo del Monte* 11). In the continued national debate, del Monte dared to oppose strong official censorship of writing on subjects related to slavery. He wrote in a letter on May 26, 1836, to Salustiano de Olázaga (1805–1873), a liberal Spanish politician and writer and a friend of del Monte, that Governor Tacón had precipitated abolitionist José Antonio Saco's exile from the island after the publication of his "extremely daring article against the slave trade" (del Monte, *Escritos* 44). Del Monte himself had experienced strong censorship in Cuba of literature containing negative views of slavery. Censorship suppressed from one of his poems the following abolitionist statement: "That I never could hear without my soul's boiling in rage the barbaric, atrocious sound of the whip on slave flesh" (qtd. in *Domingo* 14). He was writing under the pseudonym Bachiller Toribio Sánchez de Almódovar, a device that other writers also used in order to avoid controversies (Gómez del Valle 280–90). Because of his political activities, del Monte left Cuba as an exile in 1842. He would never return.

The impact of Manzano's attendance at literary *tertulias* was reflected in his ability to provide self-criticism of his poetic work. According to his self-portrait of a well-read gentleman in the romantic tradition, he managed to attain advanced literary knowledge. Proudly he mentioned that one of his literary models was the Spanish poet Juan Bautista Arriaza (1770–1837). His discussions of literary influences became one of his trademarks as a mulato fino who not only could speak correct Spanish but also produce and record abstract thoughts, unlike the field slaves.

Manzano's demeanor as a mulato fino (although a slave) was not exceptional. The Costumbrista writer José del Castillo (1786–1861) made the following statement about a booming, well-off mulatto class in Havana: "some of them with abundant financial assets, who in their style of life, in their attire, in their demeanor and in their manner of self expression were imitating the White gentlemen that still remained in Cuba, and among them there was no lack of people fond of reading serious books and even of writing verses" (qtd. in Moliner 211).

Interest in Manzano's autobiography was strong among del Monte's group of abolitionist intelligentsia, in spite of the fact that Manzano was better known for his poetry. Del Monte's admiration for Manzano's literary production was documented in their correspondence. Manzano trusted del Monte completely, as indicated in his letter of October 16, 1834, to his sponsor, in which he expressed his gratitude for del Monte's editing of earlier poems: "You have devoted yourself to polishing my verses, making them more enjoyable in the parts that needed it, you will be able to give me the title of half poet" (qtd. in Franco, *Autobiografía* 79).

Del Monte did not edit Manzano's autobiography, however. In 1839 he commissioned the Costumbrista writer and aspiring novelist Anselmo Suárez y Romero to prepare the manuscript for publication. Coincidentally, at this time Suárez y Romero was writing his articles of customs, based on his own experiences as a sugarmill administrator. Presumably there would have been some cross-pollination between these texts. Writing to del Monte, on July 7, 1839, Suárez y Romero stated his initial reaction upon reading Manzano's manuscript: "what naturalness, what grace, what sadness, what expression of horrors, what an evil owner, what a poor Manzano, always beaten, suffering, weeping!" (del Monte, *Centón* 71).

Suárez y Romero did not comment on how much editing he did of Manzano's manuscript. It seems that he saw only one version, which he worked on, in a process that Roberto Friol has described as "expurgation of errors in spelling and in prosody" (*Suite* 30). That manuscript was not to be published in Cuba in the nineteenth century. A publication in English translation appeared in 1840 to commemorate the first antislavery convention in London that year, by the abolitionist Dr. Richard Madden. It was part of a collection entitled *Poems by a Slave in the Island of Cuba, Recently Liberated; Translated from the Spanish, by R. R. Madden, M.D. with the History of the Early Life of the Negro Poet Written by Himself; to Which Are Prefixed Two Pieces Descriptive of the Cuban Slavery and the Slave-Traffic, by R. R. Madden* (Burton 2).

Madden, who had met Manzano in 1838, had received from del Monte a copy of Manzano's autobiography and other abolitionist literary pieces, among them Suárez y Romero's novel, *Francisco*. Of those works Madden published only Manzano's autobiography, perhaps because, as critic Roberto Friol stated, "He had the objective of revealing the intellectual fruits of the Blacks and of attacking slavers and the trade" (33). Madden's own epic poems denounced the crimes that the Cuban plantation owners openly committed against their slaves. Madden visited sugarmills throughout the island in his capacity as British Superintendent of Liberated Africans on the Mixed Court of Arbitration on the Island of Cuba, a position in which he attempted to restrain the slave trade into Cuba (Friol 31; Burton 3; Pérez de la Riva, "1860" 253).[3]

Although the original manuscript of Manzano's autobiography in Spanish did not appear in Cuba until 1937, the third edition of a poetry collection, *Poetas de color* (1879) [Black poets], by Francisco Calcagno, included excerpts of the work (heavily edited by Calcagno). This publication kept Manzano's manuscript known in Cuba, in spite of "mistakes" in the edited version (Friol 40). Calcagno's volume of poetry and other types of writings by Black writers was meant to raise funds for purchase of freedom of the slave poet José del Carmen Díaz in Havana (Franco, *Plácido* 10).

An important element in understanding Manzano's autobiography is the fact that he wrote his memoirs, commissioned by del Monte, from the vantage point of his own experience as a slave at the time when he was writing. Whether the production of this text was a condition of del Monte's campaign to collect money destined to buy Manzano's liberty was not documented; however, it is clear that Manzano set out to write a document that would please his distinguished mentor and, by extension, other White readers sympathetic to the abolitionist cause. Ultimately, perhaps to avoid legal problems for Manzano in Cuba, Madden published Manzano's autobiography without using his name. More importantly, his dual experience as an urban slave and a mulato fino was to become the poster image that Madden took to Great Britain, rather than that of the most numerous group of slaves: the field workers, timidly developed in Suárez y Romero's Costumbrista articles.

Manzano maintained a regular correspondence with del Monte, of which only a handful of the letters from Manzano survive (Friol 55). In those letters Manzano abundantly displays his gratitude toward del Monte, who had initiated his campaign to buy the mistreated slave's liberty: "your Grace will forgive my taking the liberty of troubling your attention in these ill arranged lines, since all the problems imposed upon me by my respect for good opinion have not been able to hold me back within the limits of hoping to see you in order to verify it with all the enthusiasm that inspires the gratitude and recognition toward the object to whom something is due" (Franco, *Autobiografía* 77). The main reason for most of his letters was Manzano's deep gratitude for his forthcoming (though not soon enough for him) emancipation, which Manzano found justified because of the injustices that he had suffered under a cruel mistress. What may seem odd to the modern reader of these letters is Manzano's emphasis on his own case alone; he did not lobby for the abolition of slavery for all slaves, mistreated or not. His case was different because of his sensitive soul "which makes me superior to some people who laugh at me without the least concern" (qtd. in Franco, *Autobiografía* 79). Manzano's reference to a soul, a concept that had been debated in ecclesiastical forums in relation to the Black, was repeated in various formats in these letters and in his autobiography.

Manzano's autobiography is divided into two periods of his life, forming a "history," according to his letter to del Monte, of July 25, 1835 (Franco, *Autobiografía* 83). That letter also describes his eagerness to embark on this project and his relief that he has finally been commissioned to do so: "I can't do less than express to you that I have not had such a notice with so much anticipation" (83). He proceeds to describe his plan, although he shows concern about the credibility of some of its content: "limiting myself to the most interesting events; on four occasions I have considered not continuing it, a picture of so many calamities, it seems to be just a thick heap of notes about lies" (83). Although an initial manuscript had been extensive but inconclusive of the totality of Manzano's life, he expected to finish his memoirs quickly and to keep them short, a characteristic that he seems to imply was requested by del Monte: "I hope to end soon, tightly limiting myself to only the most interesting events" (83). Manzano's plan to draft "a portrait of so many calamities" seems to indicate that he was aware of the production of other abolitionist sketches of customs, such as those by Suárez y Romero, who eventually edited Manzano's manuscript (83).

The first section of the autobiography covers Manzano's birth and his training as an urban house slave by a kind mistress, a position that he was born into because of privileged personal circumstances. A second stage, which includes most of his youth and his early teen years, describes his subjugation as a mistreated field slave of a different mistress. Perhaps such clear-cut divisions of happy and sad life stages corresponded to his original plan as he had described it to del Monte: "I don't know how to show deeds leaving the most terrible part in the inkwell, and I do wish I had other deeds with which to fill the story of my life without recalling the excessive strictness with which my old mistress treated me, obliging me or putting me by force into the necessity of appealing to a hazardous flight in order to relieve my poor body of the continuous tortures that I could no longer suffer" (83–84).

Manzano had chosen to highlight his special background as a house slave whose behavior was akin to that of his White masters. Transcribing his "continuous tortures," he wrote to del Monte, filled him with shame. He described himself as "a weak creature," who, at the hand of a mean White mistress, endured "the most serious sufferings, handed over to several overseers without the least regard of his being the target of their abuse" (84). Indeed, his self-characterization as a delicate being was part of his portrayal as a mulato fino, as evidenced throughout his letters to del Monte: "My present situation can confine the strongest heart, sensitivity and pride struggle in my heart, and silence about my sorrows is the best option that I have left" (86–87).

Costumbrista writers and artists, often mockingly perceived, affected the behavior of mulatos finos as part of a process of *blanqueamiento* [whitening]. In the Costumbrista writer's satirical view, some characters were shown attempting to become physically White. Some Black characters actually underwent whitening processes in order to appear White. Although whitening the skin (attempted through use of abrasive skin lotions) was impossible, codes for the appearance of Whiteness resulted in the emergence of the figure of the mulato fino. Such attempts failed miserably, as many secondary characters in Costumbrista articles illustrated. Mulatos finos dressed fashionably, attempted to speak Spanish correctly, and behaved in the manner proper for a lady or a gentleman; in short, they behaved according to the norms of mainstream culture. The whitening produced a mask that in satirical drawings of the nineteenth century became racist caricatures of characters with exaggerated Negroid features in faces of unreal white shades.[4]

Manzano would have been aware of such popular caricatures, widely available through commercial propaganda, such as the *marquillas*, lithographs on cigarette labels that often promoted negative stereotypes associated with mulatos finos (Kutzinski 54–80; González Echeverría 99–104). Often inspired by crude jokes, which Manzano as a house slave would have heard, the figure of the mulato fino was well known as a member of a booming, up-and-coming Black working class, whose financial means allowed public display of a new Black urban aesthetic. Although Manzano may have intended to construct his own version of an urban mulato fino, his decision to whiten his memoirs also resulted in marginalizing to a minimum his contact with other slaves or freed Blacks. The fact that Manzano did not complain or plead in favor of any other mistreated slave in any of his letters to del Monte demonstrated his deeply felt isolation from the Black working class.

Richard L. Jackson indicated that Manzano may not have had complete control in his choice of his peculiar self-portraiture as a faithful, cultured mulato fino. According to Jackson, del Monte may have intended for Manzano "to play down the threatening image of the rebellious slave while playing up the image of the docile and submissive slave" (29). In this purposefully well-rounded image of a mulato fino, a very revealing factor was Manzano's careful handling of the racial constitution of key characters in his life.

Manzano's self-image as a mulato fino slave may illustrate a "passive characterization" also observed in other abolitionist texts (Barreda 45). His cautious handling of the institution of slavery, as the critic Sylvia Molloy pointed out, created "a mediated text, one unavoidably fostering the *twoness* so many Black writers have described and so many members of minorities have felt" (39, emphasis in the original). Manzano's self-expression as White and Black, slave and aspirer to freed Black, created the strong duality characteristic of the mulatos finos. A byproduct of such hybridity, as William Luis has pointed out, was Manzano's "daring task of bridging through writing the cultural and historical gap between the life of whites and blacks" (85).

One of the most controversial traits of mulatos finos in a position subordinate to White men was their assumption of rather feminine traits, resulting from their passive acceptance of mainstream social values and from their determination to perfect their handling of acceptable behavior, such as their use of an "affected" Spanish. Fionnghuala Sweeney pointed out that this perceived passivity may have been part of their preferred strategy to navigate the slave system: "The expression of the feminine (slave-holding) agency anchoring Manzano's identity marks the origin of a selfhood molded in feminine paradigms of social identity, and a career that will consistently be subject to feminine will" (419). In the particular case of Manzano, the duality observed in Manzano's autobiography resulted from his perceived racial hybridity, the "twoness" resulting from his belief that he belonged to the White mainstream, which he preferred to express in terms of a feminine perspective as a privileged Black, different from the raw behaviors of many Black slaves. His claim to White heritage was strong, symbolically related to his affiliation to his first mistress, a kind woman who treated him as her son.

Manzano had claimed his status as a mulato fino from the unusual circumstances of his birth. His detailed accounts of the early part of his childhood boast about his prominent position in the household of his mistress, proudly presented to the reader as Doña Beatriz de Justiz, the Marchioness Justiz de Santa Ana, wife of Don Juan Manzano. On the other hand, Manzano does not dwell on the *nación* [nation] of the origin of his parents, information often included in reports about runaway slaves or in the newspaper ads announcing slaves for sale. This preference to ignore his ethnic ancestry went against the traditional insistence of Blacks on maintaining an oral record of their ethnic backgrounds. For example, in his memoirs, the runaway slave Esteban Montejo established early on his bicultural African ethnicity. Lydia Cabrera's ethnological fieldwork in Cuba documented such ethnic pride. One of her cultural informants, while referring to the Blacks' active desire to maintain family data, stated, "There, in my town, it was rare for a Black not to know it" (*Reglas* 2).

Manzano seldom used the label "mulato" (if indeed he was a mulato) to indicate his own race, which he set in opposition to other "Black" slaves, whom he never referred to as mulattoes. Blacks often appeared as his adversaries, and they too were not identified by national origin in his writing. There was no substantial information about them, and he did not indicate that they were experiencing the same brutal physical mistreatment as he. His self-preoccupation seemingly prevented his having concern for other Blacks, including those abused. He denounced abusive behavior toward slaves only when it happened to him; Manzano considered such punishment unwarranted for a well-behaved mulato fino slave such as he.

From the perspective of a faithful mulato fino slave, Manzano dwelled on his family's good behavior, a characteristic that the White elite and the White farm administrators admired and that the slaves around him seemed to resent. This animosity between Black slaves and Manzano was never resolved, although at the end of his memoirs he seems to imply that Blacks have become his only allies. Other than in episodes in which the slaves took part in Manzano's physical punishment, there is no mention of their impact on his life, nor does he attempt to befriend them. In Manzano's work, Black slaves remain shadow figures at best, submerged in a complex social structure based on racial castes, at the top of which White men have dominant power. Although his favorite image was that of the mulato fino as a graphic way to demonstrate that he embraced mainstream culture, he also displayed disappointment that, in spite of this cultural immersion, he would remain marginal to a power structure that he had viewed at play as a house slave.

Manzano's narrative focuses on his interaction with White people, whether members of his mistress's family or other key characters in his development as a house slave. His feeling of being different is traced back to the unusual circumstances of his birth, stemming from his mistress's strong affection for his mother, María del Pilar, who had been selected from among the most beautiful of the young women field slaves to go to live with the family in their city home.

Manzano coldly states the selection, in a process that, although rooted in an impersonal slavery practice, makes Manzano's family background exceptional to that of other slaves:

> Whenever Doña Beatriz de Justiz, the Marchioness Justiz de Santa Ana, wife of Don Juan Manzano, went to El Molino, her famous plantation, she liked to take with her the most beautiful ten- and eleven-year-old Creole girls. She took them along, providing them with an appropriate upbringing for their class and station in society. Her house, therefore, was always full of maids instructed to minister to her every need, so that one did not notice the absence of the three or four who were ill-suited for work because of age, ailments, or freedom granted. Among the chosen few, was one María del Pilar Manzano, my mother, who, as hand servant in the marchioness's later years, was one of the maids of distinction, esteemed, or *singled out for training*, however one prefers to put it. (44, emphasis in the text; trans. 45)

The Marchioness Justiz was of advanced age when she chose María del Pilar, a fact that may explain her particularly good treatment of her new choice. María del Pilar became a house slave, which Manzano described as a lady-in-waiting, taking care of her mistress's needs, including serving as *la criandera* (46), the nanny for the newborn White children of the household. These two types of slave labor appear in secondary characters in many Costumbrista essays of the time.

One of the marchioness's outstanding customs was her providing *la libertad en donación* [liberty donated] to her ladies-in-waiting, contrary to the tradition of facilitating a *coartación* [setting a price for the slaves' self-purchase of their liberty] (Ortiz, *Los negros esclavos* 285–90; Mellafe 135–36; Pérez de la Riva, *Para la historia* 163–64). After setting a slave free, the marchioness bought for her a trousseau and arranged her marriage to a free artisan of color (44).

The story of Manzano's mother was, however, different from those of all the previous ladies-in-waiting in two important ways, facts that made Manzano's case tragic. María del Pilar did not receive freedom from the marchioness, for reasons that he leaves unexplained. Perhaps the mistress had depleted the number of available slaves by granting them their liberty. The other difference was his mother's marriage to Toribio de Castro, a slave of the marchioness, stated by Manzano in a short legal statement: "a marriage took place between Toribio de Castro and María del Pilar, to whom I owe my life" (46; my translation). Although María del Pilar did not marry a working freed Black, as previous ladies-in-waiting had, her marriage was legal and not the product of *amancebamiento* [couples just living together], as often happened among both rural and urban slaves, and among freed Blacks. There was no explanation of María del Pilar's choice to marry a slave, Toribio, instead of a freed man, a more appealing choice. Manzano never spoke about love between his parents. Their marriage would have been an unusual decision for his mother, whose high standards Manzano admired.

This incident of a beautiful female slave's transfer to a city house may not have been an isolated case but a general practice among owners of sugarcane plantations. It appears almost verbatim in Suárez y Romero's article "El cementerio del ingenio" [The cemetery at the sugarmill], which suggests that perhaps the anecdotes discussed in del Monte's literary gatherings inspired the Costumbrista writer, or he picked it up as he was editing Manzano's manuscript. In Suárez y Romero's article, the female protagonist of the story is also an exceptional slave, chosen because of her outstanding beauty and her committed loyalty to her mistress. Unlike Manzano's mother, however, the beautiful slave gracefully refused the generous offer, preferring to continue working as a field worker in order to remain close to her blood family.

The strong family bond among slave family members was for Suárez y Romero an indirect abolitionist statement, but in Manzano's memoirs, his familial interaction is weak. He clearly shows a preference for portraying his mother more than his father, Toribio, who remains a figure of less importance. He had a noticeable impact on Manzano as child; a fine musician and a tailor, had he been a freed Black, he could have joined a booming Black artisan and musician community.[5] After Toribio becomes a rural slave, as a character he appears in considerably fewer episodes, and as an individual he had little impact on the development of Manzano's personality.

The father figure would be replaced by some kind White men whom Manzano served for short periods of time. They ultimately contributed to Manzano's formation as a gentleman, the mulato fino whose affected tone prevails throughout the memoirs.

Removed from the care of his natural parents, Manzano presents himself as the beloved child of the kind marchioness, who called him "the child of her old age" (46; my translation). In hindsight, however, Manzano recognizes that she "adopted me as a form of entertainment" (46; trans. 47). His father took a position second in importance to that of the child. Manzano's becoming the marchioness's spoiled brat creates tension between the mistress and his father. As the marchioness's great favorite, he even called his mistress "mama mía" (48). Manzano misbehaved, knowing that she had declared that only she should be responsible for his discipline. On one occasion, his father openly disobeyed her and punished his son, causing the marchioness to stop speaking to Toribio for several days. This behavior was more proper for a wife upset with her husband than for a mistress displeased with her slave's disobedience. Other scenes in which the marchioness behaved more as a condescending mother than as a mistress provides the memoirs with a disjointed feeling of acceptance of a "maternal" White mother and rejection of a Black father.

A confrontation between Toribio and his mistress ends on a curious note. The confessor priest lectures the marchioness about the father's duty toward his own son, and she finally forgives Toribio: "She did so only after making clear to him which parental rights were his as a father and which hers as a slaveholder who assumed the role of the mother" (48; trans. 49). It was unusual for a priest to tell a mistress that her ownership of a slave had limits imposed by the natural laws of fatherhood.

Manzano held a prejudiced view against Black culture, as it was represented in his father's noticeable "Blackness." This characteristic was also a trait of numerous writers, who emphasized and often ridiculed literary male and female mulatto characters. As a mulato fino, Manzano proudly dwelled on his unusual upbringing as the spoiled child of a caring marchioness, an atypical condition even for an urban slave, and particularly different from the life of slaves working on plantations. His disdain toward the field slaves was noticeable. After the death of the marchioness, both of his parents lived and worked on a plantation, but there is no presentation of even a glimpse of the harshness of that type of work. Manzano's memories of life on a plantation were limited to instances when his second mistress sent him there as punishment for what he considered minor misbehavior. Threatening urban slaves with harsh work on a plantation was common among city slave owners.

It was also part of a literary tradition reflected in Costumbrista-inspired, unpublished abolitionist novels.

There were divisions among Black characters, of urban slaves and urban freed Blacks in contrast to rural slaves, revealed in Manzano's stereotypical views of "Black" slaves. Similar diversity was evident in texts written by White Costumbristas. Although Manzano's perception of Black culture was altered by his psychological distortion as a slave wanting to be recognized as a White man, he wrote about several specific Black types, mainly in terms of trades or occupations specifically filled by slaves or freed Blacks.

Positive examples of Blacks are Manzano's godparents. His godfather, Javier Calvo, was a first sergeant of his battalion. Presumably, he belonged to the army division for Blacks and mulattoes, although Manzano does not make that point clear. As with his father, Manzano includes a handful of scenes involving Calvo.[6]

A highly positively characterized figure is Manzano's Black godmother. She had been responsible for his instruction in her own school, presumably a school for colored children. This type of school, although highly limited in the number of subjects that could be taught, allowed a large number of freed Blacks to serve as teachers.[7]

In the first part of the memoirs Manzano pictures a life of ease, which is contrasted with the brutal conditions on a sugarcane plantation. He highlights each section through key characters—for example, the urban *criandera* [the nanny], who nurtured and raised the White children while a Negro *contramayoral* [the Black assistant of the White plantation overseer] performed the dirty jobs, mainly flogging rebellious slaves on the rural plantations. These are characters in Costumbrista articles, but, as already stated, they are represented in small numbers and only as secondary characters.

Education and willingness to accept White customs were Manzano's (and for that matter, any other urban slave's) only way to become a mulato fino, so he accepted the White class that he faithfully served. In his creation of that self-image, he was raised in an urban household, an environment that has been defined as "feminine domestic and cultural spaces" (Sweeney 411), Manzano's humble behavior implied his submission to White cultural and political power structures. As an urban, favorite slave he had a life of privilege, but the field slaves remained marginalized to rural areas, where they suffered untold, hellish lives. He preferred to write scenes that reflected his view of being different, almost special and not meant to be subjected to slavery, or at least not to the brutal tasks performed by the rural slaves. He was, therefore, superior to other Black slaves.

In line with his proud view as a mulato fino, Manzano declares himself to have been a prodigy at age ten. Boastful description supports his self-portrait as a White-like child. These memoirs can be seen as a detailed account of Manzano's self-creation as an intellectual, in spite of ongoing practices that attempted to keep slaves marginal to learned influences. One example suffices. From an early age, at ten years, he already considered himself a poet. Although unable to write the poems that he was composing by age twelve, he found a way to preserve them and avoid the restrictions imposed by his godparents.

There are numerous examples of his ease in adapting to the White ways of a privileged life; however, unlike the traditional effeminate behavior often observed in mulatos finos, they illustrate the reasons for his vivid personality and his highly developed intellect. The scenes offered stress his view of being different, but not the passive, womanlike being that Sweeney claimed for Manzano: "Here, the male subject created in the shadow of feminine power demonstrates little if any of the kind of agency so admired of western masculinity: he is weak, effeminate, seeks escape rather than confrontation, is overly sensitive and remarkably non-rational" (412).

In one example of his being different, Manzano provides a detailed account of his elaborate baptism, an event belonging to the happy time of his childhood, described in a style reflective of self-characterization as a White boy: "I will concentrate only on the pleasant ones, and I am now wandering through a garden of very beautiful flowers, as a series of joys. They took me to the church in the same baptismal gown used for Doña Beatriz de Cárdenas y Manzano, and the ceremony was performed with a harp played by my father and with clarinet and flute music" (50; trans. 51). The literary language matches the elevated tone of the ritual, which was not part of slave traditions. A rare description of a slave baptism appears in one oblique reference in Suárez y Romero's article "Los bohíos al oscurecer" [Huts at dusk]. It is not a descriptive scene, merely an allusion to a slave baptism with no other consequence to the plot than the mere mention that the proud slave parents have come to the plantation house in order to formally introduce the newborn child to the master. Unlike at Manzano's baptism, the proud parents refuse to have the master act as the newborn's godfather, preferring to have that role filled by fellow slaves who were friends.

Another mark of the importance of Manzano's baptism (other than the fact that he was wearing borrowed clothes belonging to his mistress) was the marchioness's decision to provide *coartación*. The event was important for the future of Manzano's parents, but it was also another indication that his life had a different, higher purpose. The suggestion that through baptism Manzano had become a member of the marchioness's family was reinforced by her symbolic purchase of the child, reflected in her generous granting of Manzano's parents' *coartación*.

Although the description of his elegant baptism may suggest that religion would be a central theme in Manzano's autobiography, it takes second place to education. Although there are some mentions of religion, Manzano stresses his outstanding education—another factor that separates him from most slaves, who are allowed only basic religious instruction.

Manzano attended mass regularly with his godmother and his catechism instructor. The latter was not a priest. References to mainstream religious matters continue throughout the memoirs, but they are presented as his only comfort in an otherwise brutal existence as a slave of the evil second mistress. Religion was for him relatively unimportant, although Manzano mentions that he observed a detailed series of daily prayers. He mockingly describes his religious beliefs: "From childhood, my elders had taught me to love and fear God. My confidence was such that I would spend almost all the early hours of the evening praying to heaven that my labors be alleviated. I would recite a certain number of Lord's Prayers and Hail Marys to all the saints of the celestial court, all so that the next day would not be as injurious as the one before" (86; trans. 87). Manzano's references to the saints indirectly derided the religious belief system of his evil mistress, who faithfully observed the traditional cult of the saints as the Catholic Church prescribed: "That is how I knew the lives of all the most miraculous saints and the verses of their prayers, those of the novena of San Antonio, those of the trisagion, in short, all those of the saints, because they were the ones that reached my mistress's table" (124; trans. 125). His embracing of Catholic principles of obedience is in line with his preferred image of a faithful, trustworthy mulato fino.

Controversially, in his autobiography Manzano reveals that he also observed religious beliefs common among slaves and freed Blacks. Two episodes illustrate this point, and one of them includes a memory of his father, a rare documentation of their personal interaction.[8]

In this incident Manzano deals with *brujas* [witches]—supernatural beings that, as the runaway slave Esteban Montejo said extensively, were feared by the slaves (Barnet 20, 64, 113–14, 122). The episode is not, however, intended as a discussion of religious beliefs among the slaves; it is an anecdote about the many talents with which Manzano entertained both Whites and Blacks. Having previously described himself as a child who liked to perform in public, charming his audiences (mainly the house slaves and White visitors to the mistress's house), it is not surprising that Manzano took advantage of the drawing classes given there to the White children by learning to draw. His drawings, according to the instructor, were good, which makes the following scene somewhat puzzling. It seems that Manzano used his drawings as visual aids to his stories, so he drew "a witch giving aid to a demon; the latter had a sorrowful look, and the witch was cheerful" (66; trans. 67). The piece, according to his own statement, "prompted much laughter" (66; trans. 67); however, without any obvious reason, it caused his father's rage, although initially he too had laughed at it. Manzano continues, "I had plenty to cry about for more than two months because my father, with his austere nature, prohibited me from taking up my paint brushes as long as he lived. He took away my box of colors and threw it into the river, tearing up the same picture that had made him laugh so much" (66, 68; trans. 67, 69).

The reasons for his father's behavior are left unexplained. Perhaps Manzano had drawn the witch after the likeness of his evil mistress. The more puzzling factor is, however, that this event is rare in the autobiography, in that it is not about his mistress's raging behavior, but about punishment by his father, who has been an absent father through most of the memoirs.

The second episode depicting Manzano's belief in supernatural beings takes place as part of the numerous examples he gives of the cruel behavior of his second mistress. The episode, which occurred when he was between twelve and fourteen, illustrates an incident of brutal punishment for the "least childish mischief" (56; trans. 57). He was locked up for a day in a dark coal cellar, without food or cover during the chilly night. The circumstances made a terrible impression on him. Besides the cruel physical punishment, the enclosed quarters brought to his mind frightening images, which he describes: "Since my head was filled with stories of evil things from other times, of ghostly souls from the afterlife, and of the enchantments of the departed, when a troop of rats came out making noise it seemed to me that the cellar was full of ghosts" (57–58; trans. 57–59). In retrospect Manzano recognizes that his fear of the wandering souls of the dead was due to his overactive imagination as a talented storyteller, as his many previous anecdotes boasted. Writing as an adult, Manzano has abandoned such beliefs in order to associate himself with a behavior in line with White culture.

The alignment to White culture may explain Manzano's close relationship with his mother, who, unlike his father, has a central role in the memoirs, but only after he begins to experience the cruel behavior of his second mistress. The presence of his mother, characterized as a mulata fina, is particularly obvious in the section covering his teenage years, in which he describes in detail their close relationship. Manzano's distance from his father was so complete that there is no reference even to the circumstances of his death. The reader must infer that Manzano's preference for his mother was based on their likeness as mulatos finos, a trait that was denied to his father. Other than statements that Toribio was a hardworking slave and highly respected by other slaves, Manzano kept quiet about his father's race and character.

Manzano's portrait of María del Pilar as a special case among other, "Blacker" slaves may have its roots in the previous special circumstances that set her and, consequently, him apart from the rest of the *negrada*, the group of slaves. Keeping oneself apart from the damaging influences of other slaves is a recurrent leitmotif in the autobiography, beginning with Manzano's marchioness's request that he remain as close as possible to her. Manzano's high esteem for his mother is clear. He boasts about her higher status as head housemaid and ultimately the marchioness's last servant. In one scene Manzano writes of María del Pilar's "other pregnancy," for which the mistress promised freedom to the child prior to birth. Although it would seem that Manzano would be jealous that he, the first-born, had not received this, he presents this simply as an example of the absurdity of laws controlling slavery. When María del Pilar delivered twins, a legal case developed: "Because of this, there were some legal contradictions, but the decisiveness of the document forced the courts to grant freedom to both of them because they were born at the same time" (52; trans. 53). The future of the Manzano family was looking promising then. Manzano had previously stated that his parents had had news about their emancipation, and now his siblings had been born free.

Manzano's portrayal of his mother as a refined slave and, therefore, a mulata fina, continues as part of his case against his harsh second mistress. María del Pilar had lost her status as an urban lady-in-waiting: "Even though she lived on the plantations, as the wife of a slave who knew how to conduct himself and command respect from everyone, she was exempt from work" (72; trans. 73). The contrast between a good (slave) mother with ladylike status and an evil (White) mistress is evident in an episode in which Manzano seems to explore the theme of unfair treatment of the good slave. This was one of a series of examples of Manzano's mother's strong affection for her son, who was often subjected to brutal punishments by the plantation's overseer and his subordinate slaves under the mistress's orders. It detailed the maternal behavior that led to María del Pilar's first (and perhaps only) flogging in her life. This type of punishment, although often applied to female slaves, was shameful for a slave with White manners.

María del Pilar's behavior is carefully presented as proper—the expected demeanor of a ladylike slave—but she attempted to stop mistreatment of her son by the overseer, Silvestre. Her refined approach made this brutal man listen to her requests for leniency for her son, even though the orders came from his mistress. On this occasion, however, Silvestre was irritated because they had made him get up early, so he hit María del Pilar with his whip (70). What follows is a self-description of an angry child in defense of his mother, in a scene that goes against his previous self-portraits as a meek slave: "All at once I screamed and was transformed from a gentle lamb into a lion. I wrenched myself loose from his grip with a strong yank of my arm and I attacked him with teeth and fists" (70; trans. 71).

Because of his daring action, both María del Pilar and Manzano were held incommunicado for a day, under instructions (presumably from the mistress) to flog both of them the following day. The manager had two assistants, known as *contramayorales*, described as *morenos* [Blacks], "each one of the mulattoes leading his prey to the sacrificial site" (70, 72; trans. 71, 73). Details of the horrifying scene have a strong suggestion of religious martyrdom:

> Bewildered, seeing my mother in this position, I could neither cry nor think nor flee. I was trembling as the four blacks shamelessly overpowered her and threw her on the ground to whip her. I prayed to God. For her sake I endured everything. But when I heard the first crack of the whip I became a lion, a tiger, the fiercest beast, and I was about to lose my life at the hands of the aforementioned Silvestre. But let us pass over the rest of the painful scene in silence. (72; trans. 73)

Although it may seem that Manzano's contrast of the doting mistress versus the sadistic mistress is at the heart of his memoirs, Manzano's frequent descriptions of the severe punishments for his teenage misbehaviors (on one occasion, for example, for pulling a leaf off a geranium plant) bring forward deep reflections in his self-analysis as a refined mulatto. Although Manzano does not use this term in reference to himself, there is one scene in which another Black, whom Manzano plainly describes as "a free house slave," wonders why Manzano allows such mistreatments in spite of his higher status as a whiter slave: "Look, young man, aren't you ashamed of being so mistreated? Any African is treated better than you. A mulatto youth like you, with as many skills as you have, will find someone to buy him in a second" (130; trans. 131). Manzano endured most of his youthful years as an abused slave, although there was a legal way out, which Manzano refers to as "paper to solicit a master," a permission that would allow him to work for another master. He had attempted once to take this option and requested it from his harsh mistress, but he was discouraged by feelings of guilt, common to people subjected to bondage: "I was sorry for having bothered her in such a way" (108; trans. 109), and he had abandoned this option.[9]

Eventually, Manzano's psychological state becomes so compromised that, unlike the proud mulato fino of the first part of the memoirs, he uses racial slurs in describing himself. He states that he became a common urban-born slave, or "an object known as the little half-caste, or María's little mulatto" (112, 114; trans. 113, 115). The refined mulato fino, who coveted the life of the wealthy plantation owners in their luxurious city houses, found himself immersed in the harsh environment of the plantation, a state that was completely foreign to him. It is, thus, not surprising that Manzano offers no information about rural slave culture, even at the most basic level, such as references to food or music—items often mentioned in travelogues by foreign visitors. Like the Cuban Costumbrista writers, Manzano preferred to write about the Black musical scenes available in Havana. Boastfully, he says that he prefers operas to the street Black musical performances, including no reference to having attended dances in *cabildos*, or dance halls with a membership composed of freed Blacks. Other examples of how his upbringing kept him away from rural slaves include his use of standard, refined, literary Spanish; he is clearly avoiding the use of bozal or the Creole forms of Spanish used by plantation slaves.

Manzano's fall from fortune, as he labeled his dark period as the slave of his second mistress, appears in theatrical terms that reflect his desire to express his sensitive spirit:

> From the age of thirteen to fourteen, the joy and vivacity of my charac-
> ter and the eloquence of my lips, dubbed "the golden beak," all changed
> completely into a certain kind of melancholy that, with time, became a
> personal trait of mine. Music enchanted me, but, without knowing why,
> I would cry, and enjoyed that relief, so that when I found an opportunity
> I sought solitude in order to allow my grief free rein. I would cry rather
> than sob, but I was not faint of heart except during certain states of de-
> pression, incurable to this day. (58, 60; trans. 59, 61)

His long list of tasks performed under the commands of various masters and mistresses provided Manzano space to do in-depth self-analysis of his failed potential, not as a worker but as an intellectual. Nonetheless, his performance of manual tasks, as he observes, were the kind that gave him prestige as a well-rounded house slave. He remembers, for instance, that he was a good tailor, and, had his father not opposed it, according to a teacher of art, he would have become a good portrait artist worthy of painting for White patrons. After he was granted his freedom, Manzano even became a well-known pastry chef.

Although Manzano's house chores were manual tasks, his self-portrait is that of a thinker with a sensitive soul, whose rather existential considerations dwell on less mundane subjects. His inclination to ponder the abstract may explain the scarcity of passages dealing with physical descriptions of his body. They remain for the most part limited to revelations about his elegance in attire (when he served as house slave). As a proud mulato fino, in two key scenes he apologizes for his short height, which he attributes to his "weak constitution [due] to the bitter life I have had since the age of thirteen or fourteen" (58; trans. 59). This unflattering portrait contrasts with the highly positive descriptions of field slaves in Suárez y Romero's Costumbrista articles; their physical strength often stands out as their main defense against brutal treatment. Manzano presents himself as a man of unprepossessing appearance, perhaps to elicit pity from his sympathetic White readers: "always thin, weak, and emaciated, and my face constantly betrayed the paleness of a convalescent, with enormous rings under the eyes" (58; trans. 59).

In spite of his efforts to appear defenseless, according to his perception, White people around him viewed him in a different light. Manzano claims that he often ate like a glutton: "I would stuff myself and gobble the food down almost without chewing, so I frequently had indigestion. That made me have to take care of certain necessities often" (58; trans. 59). These absences from his post brought him more punishment: "My usual offenses were not hearing the first time I was called and missing one word when I was given a message" (trans. 58; 59). That barely disguised scatological reference to his constant need to relieve himself becomes a repeated leitmotif, a veiled commentary on the impact of slavery on his body and, by extension, on his developing personality.

A more puzzling silence is Manzano's lack of description of his skin color, and he gives no indication of the degree of coarseness of his hair. Both traits, particularly statements about the *pasas* [kinkiness] of the Black characters' hair, are present in many Costumbristas writers' descriptions of Blacks. Often the closeness of Black characters to White physical traits defined the degree to which they could be trusted. About his hair, Manzano makes only one reference: His evil mistress had the custom of stripping him of his clothes, which were replaced with a coarse pair of overalls, and having all his hair shaved off. Not bragging about straight hair (produced after painful, damaging artificial processes) went against the traditional image of mulatos finos, particularly evident in proud light-skinned mulattas, whose literary characterizations often indicated their fixation on the straightness of their hair as a mark of their Whiteness and, therefore, their acceptance into mainstream Cuban society.

In lieu of physical descriptions Manzano frequently documents his mental state, which, he stresses, is that of an extremely nervous person, so that "as soon as they called me I would be overcome by such intense trembling that my legs could barely support me" (58; trans. 59). He became melancholy, another indication that he was framing his life within the romantic literary models to whom he later enjoyed listening in del Monte's literary gatherings in Havana: "since melancholy took root in my soul and had physically become part of my existence, I took some pleasure in composing verses, all sorrowful ones, by memory under the guásima tree whose roots formed a sort of pedestal for those who were fishing. I did not write the verses down since I did not know how to, but I possessed a mental notebook of verses and improvised anything" (62; trans. 63).

Manzano refers often to his poems, but he offers no descriptions of their content nor does he give their titles. They are his most tangible demonstrations of his possession of a marked spirit, a sensitive soul in opposition to the raw nature of other Blacks. He had been, according to his testimony, a child prodigy who found unusual ways to provide himself with written materials, which he describes in scenes that echo other such desperate writers: "From early childhood I was in the habit of reading everything legible in my language. And when I walked down the street, I always went along picking up pieces of printed-paper, and if it were in verse I would not pray again until I learned it by heart" (124; trans. 125). Throughout the text he refers to Spanish as his native language. Advanced, skillful use of the language was a most difficult task for a mulato fino. The stereotypes of such "learned men" would became common objects of public scorn, particularly in theatrical productions that presented an affected, almost effeminate man who distorted the Spanish language by means of convoluted use of grammar and misuse of vocabulary.

Manzano's cultivated image as a learned, refined mulato fino conflicted with his constant struggles with an evil mistress, who displayed an unstable mental condition. His highly developed skills as a house slave failed to please the woman, whose unrealistic expectations became examples of abusive mistreatments of slaves under the cover of Cuban laws. He brings to the reader three incidents that in a linear sequence foretell his necessary escape from his mistress's control in order to save his life. This ending is foreshadowed at the beginning of the memoirs. The final scene is brief. Immediately after a nasty physical encounter with his mistress, Manzano swears, he heard an ominous sentence announcing his tragic end: "'I'm going to kill you before you come of age'" (84; trans. 85)."

Although Manzano escaped from that dark fate, there was a price to pay. The strain on his relationship with his family inspires the most passionate of his statements. After his mother's sudden death, he expresses his loving thoughts: "As her son and one who loved her, I showed for her every possible emotion that one can imagine" (114; trans. 115, 117). Furthermore, he finds out that the mistress effectively had controlled María del Pilar's possessions, which surprisingly included jewelry that the slave had kept hidden. The events that follow are even sadder. Three months before she died, she had presented money to her mistress to buy Manzano's liberty, a transaction that the evil woman would later deny. This provoked his decision to escape the grasp of the mistress. She had violated the motherly bond often found between the owner and the faithful slave, so he felt justified in his desire to escape: "As for me, from the moment I lost the illusion of my hoped-for freedom, I was no longer a faithful slave. I was transformed from a meek lamb into the most despicable creature. . . . All my feelings of gratitude were weakened, and I thought only about fleeing" (118, 120; trans. 119, 121).

Manzano had finally accepted openly his dissatisfaction with his condition as a tame slave: "Despair had occupied the place of all my feelings. My mother was the only thing I had there, and she was gone" (120; trans. 121). His sentimental ties with the wicked mistress broken, Manzano decided to run away—an action that went against his White frame of mind. The *cimarronaje*, or the strong tendency to become a cimarrón [runaway slave], indicated in legal documents of the time, was present in Manzano's family. He mentions in passing an uncle (left unnamed), who had "bad luck," after having run away. "He was brought back like a true runaway slave" (134; trans. 135). Although that was not a very good example, Manzano became a runaway. In a statement he placed faith in his destiny: "I was, nevertheless, resolved to try my luck and suffer the consequences" (134; trans. 135).

Other factors in Manzano's decision to become a *cimarrón* may have been his frequent punishments and his feeling of alienation from the other field workers. His characterization of them reveals the deep social divisions between the house slave, whose behavior was more akin to White culture, and the rustic slave culture of the plantations. Manzano resented being equated with the field workers. He describes his strong displeasure at the wicked mistress's frequently pretending that Manzano had been born on the plantation: "She always painted me as the worst of those born at El Molino, of which she said I was a native son. This was another kind of mortification for me. I loved her in spite of the harshness with which she treated me. I knew very well that I was baptized in Havana" (122; trans. 123).

Manzano's loneliness on the plantation was aggravated by what he perceived as the field slaves' hatred for him. His self-portrait as a White-raised Black set him apart from the field slaves: "I saw myself at El Molino, without parents or even relatives, and, in a word, a mulatto among blacks. My father was a bit proud and never allowed small groups in his house or that any of his children play with black children from the plantation. My mother lived with him and his children, which is why we were not very well liked" (132; trans. 133). This description, however, goes against his previous statements that both his father and his mother were respected by the field slaves.

Despite the importance of his decision to escape, in his description of the actual scene of his becoming a runaway slave, Manzano fails to offer a thrilling portrait. Perhaps it was because such an action illustrated his White aversion to breaking the law. He was to become a rough runaway at the mercy of his skill to survive in the wild (of which he knew very little). The actual scene of his escape is rather anticlimactic. He saddled a horse for the first time in his life. Before he mounted the horse, he said: "I got on my knees, entrusted myself to the saints of my devotion, put on my hat, and mounted" (134; trans. 135). His flight from the dreaded plantation prompted an indirect apology for his negative portrayal of the field slaves. As he mounted, he heard a voice that cheered him on: "God be with you. Hurry along" (134; trans. 135). This apparently divine intervention had an explanation. The mysterious voice came from one of the many slaves who had been observing Manzano. In retrospect, he realizes that the slaves had observed his preparations to escape and had concealed his escape from the supervisors: "I thought that nobody had seen me when everyone was watching me; but, as I later discovered, nobody tried to stop me" (134; trans. 135).

The concept of an extended Black family, from which he had excluded himself, was, at the end, vindicated. It was his hated *negrada*, the Black slaves, who protected him, not the White characters, whom Manzano previously offered so many descriptions of, as proof of his devoted service to them. He went into the roads leading to Havana, a route that he had gotten to know well, when he had served as a page for the kind mistress's coach, but unlike those fancy trips to the country, he was now traveling as a runaway slave.

His decision to escape, so far from his preferred image of a learned mulato fino, went against his knowledge of Cuban regulations about the mistreatment of slaves. If there were lessons learned from his probably traumatic experiences as an urban slave turned into runaway, they were lost in the misplaced second part of the manuscript of the autobiography.

In June or July of 1836 (Friol 31) Manzano finally received his freedom and, therefore, symbolically became the White gentleman that he had yearned to be since his privileged childhood as a house slave. Despite being part of an impersonal, demeaning commercial transaction, in which he was objectified and priced at five hundred pesos, he must have felt that he was playing the "White" part right (Láscar).[10] After all, eventually he would meet with reputable intellectuals, such as Madden, whose personal interaction with Manzano may have influenced both the direction of his abolitionist campaign in Great Britain and the content of Madden's *Poems by a Slave in the Island of Cuba.* The British superintendent of liberated Africans on the mixed court of arbitration, who translated into English and published in Great Britain Manzano's memoirs, as Roberto Friol has pointed out, had, however, a specific political goal: "to reveal the fruits of the intellect of the Black and to charge with crimes the slave traders and the slave trade" (33).

On the other hand, Manzano had considerably less elevated sentiments than Madden. For Manzano, the humble slave, who had already started writing his memoirs, his first choice was not an autobiography; he would rather be writing a novel. As he confessed to del Monte, in his letter of September 29, 1835, he had designed a plan to set aside "one part of my life," which would be part of a future "real Cuban novel" (qtd. in Franco, *Autobiografía* 85). Although such was not implied in this, Manzano might have been referring to slaves' narratives, a genre that he would have been familiar with through his conversations with Cuban abolitionist writers in their meetings at del Monte's gatherings (Bremer 496).

Richard L. Jackson has pointed out the intrinsic importance of Manzano's memoirs as an example of slaves' narratives, which had impacted the Cuban abolitionist and literary scenes through "unique statements about identity" (33). In the case of Manzano, the racial identity that he so strongly subscribed to in his autobiography went against that of the public view of his persona. While others saw in him only a Black house slave at best, he sought to be considered a mulato fino and thus a "Cuban" whose human rights had been violated.

Manzano self-described himself to del Monte as a *mártir*, an image of religious sacrifice that permeates his memoirs (qtd. in Franco, *Autobiografía* 84). Whether del Monte offered specific instructions to Manzano cannot be ascertained from Manzano's surviving correspondence with his literary mentor. Presumably, however, del Monte, well-known as the precursor of "the art of prose," would have suggested stipulations about his commissioned autobiography (de la Cruz, "El guardiero" 81). A clue to understanding what del Monte might have been expecting from Manzano may be reflected in his article "Dos poetas negros: Plácido y Manzano" [Two Black poets: Plácido and Manzano].

Writing from exile in Paris in 1845, del Monte presents the poetry of Cuba's most notable Black poets, whom he contrasts in terms of their opposite racial identities: "Plácido was never a slave, and of course, his color was almost White. For that reason he did not have to struggle in his life, as did Manzano, who was almost Black and a slave from birth, with the insuperable obstacles of his condition, in order to develop the natural talents of his imagination, which was really poetic" (*Ensayos* 84–85). That poetic constitution may have been the source of Manzano's desire to produce his version of a mulato fino, proof of his adherence to mainstream cultural values.

Del Monte reveals his preference for Manzano's poetry over Plácido's. His reasons are simply put in terms of Manzano's overcoming the difficulties of a life full of hardship: "Manzano cannot repeat in his linked lyre, any theme other than the anguish of a hazardous life filled with terrible ups and downs. But I preferred the sad chants of the slave, to the nugs canors (simple, but harmonious verses) of the free mulatto, because I noticed deeper feeling of native humanity" (85). Indeed, in an indirect reference to his unstated "principles of my aesthetics and of my philosophy," del Monte presents those as the reasons for having an affinity to "the lament torn from the heart of one oppressed" (85).

Manzano's self-image as a mulato fino prevented his producing the abolitionist text that del Monte might have expected. Manzano frequently explains to del Monte in their correspondence that in drafting his memoirs he intended to produce a realistic document. In a letter dated December 11, 1834, Manzano summarizes his life: "my slavery has been only a collection of calamities and pointlessness" (Franco, *Autobiografía* 81). Although in that letter Manzano displays determination to gain his freedom, framed as "my love for freedom," he wants it as "a natural principle" that must be available to all slaves (81). In spite of such a progressive view of the horrors of slavery, Manzano's emphasis on his own case, based on what he considered violations of his human rights as an integrated mulato fino, could have invalidated his memoirs as an effective abolitionist text.

Instead, as Manzano fully describes to del Monte, he had intended to write a more personal account of the impact of slavery upon his sensitive soul, and in particular, of his uncalled-for mistreatment by a mentally disturbed mistress. This was his view of slavery as a mulato fino. Slavery became a sort of catalyst to heighten his emotions, as he indicated to del Monte in a letter dated October 16, 1835: "My present situation can make helpless the strongest heart, sensitivity and sense of pride conflict in my heart, and the silence of my sorrows is the best that remains in me" (Franco, *Autobiografía* 86–87). Puzzlingly, he preferred to maintain silence about most of his cruel experiences as a mistreated slave, because if he were to write the complete version of such tragic experiences, the resulting product would have been "an extensive protocol of lies" (Franco, *Autobiografía* 83). He refers to the legal protocol used by his mistress to make him suffer.

Unlike a runaway slave whose escape into the wilderness graphically intended to show a break from both slavery and the unjust legal system that allowed such a terrible practice, Manzano maintained a psychological profile of acceptance typical of the mulato fino. He spoke about his humble condition as a faithful slave, who placed himself at the mercy of the system, as he indicated to del Monte, in his letter of June 25, 1835: "I am a slave and the slave is a dead being before his lord" (Franco, *Autobiografía* 84).

As a submissive mulato fino, in this surrender to del Monte, who was kind but ineffectual against the slavery system, Manzano trusted that he as a "White" gentleman now could find a place for himself within a racially divided society. He considered his life as a refined slave implicitly incorporated into the mainstream, not into the life of other, more raw slave experiences, such as those of the field worker. He saw himself as a prime example of a system that violated his rights as a self-proclaimed mulato fino. Such a privileged status provided him, according to a letter from Manzano to del Monte, Cuban citizenship, as reflected in his proud reference to Cuba as "my fatherland" (Franco, *Autobiografía* 85). From that perspective he produced a nationalist discourse that provided him the right to speak against the evils of Cuban society.

# 3

. . . . . . .

# Urban Slaves and Freed Blacks

## Black Women's Objectification and Erotic Taboos

Cuban multidisciplinary texts documented in detail Blacks' ordinary activities, making it possible to picture their changing status throughout colonial society. One of the earliest sources of Cuban slaves' public activities is the Actas capitulares del Ayuntamiento de La Habana [Chapter minutes of the city council of Havana] at the City Hall of the city of Saint Christopher of Havana on the island Fernandina (the name of Cuba given by Christopher Columbus) meetings. The Minutes are available in two volumes from 1550–1565 and 1566–1574 (Roig de Leuchsenring). Most of these records were of city ordinances or regulations imposed on slaves or freed Blacks. They covered the types of manual work allowed in public and private spaces as well as living arrangements, including restrictions on their location and on materials that freed Blacks could use. There were limits on their participation in public activities, and certain types of clothing were banned.

There are also glimpses of the impact of Blacks on daily life in Havana. These prohibitions revealed the Blacks' tenacity in re-creating regional African customs or in developing so-called Black Creole products.

The meetings at the Havana City Hall fully addressed customs of slaves, and eventually they documented the presence of freed Blacks, known as *horros*, and the activities associated with their socioeconomic positions, first as enslaved individuals and later as freed Blacks in a highly structured ethnic society. In spite of the highly regulated lives imposed upon slaves and freed Blacks, they managed to preserve their popular customs (against restrictive monitoring of their activities), which were often viewed as illegal. Of much interest to literary critics are the images of emerging Black urban "types," who became popular characters in the Costumbrista literature of the nineteenth century.

The most common entry in the City of Havana's Minutes is Black street vendors, who were either slaves or freed Blacks. The city closely regulated the kinds of merchandise they were allowed to sell and the prices of their goods. They dealt with specified goods, such as root vegetables and other vegetables, fruits, casaba bread, eggs, and poultry, to be sold at fixed prices and in certain locations within the city limits. This commerce gave rise to a booming Black social class, and from it came a literary character, the *pregonero*, or street vendor, whose selling style and advertising methods of yelling about his or her goods (as a *pregón*, or screamer) became a subject of Costumbrista literature.

Violations by Black vendors were common entries in the City of Havana's Minutes. One violation was the establishment of illegal taverns and other places of entertainment, which often included sleeping quarters, a coded reference to a house of ill repute. For example, on August 21, 1570, there was a hearing against Margarita Hernández, a Galician woman, who had been accused of selling wine to Blacks from her house turned into a tavern. Black freed women were by law forbidden to "sell wine in a public tavern since it is gravely damaging to a republic, because after getting drunk many Blacks would get killed" (I:286).

White and Black men frequented taverns, which were one source of African-based music within an establishment that was often described in negative terms: "in the said house [ . . . ] there occurs much immodest and roguish behavior" (II:201). The constant references to Blacks in attendance and the veiled references to the kinds of activities that took place would also be reflected in nineteenth-century Costumbrista literature.

Another common theme in the Minutes was the City Hall's handling of lands used by freed Blacks. The creation of areas specifically for the construction of houses for freed Blacks came about as the result of formal requests from freed Blacks. Granting such petitions, as stated in one case, seemed to have been in recognition of extraordinarily good habits. Permission to build permanent dwellings contrasted with the negative portraits mentioned previously. The freed Black asking for land to build a dwelling appeared named, often with first and last names, and there was a positive reason stated for his or her request.

There seems to have been a concerted effort to restrict areas specifically geared to incorporate land under petition by freed Blacks. There were many requests by Blacks to inhabit lots next to properties owned by other freed Blacks. The rejection of land petitions seems to imply that the land requested was restricted to White inhabitants only. In Costumbrista essays these Black neighborhoods served two significant purposes. First, they were the stages of dangerous and forbidden scenes. Second, they would be the last bastions of "traditional" customs, mainly represented in foods, which have not disappeared yet under the influence of modernism.

There were two matters obviously left undiscussed in the City of Havana's Minutes: any recording of religious observances by slaves or freed Blacks or any celebration of musical activities. Other than a request from a church for permission to purchase slaves to be used in construction, there are no entries about Blacks' connections with any official religious organization. There was also no discussion of the underground practices of native African religions in Havana. The Minutes did not record the presence of folkloric music so common among slaves and freed Blacks, particularly during religious performances. "Noises," in one of the Minutes referred to as "scandals," may point to the adherence by Blacks at the time to such religious music, related to a *cabildo*, or an all-Black social organization.

Alcohol was a source of amusement for Blacks and Whites alike (II:54). This type of entry was often detailed in references to illegal taverns, which, as indicated earlier, were places for sexual entertainment. Forced prostitution, as masters engaged slaves in a sexual market, became a frequent complaint cited in the Havana City Hall Minutes, and it was the subject of legal restrictions issued by Spanish law (Hall, *Social* 91). The numerous statements that White men were often present in taverns, participating with Blacks in violations of proper social conduct, implied a special type of multiethnic marginal community. This group of "criminals" would also be a topic of interest to the Costumbrista writers.

Historical texts continued to offer portraits of Black figures based on their specific place within the highly structured and controlled, colonial, slavery-based society. The earliest of such historical accounts is found in *Descripción de la Isla de Cuba, Con algunas consideraciones sobre su población y comercio* [Description of the island of Cuba, with some observations about its population and its commerce] by Cuban-born Nicolás Joseph de Ribera. Written in Spain in 1760, but never published, this first-person account of the conditions of Cuban society provided information about the island's judicial management as a Spanish colony, including the effects that limitations on the slave trade had had on commerce.

As part of his historical overview of the Cuban population, de Ribera's chapter entitled "De sus gentes" [About its peoples] begins a condensed account of a national racial profile. He omitted any serious attempt to memorialize the native inhabitants, who had disappeared by the time of his writing: "in some other towns one sees such descendants of them, they are of mixed race and they are quite few" (101). Using a descending scale of racial components, de Ribera divided the population "by color" into three distinctive groups: Whites, mulattoes and Blacks. "The Whites are from Europe or they are descendants of Europeans. The Blacks are brought from Africa or they are descendants of Africans, and the mulattoes are a mixed race of Black and White" (101). De Ribera was a declared supporter of the slave trade, which, he wrote, must be increased in order to support Cuba's booming agricultural industry of the late eighteenth century.

His discourse on Black racial classifications was based on their "condition," inherent in their birth, as "free or slaves." He explained that dichotomy: "All the Whites are free, and those Blacks and mulattoes who by their own labor or by the generosity of their masters acquired freedom. And the slaves, those subjected to such an unfortunate condition, as a prize of war or by another legitimate title in Africa, were transported to that Island, or were born there of captive mothers brought there" (101).

De Ribera offers glimpses of a highly structured caste system among slaves. This caste system of African-born slaves and their descendents, known as criollos [Creoles], are at the heart of the rigid Cuban slavery system. His final observations on the racial constitution of the African ethnicities, whose origins he divided into "fifteen or twenty different nations," none of them named, provided a subcategory: Cuban-born slaves, or criollos, and those natives of Africa known as bozales (102). This division, as with Whites and freed Blacks, provided de Ribera grounds for explaining an animosity that kept them apart: "Criollos are those who are born on the Island, and the bozales came here after their birth. The former speak Spanish as the Spaniards do, which is the only language of the whole Island. And the others, more or less, according to their intelligence, and the time that they have heard it" (102).

Although de Ribera clearly preferred the Creole slave over the bozal, he also commented on a special consideration for the bozal slaves: "one tries then to instruct them in our religion and in our laws, and equally in the language of the land" (102). As many eyewitnesses stated, however, often this regulation was not observed, particularly in rural settings, such as the plantations.

Creole slaves were not afforded any special privileges. De Ribera had a sympathetic view toward them, perhaps simply because, unlike the bozales slaves, they had been born in Cuba. He referred to an immediate need for new laws on slavery, an update that was necessary because "they were formed a long time ago in Havana, they are antiquated now . . . and at every step they show that they were made with extremely little knowledge of the whole Island" (144). Such legal reform was necessary for differentiation of the rights of the three main racial components on the island: "It seems to me that on the Island, there is a need for municipal ordinances that distinguish the rights of Whites, and of Blacks, and of mulattoes" (144). The subject of mulattoes, the island's third racial component, to whom de Ribera presumably was willing to grant rights, remains unexamined throughout the text. His lack of interest in further exploration of the freed Black may be explained by the mulattoes' disassociation from slavery-based tasks on plantations; however, his mention of them indicates their increasing importance as a component of the Cuban social fabric. He makes no effort to illustrate such a role, for example, by indicating their fields of work or places where they were allowed to live.

José Martín Félix de Arrate (1701–1765) offers a different view of slavery in his *Llave del Nuevo Mundo, Antemural de las Indias Occidentales, La Habana Descripta: Noticias de su fundación, aumentos y estado* [Key to the New World, defense of the Western Indies, Havana described: news of its foundation, growth and condition] (1761). This is a more comprehensive study of the emergence of Havana as an urban center of a booming economy. In a text considerably longer than de Ribera's, de Arrate, writing as a member of the City Council of Havana, states his hope for an increase in the importation of Africans onto the island as slaves, the only means for fulfillment of Cuba's economic potential. Understandably, his prejudiced view toward slaves stemmed from his promotion of slavery itself, a business from which the city of Havana derived many economic benefits.

De Arrate characterized Blacks as barbaric, compared with the late native, indigenous peoples, whose demise had been a reason for the importation of Blacks. His portrayal of the indigenous people, summarizing an unnamed chronicle, was set within the tradition of the noble savage: "they were peaceful in nature, docile and shy, very respectful toward their superiors, with great skill and aptitude for instruction in the Faith, willing to help, of good disposition and personable, and pleasing in form and beauty" (18). This was in contrast to the African slave, delineated as a "barbarian" (18). He lamented:

> It is indisputable that in this country and in others like it, the preservation of the Indians would have been incomparably more desirable than the entrance of the aforesaid Blacks, because that people being less barbaric, as our historians suppose, they would serve with more intelligence and skill in their work in sugar and tobacco, in sowing and in the harvests of the rest of the products that the Island offers, which do not demand so much strength as the work in the mines. (40)

De Arrate did not record details concerning the booming sugar market that he indirectly refers to in the preceding quotation, preferring to dwell on data dealing with the city of Havana.

Havana had begun to contend for the luxurious life of the capital cities of the viceroyalties of Mexico and Peru. De Arrate recorded the existence in Havana of a trade class, composed of freed Blacks, whom he labeled as "brownish-grey or Blacks" (76). He developed a positive portrait of freed Blacks in his description of the militias for Blacks and mulattoes (*pardos*), whom he presented as "so fit, sharp and talented for this purpose as for other different ones of royal service" (76). Arrate continued to express, however, a preference for the Cuban-born White of Spanish descent, whom he called criollo, and described in a highly optimistic terms: "Both men and women are in countenance and body of good proportion, kindness and skill" (105). References to violent behavior in the relationship between the Cuban White Creole and Blacks remained unsaid.

In contrast to this early, positive portrait, throughout the nineteenth century there would be dissenting voices that presented urban freed Blacks in a negative light. One example is *Memoria sobre la Ciudad de San Felipe y Santiago* [Memoir of the city of San Felipe and Santiago], published in 1830 by Manuel Mariano de Acosta at the request of the Patriotic Society of Havana. He described in negative terms "a mixture of Whites and Blacks that produces mulattoes" (51). His description of the colored population makes no clear differentiation among groups, but he openly preferred the freed Blacks, whom he called *pardos*.[1] The memoir does make clear distinctions between workers by gender—a detail that Cuban Costumbrista writers imitated: "Mulatto women and freed Black women attend to their housekeeping and work for a whole year in order to spend all their savings on one get-together and one dance, with the object of surpassing that day the luxury and brilliance of White women, but, nevertheless, there are many that are estimable" (430).

Another type of historical approach ignored altogether the origin of certain established cultural traditions documented in Costumbrista articles as African. If the names so denoted, the reader may have suspected that they had a Black background. Examples of these two types are evident in José María de la Torre's nostalgic memoir of the city of Havana, *Lo que fuimos y lo que somos o La Habana antigua y moderna* [What we were and what we are or the old and modern Havana] (1857). He demonstrated the fluency with which chroniclers often erased Black contributions to mainstream cultural practices.

One case referred to by de la Torre was the sale of tortillas de maíz, a kind of corn fritter, known in Havana as tortillas de San Rafael because they were prepared on October 24 in celebration of the feast of the archangel Rafael. He fondly remembered the tortillas. He acknowledged the popularity of this food item, as indicated in an ordinance of the City of Havana that regulated its sale, but de la Torre failed to mention that Black women cooked them (164). His description of that popular delicacy was surprisingly bland: "The corn fritters were sold, in October, each rationed to ten ounces, and thus the City Council ordered that they be sold at three for one real, and when two were given, they should weigh fifteen ounces" (164).

In contrast to de la Torre, José Victoriano Betancourt offers a vibrant report of the fair of San Rafael in the article "Las tortillas de San Rafael." In the tradition of the Costumbrista article, it is a first-person narration by a speaker who was nostalgic about the celebration. The corn fritters were a staple of the feast of San Rafael, celebrated by large crowds in a popular neighborhood well known in Havana. Betancourt hailed this native food item as one element of a dying tradition worth preserving. Although the essay was not completely positive, Betancourt presented a portrait of events at the fair, which included a combination of religious and popular festivities so commonly seen in large Cuban street parties.

Two temporal perspectives were at play in Betancourt's essay. In the first part of his article, he traced his recollection, as a teenager, of his first visit on his own to the neighborhood known as El Angel, in honor of the archangel whose church dominated a hill. At the time of the drafting of this article, the neighborhood came to life once a year, "where for eight days with fraud and shamelessness," they celebrated the feast of the archangel Rafael (225). The open-air fair brought, according to Betancourt's article, "peasants, soldiers, Blacks and boys of all colors" seeking, among other activities, gambling games and, of course, the tortillas de San Rafael (218). These multitudes of dissimilar characters were the center of attention of an article of rather bland plot delineation and character development.

In spite of the presence of male figures of ill repute, racial types possessing highly negative character traits, there were popular components that the adult perspective of the essay declared part of Cuba's national folklore. This was true of tortillas, which were discussed at length:

> In the epoch to which I commit myself and until the year '34, such was the consumption of tortillas, that the preparers of note spent the night producing them, and they could not cope with the orders, so it was necessary to arrive at dawn in order to obtain enough of them, and so great was the number of buyers who flocked there that they formed a line, and at times, one needed two hours to reach his turn. The truth is that they made them of such exquisite taste that it was worth the nuisance of the wait, in exchange for the pleasure that they offered. (222)

Although the absence of a direct mention of the race of the preparers appears to be part of Betancourt's project to set forth a national folklore, at the end of the article he provides names of cooks, presumably those who attracted the longest lines for buying tortillas: "only missing are María de la O and María Belén, the queens of tortillas" (227). Their names indicate Black women, as these same names often appeared in other Costumbrista essays about Black or mulatto women.

Ultimately, as other Costumbrista writers remarked, a more moral character overtook the celebrations. Although this new phase appeared to be the best option against wild behavior (of male characters) fully described throughout the text, Betancourt seems to miss that free-for-all, which he associates with his teenage years: "Thus civilization, slow but sure, goes along modifying popular customs and bringing them into harmony with morality and reason; all the grotesque and harmful accessories disappear; the base remains and appears more beautiful, although the outlines may not be so pronounced and brilliant" (226).

Another example that points to ways in which Black contributions were ignored in memoirs intended as historical recollections about a developing Cuban identity was discussed in de la Torre's *Lo que fuimos*. At the time of its drafting, he mourned the decline by 1803 of the custom of street vendors' selling a popular drink, with a colorful, whimsical name of *frucanga* or *sambumbia* (166). The drink was an example of a food item available at the "very famous booths of Peñón" (166). De la Torre does not indicate, however, an African source of the drink. The *sambumbia*, as described in *Nuevo Catauro de Cubanismos* [New basket of Cubanisms] by the Cuban ethnologist Fernando Ortiz, was a "fermented drink made of water, sugar-cane syrup, and pepper" (443). Because of the slightly dark color of the drink, Ortiz expresses his opinion that the name may have come from "sambo [mulatto], 'amulatado,' [mulatto-like] 'medio oscuro' [half-dark]" (443). A stronger connection with African culture, Ortiz discloses, was that in the Calabar area the word *mbubiam* referred to "dirtiness, filth, lack of cleanliness," qualities that the word *sambumbia* took on in Cuban popular speech.

Cuban Costumbrismo followed a national historical trend to "whiten" urban folklore, in a process that Roger Bastide described as initiated "by the Negroes in their drive to achieve assimilation and social betterment" (171). In Spain, Costumbrista writers also demonstrated an early interest in documenting city dwellers. The critic José Escobar pointed out that initial publications in Spanish newspapers owned by José María de Cernerero, beginning in 1828, were part of a national campaign to picture "in imagination the national character endangered supposedly by historical circumstances of revolutionary change" (Escobar 125). At the core of this campaign was the documentation of socioeconomic types or "figures representative of all sorts of social phenomena" (Montesinos 110). Referring to Spanish and to Latin American Costumbrista literature, the

Cuban critic Salvador Bueno observed that the "pictures [ . . . ] express the life-styles and the social psychology of these people" (*Costumbristas* ix).

In the nineteenth century the question of who was to be considered a type worthy of inclusion in a Costumbrista article was a subject of heated debate among Spanish writers. Spanish Costumbrista writer José María de Andueza stated that the importance of the socioeconomic "type" of character is found not so much in his or her personal traits as in the unique story line associated with that particular character:

> A type is an individual member of society who represents a class that shares common customs that in no way belong to any other class. It is clear as daylight that the gypsy woman, the guerrilla fighter, the house-keeper, the Spaniard who returns to Spain with a fortune made in South America, and the night watchman eat and sleep; for that very reason one should not present them in bed or at the table, but in those scenes of their particular life of which the outstanding element is the character that really belongs to them. (Qtd. in Montesinos 111)

The involvement of such types of characters into a plot was at the core of the Costumbrista article, in a process of reproduction that often was seen as intrusive.

The famous Spanish writer Ramón Mesonero Romanos avoided criticism of intrusion into the privacy of a particular, identifiable person by pointing out the rather generic character development of his depicted types: "Nobody will be able to complain about being the direct subject of my discourses, since they must bear in mind that I paint, I do not picture" (qtd. in Romero Tobar 414). This image of "painting" and the degree of accuracy that the portrait intended to represent was to become a leitmotif of many Costumbristas. This was observable, in particular, when the article dealt with a morally controversial or taboo (sexual) subject.

Literary critics have also discussed the degree of accuracy of a "character type." Montesinos observed that the function of a Costumbrista writer was to display traits associated with a portrayed character: "it has been possible to construct the traits of a character from folklore in a certain way, by the author's collecting around a fictional being folkloric features deduced from similar types" (131, emphasis in original). The self-imposed role of the Spanish Costumbrista writers, and of Mesonero Romanos in particular, as collectors of customs was, as Romero Tobar stated, part of a documentation of "customs of great worth to anthropologists and to folklorists" (422). A final byproduct of this anthropologically oriented research was an archive of representative Spanish national customs.

Critic Evaristo Correa Calderón set the parameters of the Costumbrista essay as: "to paint a small, colorful picture, which reflects with great charm and fluency the lifestyle of an epoch, a popular custom, or a representative type" (xi). Early Costumbrista productions in painting and in other media (such as engravings and drawings) inspired Costumbrista writers. Some of them, like Mesonero Romanos, expressed an overwhelmingly positive view: "the picturesque exterior of things, smoothing every possible harshness with mild concealment and amusing charm" (qtd. in Correa Calderón cl).

In Cuban slave society of the nineteenth century, however, the documentation of urban Black types took on a different sociopolitical intention. Although Cuban Costumbrista writers inserted their essays as part of discussions about the developing national project of national identity, their portraits of Blacks as literary "character types" were severely limited. Slavery continued to be a highly controversial subject, discussed in print in Cuba mainly in texts that hailed that institution as absolutely necessary for the economic boom in sugar production. The writer's personal stand on issues related to race, on the other hand, reflected not only racist views, but also the question of how much of Black culture was worthy of providing proper themes for publication.

Cuban Costumbrista writers displayed hesitancy in recording in depth street scenes related to an extensive, colorful Black culture observed in Cuban cities. For example, the earliest Costumbrista publications in the Havana newspapers *El Regañón* and *El Nuevo Regañón*, published in anthologies by the Cuban poet José Lezama Lima in 1965, contained only two articles pertaining to recognizable urban Black types: two untitled essays, one on the calesero, the colorful Black coach driver (*El Regañón* 216–19) and the other on the *mataperros*, or street boys, "little Blacks, mulattoes, and even Whites," known in Havana for interrupting religious ceremonies (such as baptisms and funerals) and for begging for money (*El Regañón* 86). Both of these types would appear mainly as secondary characters in numerous Costumbrista articles.

Oddly absent from these early Costumbrista articles were references to Black street celebrations. Such activities included dances in honor of the kings and queens of *cabildos*, associations of specific African groups; Black dances that took place in private homes; and parades of Black characters associated with Roman Catholic popular celebrations. These Black characters as Costumbrista writers and artists handled them were often caricatures, mere sketches of deeply rooted social divisions inherent in the powerful caste system of the time in Cuba.

To say that the Costumbrista writers exhibited a careful selection of national racial types as potential representatives of a developing national identity is an overstatement. In the collection *Los cubanos pintados por sí mismos* [Cuban self portraits] (1852), for example, of thirty-eight essays none had a Black character type as protagonist. More striking is the fact that, although there were characters directly associated with Black types, such as *mataperros, curanderas* (herbal medicine woman), and *galleros* (handlers in cockfighting), all of them are characterized as White, or there is no reference to their racial background, so that the reader assumes that they are White. This is an interesting choice of characters, perhaps the result of a political censorship. The collection carefully limited references to slavery practices to only two types: "el administrador del ingenio" [the sugarcane plantation's administrator] and "el peón de ganados" [the cattle handler]. The latter task, associated with activities of the *guajiros*, the Cuban peasants, was hailed as representative of "customs worthy of occupying the pen of their writers" (Hernández Chiroldes 119). Correa Calderón observed in his study of Spanish Costumbrista writers that the Costumbrista character type was often related to a retrospective view of national history, leading to a "historical digression, in many cases necessary for comprehension of what was brought to view" (lxxiv). For Cuban Costumbrista writers focusing on Black characters, such a historical exploration would necessarily have included an analysis of slavery practices or of laws concerning freed Blacks in order to explain the specific behavior of that particular character.

Blacks were rarely the protagonists of Costumbrista articles. They usually were presented as antagonists of White characters. The undertone of Black characterization was too often racist, a representation that has been labeled "stigmatized" (Castellanos 4:91). Black types, as indicated in Juan Francisco Manzano's memoirs, were identified as rural slaves, urban slaves or freed Blacks; these were important factors in the biased Costumbrista portraits of Black traditions.

In spite of the limits on the representation of slaves as literary characters, glimpses of rich Black cultural backgrounds are evident. Rafael L. López Valdés observed that a high percentage of the workers in manual or service professions were *pardos* or mulattoes: 61 percent in transportation, 60 percent in construction, 63 percent in service occupations, such as barbers and laundresses, and 79 percent in music (*Pardos* 93, Note 82). Freed Blacks had an impact on the Cuban economy of the nineteenth century in jobs that were often reserved for them as people of color. The Cuban historian Pedro Deschamps Chapeaux reported such workers as: members of the militia for Blacks (El negro 59–86); workers on piers (89–102); musicians (105–18); teachers (121–32); tailors (135–49); barbers, bleeders, and healers of phlebitis (153–65); and midwives (169–84). In numbers midwives were overwhelmingly women *de color* [of color]. In 1841, for example, there were 12 registered midwives in Havana, only five of whom were White women (Gómez del Valle 396; Deschamps Chapeaux, "Las comadronas" 67–82). Perhaps this high number of Black midwives moved Dr. Domingo Rosainzs to state in the introduction to the first manual for midwives, *Cartilla de parteras* (1824): "Certainly, one would not write in this way a manual for midwives in London or in Paris, but among us, perhaps from the way that mine is written, not a few times it will appear unintelligible to those who must use it" (qtd. in Gómez del Valle 396).

Manuel Mariano de Acosta and Antonio Pérez de Guzmán documented in 1830 the dominance of freed Blacks in manual labor in the city of Havana: "Of the mulattoes and freed Blacks and slaves of both classes who live based in a town, the first work as artisans in the diverse manual jobs that they have learned; and the second, in domestic service, or in daily jobs in manual work as bricklayers, ironworkers, water bearers, or as day workers for anyone who pays them" (438–39). The freed Blacks were held in higher esteem, according to these authors, because: "The mulattoes and the Blacks live quietly in their shops, but slaves are prone to drunkenness and to licentiousness" (439).

Manual work was seen as the domain of the Blacks. White people, even those of the lower classes, or "a white man of plain status," preferred to stay away from manual work, considered to be degrading (Deschamps Chapeaux, *El negro* 49). An example of such clear-cut social division was a legal statement of 1823 about the racial background of a woman seeking to marry a White man. It was decided that she must have been of Black ancestry, because her family trade was tailoring: "generally speaking, in this country the people who work as tailors either are mulattoes or are suspected of being so" (qtd. in Deschamps Chapeaux, *El negro* 189).

Of particular importance in a study of the literary production of Cuban Costumbristas is the strong gender-based division in their representation of Black customs. Although Black women characters appeared in Costumbrista essays in a rather sympathetic light, they were not frequently protagonists. As members of the lower classes, Black women, like representatives of popular classes in Spanish Costumbrista production, reflected the authors' concern that those characters could exert a pernicious influence on well-behaved women (Pozzi 255). For the Costumbrista writer, Black women characters had two main functions: (1) they illustrated the legal regulations imposed upon their occupations, so that the characters were identified with their occupations and (2) they offered opportunities to explore Black sexual dynamics, or rather, they revealed what Costumbrista writers believed Black and White men were allowed to do under the screen of the so-called freer sexual code of behavior. Ultimately, although biased, the presence of the Black female characters in Costumbrista articles demonstrated the mechanisms implicit in the construction of gender, or "the physical presence of bodies and the diverse representations of these bodies as gendered, violated, fragmented, marginal and central, and the objects that surround the body (clothing and ornaments)" (Amador Gómez-Quintero and Pérez Bustillo 6).

## Cuban Costumbristas' Multifaceted Portraits of Black Women

The importance of freed Black women in the urban Cuban economy was notable. Great numbers of them fully incorporated themselves into the job markets of Havana. For example, they were owners of land and cultivated minor products, or they served as cooks, maids or laundresses in White households. They were particularly involved as owners of boardinghouses and cafes near the port of Havana (Castellanos 1:84). This association with boardinghouses and sailor crews contributed to the development of sexual trades. D. M. Estorch, historian and member of the Havana City Hall, writing in 1856 about Havana, made a not very subtle allusion to sexual trades associated with freed Black women: "What is the role in cities of this great number of Black women destined, not to domestic services, but to the demoralization of White youth, and often of the children of Whites" (29). In Costumbrista essays such sexual encounters were often suggested without being fully revealed.

In their role as archivists of national historical memoirs, Costumbrista writers documented various kinds of Black women. With a handful of exceptions, they appeared as minor characters, mainly as servants or as street vendors. The emergence of specific Black women as literary characters was confined within the patterns of the sociopolitical organization of slavery, such as the limitation of areas that slaves and freed Blacks were allowed to inhabit, and to the economic spheres within the tightly closed structures of Cuban colonial society.

The images of Black women, either as hardworking women of a trade or as sensual beauties, also became themes in representations by graphic artists, whose works reached large populations in Cuba and abroad. One example is the lithography of the *marquillas cigarreras*, the colorful covers of cigar boxes, produced in Cuba as advertisements throughout the mid-nineteenth century. Critic Vera M. Kutzinski made a detailed study of the *marquillas*, a booming popular art form devised by the many cigar companies in existence in Cuba throughout that century. The large number of satirical, racist representations of Black life or culture in the graphic art of the *marquillas*, Kutzinski argued, became part of a national "'theater' of representative life that formed an important part of these lithographs' standard repertoire" (54–55). Kutzinski's survey of the *marquillas* indicates that the Black character in visual art form, as in Costumbrista articles, was often portrayed because the figure prefigured a plotline.

Black women were the interest in the lithographs of the *marquillas*. Kutzinski highlights some examples. One was a Black dance, set against a background of what appears to be a sugarcane plantation, in mockery of such *bailes de negros*, Black dances at private houses or in dance halls in major cities, particularly in Havana. Another was the depiction of mulattas, who appeared in envious imitation of White women. Mulattas were characters of significance as examples of "the erasure of all images of blackness" (Kutzinski 73) or merely as representations of the sexual voyeurism of White male artists, "whose design serves to induce circumstances that allow writers to highlight or critique sociosexual, moral, and nationalistic concerns" (Duke 25).

The mulatta's prominence as a racial type was a subject of historical accounts. For example, the Spaniard Antonio de las Barras y Prado's *La Habana a mediados del siglo XIX. Memorias de La Habana a mediados del siglo XIX* [Memoirs of Havana in the mid-nineteenth century] dealt at length with the mulatta's sensual allure:

> Mulatto women form here in Havana a special type, since they are very charming in conversation and in movements, and they enjoy much favor among Europeans, whom the women almost always prefer for financial reasons.
>
> In general they are indolent and their only thought is to place themselves where they can enjoy diversions and luxury. They are usually spendthrifts and conceited. Their taste for dances amounts to frenzy, preferring it to all other entertainments. (114)

Although not stated in the text, de las Barras y Prado's sexual fixation on mulattas was a trait that became associated with Spaniards. The stereotypical view, as reflected in Costumbrista articles, was of old Spanish men, usually unattractive but with financial means, who forced young, beautiful mulattas to enter into a domestic and sexual partnership.

Costumbrista writers followed similar trends observed in popular Cuban visual art, seeking to classify Black women in terms of their supposed oversexualized behavior, of their acculturation into Cuban mainstream culture, or of the specific jobs in which they were allowed to engage. Markers that indicated the degree of a Black woman's incorporation into mainstream culture were the color of her skin and the range of her ladylike public behavior. Thus, one common character was the mulata fina, a figure that acquired different meanings, including most prominently that of the proud woman who abandoned and mocked African-based customs in favor of mainstream culture. This was reflected in her insistence on speaking Spanish correctly and dressing in the fashions of White women. As a first-generation Cuban, the mulata fina handled the transition hesitantly, so she was mocked, which happened also to her male Black counterpart. Often, the mulata fina represented a bicultural background, and she had to struggle to gain acceptance in either group, White or Black, although she usually did not care about opinions of her by members of the Black community.

In her overwhelmingly sexualized portrait, all men—Whites, Blacks and mulattoes—pursued the beautiful mulatta. Highly eroticized in portraits, perhaps she represented the excessive sexual drive attributed to Blacks (male and female). A feminist critic described that sexual objectification as "an imposed literary device that results in an ambiguous character" (Duke 26). Although it would seem that the mulata fina's position within two opposite worlds would make her an ideal cultural bridge, Costumbrista writers often drew her as a despised character, subject to suspicion by both Blacks and Whites.

The mulata fina's antagonist was the Black woman, who, unlike the mulatta, displayed no identity crises. She did not have aspirations to engage in behavior or speech similar to that of the White ladies that the mulatta desperately tried to imitate with unsuccessful but "comical" results. The Black woman maintained her sentimental relationships with Black male suitors, who, although they may have initially expressed interest in the mulata fina, often returned to the Black woman, whom they viewed as a true representative of Black culture. Finally, the mulata fina, unlike the Black woman, would remain alone, because her White suitors would not marry her. The only tangible proof that such illicit partnerships ever existed was the birth of biracial children.

Three types of characters emerged as the most commonly assigned roles for Black women in Costumbrista essays: the sensual mulatta, the street vendor, and the medicine woman. The latter two occupations were assigned mainly to older Black women. These characters underwent transformations in reaction to political changes in regard to the emancipation of slaves and, in the case of freed urban Black women, society's appreciation of their services or rejection of their presence as citizens.

Although most Costumbrista writers made these Black characters subjects of their essays, more often than not they appeared as secondary characters subservient to a White protagonist. One exception was the writer Francisco de Paula Gelabert (1834–1894), who explored female Black figures as protagonists in four articles: the sensual mulatta in "La mulata de rumbo" and in "Un chino, una mulata y unas ranas," the street vendor in "El puesto de frutas," and the medicine woman in "La vieja curandera." These articles appeared in a collection entitled *Tipos y costumbres de la isla de Cuba* [Types and customs of the island of Cuba] (Havana, 1889) by various writers. These Costumbrista essays displayed testimony of the emergence of Black female "types" as representatives of native Cuban popular cultures. Notably, Black males would remain for Costumbrista writers examples of marginal criminal groups that must be eradicated.

Gelabert, well known in Cuba for his Costumbrista articles, was also a poet and novelist. He often signed with pseudonyms, such as Aben-Omar, and he wrote for newspapers, initially for the reputable *Diario de la Habana* (*Diccionario* 372). As editor of literary journals that published Costumbrista articles, he had an important role in the development of Costumbrismo in Cuba. He also wrote a Costumbrista novel, "Un secreto y un secretario" [A secret and a secretary], published as a serial in the Havana magazine *El Siglo* [Century] between 1867 and 1868. His articles traced Havana's traditions, including reproduction of representative social speech patterns (Day Corbitt 43).

Gelabert often linked his characters to popular activities associated with Cuban social or religious traditions, which led him to not very subtle critical comments. Juan M. Villergas, a fellow Costumbrista writer, in his 1875 introduction to Gelabert's collection, *Cuadros de costumbres cubanas* [Sketches of Cuban customs], expressed high praise for "an inspired painter of Cuban traditions" (6). In "clever" articles, Villergas stated that Gelabert's articles had strong public acclaim "for the photographic truth of the portraits and the characters sketched in them and for the extraordinary knowledge of words and idioms of local usage revealed by the author" (qtd. in Gelabert 6). Although he did not specifically mention Gelabert's strong interest in documenting Black characters and settings, Villerga's initial definition of the role of Costumbrista essays seems to corroborate the reasons behind Gelabert's multitude of Black characters: "the reader takes pleasure in the animated painting of human types, penetrating into the dwellings of various social classes that, not because some may be of those whom writers generally forget, fail to deserve privileged study if one pays attention to the fact that in them is enclosed what is most characteristic of each people" (5).

Critics today are divided about Gelabert's literary contributions. Aurelio Mitjans called his works "curious, pleasant and interesting collections of humorous criticisms" (354). Another critic has stated that Gelabert was known for the "simplicity of his style, the grace and facility with which he handles dialogues" (Roig de Leuchsenring, *Los escritores* 210). The titles of his Costumbrista articles reflected his desire to document popular types regardless of their racial origin. This was the opinion of another critic, who pointed out that "Gelabert's criticisms . . . were directed more at classes than at individuals" (Day Corbitt 43).

His Black characters were, however, often a representation of stereotypical views common among his White readership (Castellanos 4:91–92). In spite of his highly negative views of urban Black life in Havana, Gelabert's articles presented a large number of Black female characters as protagonists. For most Costumbrista writers, female Black characters were mere shadow figures, but Gelabert developed numerous women house servants, working as nannies, cooks, and cleaning ladies, among other menial workers, with whom his upper-class readership would have been in touch. These articles stood out, therefore, for their use of Black "types" and their interaction with White characters easily recognizable to their readers. In terms of gender dynamics, these Black types presented the tensions inherent in the sexual constitution of the urban Black community, including an open exploration of the sexual exploitation of Black women, particularly the sexualized mulata fina by upper-class White males. Clashes in gender relations were often expressed in animosity between two Black female characters: the Black woman and the mulatta.

Among a plethora of female characters, mainly street vendors and maids, a mulata fina is the central character in Gelabert's Costumbrista essay "La mulata de rumbo" [The social climber mulatta]. In an essay that Black characters dominate, this was a study of Black mistresses kept by wealthy White men in Havana. Leocadia, the protagonist and representative of a mulata fina, is introduced in a rather negative light: "In her class, in her sphere, among people like her, she may be as worthy as any other woman. But the heterogeneous element that seduces her, that conquers her, that corrupts her and perverts her, is responsible for her faults, her vices, her nonchalance" (Bueno, *Costumbristas* 435). A detailed analysis of such a case is Leocadia as a *mulata de rumbo*, a colloquial phrase used in nineteenth-century Cuba to describe a freed Black woman whose financial circumstances had improved through sexual contact with wealthy White men.

The Cuban anthropologist Fernando Ortiz had another explanation for the origin of the term *mulata de rumbo*. In his study of urban Black thugs, *Los negros curros*, Ortiz indicates that upon the disappearance of the *curro*, this peculiar group made new socioethnic manifestations: "The little Black thug was becoming a pimp, Black or mulatto, and the young female Black was a social climber" (35). Although not sufficiently clear, implicit in Ortiz's statement is the fact that the male Black as related to criminal activities remained associated with illegal acts, such as becoming a pimp, while his female counterpart extorted White males by becoming their kept lover. Unlike the mulata fina, the *mulata de rumbo* maintained sexual relationships with White men for money, while preferring to spend her spare time within the social spaces allotted to Blacks. Although the mulata fina enjoyed the financial advantages of her association with a White man, her ultimate goal was to marry him. This, as it was emphasized in the unpublished abolitionist novel, never took place (Cámara 122; Fraunhar 161).

Gelabert's essay daringly explores taboo sexual practices, particularly the public custom of Black "kept mistresses." *Mulata de rumbo* must have been recently coined. A secondary character, Juanilla, indirectly illustrates its meaning. Leocadia, the mulata fina protagonist, was living an easy life, surrounded by fine furniture, fine clothes and expensive jewelry that her White lover, Gerardo, provided her as his kept lover. It must have seemed to Juanilla, presumably a Black woman, that Leocadia should feel happy, and she verbalizes the theme of the article: "Why not! With such an abundance of rich things, with so much improvement in your life, what is the use of your complaining?" (435). As a hardworking woman, for Juanilla, Leocadia's complaints of boredom with her easy life was a sign of the mulata fina's pretentious pseudonature as a "White" woman.

Leocadia foolishly complains to Juanilla that she is not satisfied with her easy life: "Everything tires in this world, Juanilla, everything bores and cloys" (436). She yearns to attend all-Black dances, in which the sensual rhythm of the rumba, a dance of African origin, takes central stage. These Black dances were well attended by mulattas. As the Spaniard Antonio de las Barras y Prado stressed, the voluptuous mulatta was at central stage: "In dances they are possessed by a burning of vehemence that they show in voluptuous and provocative movements, not as deliberate affectation of shamelessness, as seen in women of loose habits, but because of a natural, impatient impulse to liveliness and fire in their blood" (114–15).

An unsympathetic narrator displayed a similar negative view; he mockingly describes Leocadia as a "well-to-do mulatta of rumbas" (435). Juanilla, the poor neighbor with several children to feed and no mention of a husband, was clearly the opposite of Leocadia. She was jealous of her neighbor's position, a common theme in the dichotomy of a Black (unattractive) woman versus a (voluptuous) mulatta with White suitors. Although the narrator displays animosity toward Leocadia throughout the article, he has kind words for her. She might have been forced to enter into a sexual affair with an older White man: "She was still very young when Gerardo met her. He was rich and he dazzled her with his gifts. She succumbed as so many women do . . . in such cases, and Leocadia began a life of indolence, of disorder, of abuse, and of immorality" (435). Absent from this statement is Gerardo's age at the time of their meeting; presumably, he was a much older man, married and with adult children—facts that were revealed at the end of the story.

The rest of the plot seems to contradict, however, the narrator's initial defense of Leocadia's sexual choices. Bored and isolated, "alone in her house, crammed with luxurious furniture, with gaudy pictures, with a thousand superfluous objects" (435), Leocadia attended (behind Gerardo's back) Black parties. They were her joy, as she described them to Juanilla: "Look! I enjoy more and I have more pleasure in one little dance with women of my own color and of my class, joined by young people of good family, where frankness and joy and animation reign" (436). These dances, which were celebrated in various locations in Havana, were well attended by Black men and women, and by White men seeking sexual favors from Black women. Tensions between Black and White men often arose, as Black men resented the White men's sexual advances toward Black women.

Censorship curtailed Leocadia's speech about the sexual atmosphere readily available at these Black dances. She mentioned her favorite musical pieces, two *danzones*, the "Oligamba" and the "Yabú." There is no indication in the text that she was unfaithful to Gerardo. Her descriptions are limited to her enjoyment of the Black dances and of the camaraderie among the dancers. The music was nonstop: "One dances with harp and violin and flute until one drops" (437). There was plenty of food and alcohol, especially a drink that Leocadia called "damsel's blood." The feast took place outside, to her pleasure: "On the grass one eats chicken with rice, fish with cheese and one drinks damsel's blood until one gets drunk" (437). The musicians, presumably Black men, were also well known throughout Havana as consummate musicians (Serviat 151–52).

The memories of the Black dances are provided in the text for the benefit of a new character, Camilo, a male friend of Floro, whom the narrator carefully describes as one of Leocadia's "rumba friends" who had come to visit her at her house (436). There are constant references to Leocadia as a sensual mulatta— "heavenly black woman," for example—but there is no indication of the race of Camilo or Floro.

Floro knows Black culture well, as indicated by his enjoyment of one particular custom that attendees at these parties performed before arriving at the scene: "But earlier there is that bathing in the river" (437). This remark is left uncommented on. There is no sexual innuendo here, although there had been in previous statements regarding the dances. Leocadia's short response to Floro is given in "Black Creole," one of the few times that her speech was not in mainstream Spanish: "Well, the sea with all the islands and nearby cays" (437).[2]

The reason why Floro brought Camilo to meet Leocadia goes unexplained, but it is clear that Floro, her usual dancing partner, has a crush on Leocadia. His descriptions of Leocadia's sensuality in dancing the *danzón*, as he tells Camilo, given partially in Black slang, reveal his open sexual admiration: "In dancing the danzón, she has no equal, buddy, observed Floro—and when she dances the Similiquitron, she has a bustle at her waist that sends out fire" (436–37). This is the first indication that Floro is a Black man—a fact that would become an important component of the plot's resolution. At any rate, it appears that Floro brought Camilo to Leocadia's place in order to entice her to attend a dance with him.

A twist of the plot seems to confirm that Floro indeed had an ulterior motive in bringing together Leocadia and Camilo. Camilo was the nephew of Gerardo, with whom he also lived. Puzzled by her discovery of the relationship, Leocadia asks Floro whether he had known about it, but there is no answer, just loud, uncontrollable laughter. Camilo, sensing that Leocadia had indicated a sexual interest in him, decided to continue his quest, in a description that the narrator expressed in veiled sexual terms: "he was amused by the idea of conquering somebody who was presented to his eyes under such auspices and in such unusual circumstances. So from that moment he considered himself the triumphant rival of his uncle" (438).

After the party, Leocadia and Camilo become lovers, veiled in a censored statement that "between Camilo and Leocadia the most complete intimacy had been established" (438). She shares with her confidant, Juanilla, details about the relationship. Her main reason for her new love affair was the difference. She wanted to love and to feel loved, quoting her desire to live life in terms of literary characters: "And that one might die of sadness in the meantime and not feel, not enjoy the sweetness of shared passion like Paul and Virginia. . . . Here where you see me, I have loved a lot in this world; but I have been very unfortunate" (438). Whether Juanilla, who is portrayed as an ignorant Black woman, indicated by her Black speech, understood the reference to *Paul and Virginia* (1787), the Romantic novel by Jacques-Henri Bernardin, is not explored; however, her answer to Leocadia's complaint arose from the core of a utilitarian common sense, expressed in her characteristic Black Creole slang: "All that flies away on the wind, Cayita, while ounces of gold, in sufficient number, serve as a counterweight and they prevent your having a disaster" (438). Juanilla, the poor Black woman, indirectly expresses a wish to have the ease which her friend provided for herself, even if it meant through sexual favors. This silent envy, which was not often so concealed as in this case, appeared as a common leitmotif in narratives of confrontations between mulattas and Black women.

Emphasis on mulatta women kept as lovers of wealthy White men appears in the surprise ending. An unnamed friend of Gerardo, who had himself tried in vain to have a relationship with the beautiful mulatta, eventually tells Gerardo about his nephew's sexual encounters with Leocadia. Enraged, Gerardo confronts the lovers. He severs his ties with both and ends financial support of them. A curious detail is the fact that Leocadia convinced Camilo not to blackmail his uncle with a threat to tell his aunt about Gerardo's relationship with a Black woman. At any rate, it seems that Leocadia accepted the end of her relationship with a rich old man and settled into her new condition as the lover of a young, poor man.

For money to celebrate her birthday, Leocadia asks Camilo to pawn her jewelry. Returning from the pawnshop, he is robbed—a turn of events that brings forth a final scene. To prove to Leocadia that, indeed, the robbery happened, Camilo forges his uncle's signature and obtains a large amount of money. The plan works well, including a celebration in a party for Leocadia. It finishes abruptly, however, when the police, alerted by Gerardo's best friend, come to arrest Camilo for the forged signature.

At the end of the article, in customary Costumbrista style, the narrator presents a summary of the lessons to be learned. After Camilo's arrest Leocadia had appeared to be a desperate woman, crying and screaming, but a week later she landed herself a new lover. The closing scene of a proud Leocadia, a mulatta walking the streets of Havana, is a direct reference to an engraving by the artist Landaluze: "Suffice it to say that a new protector, a man of means, had assumed the task of restoring to her all her pawned jewelry and pretty things, and when she went out, she bore such a satisfied air and that highly provocative mien with which the skillful and ever inspired Landaluze painted her" (442). The mulatta's "satisfied air" was often her expression of superiority over the Black woman's low condition, based on her skin color and the texture of her hair. That superiority, illustrated in one of Landaluze's portraits, is suggested by the contrast of two Black women: one older and darker (presumably her mother or, as in Gelabert's essay, an envious Black neighbor) and a defiant, sexy, light-skinned mulata fina.

Gelabert's Costumbrista essay "Un chino, una mulata y unas ranas" [A Chinaman, a mulatta and some frogs] continued with the subject of the calculating *mulata de rumbo*.[3] Although the handling of the figure of the mulata fina is similar to that in the previous article, there are obvious differences in the intention of this article.

The protagonist, Madalena, the Black pronunciation of Magdalena, was a mulatta *married* to a Chinese man, although in the text the word "married" was in italics. Her husband, Pepillo, as Madalena called him, uses his few lines of dialogue dealing with Madalena's complaints, which, unlike those of Leocadia, were not demands for a more appealing sexual life. A curious detail of this article is a lack of sexual intimacy between Madalena and Pepillo, although as a married couple they had a child. The typical mulatta's oversexualized demeanor is replaced by an emphasis on Madalena as a materialist woman, interested in climbing up the social ladder through her relationship with a hardworking Chinese man. She was, after all, a *mulata de rumbo*, whose interest in social advancement provides the plot with some interesting twists.

Pepillo is a cook and a good provider, but Madalena complains of scarcity in the house, particularly of luxurious items associated with upper-class White women, such as jewelry and fine clothing. Their conversations, consisting mostly of Madalena whining, are transcribed phonetically, in reflection of the Black speech of Madalena, who the reader must assume was Cuban-born, in spite of her poor use of the Spanish language. Her opposite is Pepillo, whose Spanish reveals the difficulties of a Chinese speaker attempting to master Spanish. These are the funniest sections of the article, because Madalena uses plays on words in order to confuse Pepillo, and also because their interaction reflects the stereotypical view that each had of the spouse's racial qualities.

Madalena declares that Pepillo "like a good Asiartic [*sic*], thinks only of making money; I, on the contrary, need pleasure in my soul; let the magical accents of celestial, divine music move my heart and sweeten my ears: poetry is my strong point" (Gelabert 459). This overly romanticized pronouncement comes in answer to Pepillo's indications that she should stay put in their house in El Cerro and away from the city of Havana—the center of Madalena's daydreams of walking around parks while listening to street music. Pepillo would rather have Madalena clean the house, which was unkempt because, she claimed, she must not get her feet wet in order to avoid catching a cold.

Ordering him to clean the house because, she declared, "I have not bound myself to you in order to work like a Black woman, you Chinese rascal" (460), Madalena reveals indirectly the reasons behind her starting to live with a chino (*culí*), rather than setting up house with a White man, as did other *mulatas de rumbo*. Madalena is not happy with her choice, as Pepillo barely earns a living. He works as a cook in a private home, to Madalena's displeasure. She would rather he work as a street vendor—a more profitable task, as lithographs of the time show: "And who orders you to be a cook? Is it my fault that you know nothing more than going around with charcoal and casseroles? Why don't you go out on the street with your two baskets on your back to sell foods, which brings in a lot of money" (460).

Not able to convince him to become a street vendor, Madalena has another plan for Pepillo. She wants him to steal from the mistress of the house where he is a cook. After all, according to Pepillo, the house servant, *el negrito congo* [the little Black Congo], was often blamed for mishaps around the house. Madalena's plan was calculated and indicative of the socioeconomic tensions at play:

> Pepillo, don't be a fool, that is not stealing, but like brothers sharing super-fluous things. If the lady has many earrings, grab some hoops, since they will come in handy for me; grab a dress, of the many that she probably has in the wardrobe; some silk handkerchief; and even some frilled stockings; and in this way I will accumulate outfits, since I am in rags. Don't you say that they blame the little Black Congo for everything? Just stand strong, and he will get out of a tight spot, with three or four slaps to his face, and that's that. (461)

The plan for theft indicated that she was a *curra*, as the Black street thieves of Havana were known. Perhaps this explains why she had chosen not to become the mistress of a White man, preferring to maintain marginal living arrangements, while, at the same time, in her association with a *culí* she expected a life free of financial need.

In spite of Madalena's speaking softly, her neighbor overhears the plan. This detail is important in the development of the major part of the story's plot. The neighbors had won the lottery—a fact that they intended to keep to themselves, fearful that somebody would attempt to rob them. They forgot, however, that their neighbors could overhear their conversations.

Madalena plots with her brother, Jesús Macario, whom the narrator describes in rather satirical tones as "a worn out rascal, who had suffered several imprisonments only because of the rumored vice of appropriating other people's belongings against the owners' wishes" (461). This is another indication that both Jesús Macario and his sister are *curros*, a negative characterization that plagued this marginal ethnic group well known as thieves. Right away they plot to get the money from their unsuspecting neighbors. They know where the neighbors have hidden the money, and they figure that if the neighbors suspect them, Pepillo could be blamed for the crime (he would be their *negrito congo*). They plan to steal the money the following day.

That day it rained a lot, creating puddles that attracted frogs. At night Madalena, who feared frogs, sees two "enormous frogs here in my bed" (463), and orders Pepillo to get rid of them. Half asleep, Pepillo inadvertently ignites the mosquito net on the bed, setting his and their neighbor's houses on fire. Luckily, everyone escapes, including the neighbors, carrying their lottery money. The following morning, when Jesús Macario arrives at his sister's house to commit the crime, he finds that the neighbors have left their house and that his sister is homeless.

The narrator offers no formal indictment against Jesús Macario. In other Costumbrista articles there would have been a moral to the story, usually a warning to stay away from the turbulent Black community, which often attracted curious but naïve White male passersby looking for a cheap thrill. An indictment of the failed plan is summarized in the narrator's exclamation about the neighbor's rage upon hearing about the origin of the fire: "Oh, Eladio never found out that he was in debt to two of those black and greenish reptiles for having preserved intact his winnings from the lottery!" (463). The closing line, the moral of the story, is left open ended in an ambiguous refrain that even today is popular: "So it has been said much to the point that nobody knows for whom he is working" (463).

In spite of these two overwhelmingly negative articles, Gelabert also displayed a rounder view of urban Black folklore. In his "La vieja curandera" [The old herbal woman], an old herbal medicine woman is the protagonist of a story that, in the opinion of an opinionated narrator, highlights an old tradition that was rapidly dying in Cuba. Unlike in other of his articles in which there is a nostalgic view of old traditions, "La vieja curandera" made this character a rather unsympathetic figure. Doña Amparo del Apazote y Malvabisco, whose title imitates the pompous names of upper-class women in Havana, is introduced without the fanfare that her name suggests, as "that sort of witch, on whose charms and spells are based the hopes of a good number of unhappy people lacking all discernment and all culture" (Gelabert 472). She was also a *milagrera* [miracle worker], a mocking title for the kinds of jobs she performed, including curing domestic and farm animals. That title was, of course, fake, as the nonbeliever narrator sets out to prove to a gullible reader, perhaps a superstitious woman.

Doña Amparo's residence is a hut in the neighborhood of Jesús del Monte, a popular area that often appeared as the setting of Costumbrista articles dealing with Black culture. The fact of her living there was one of the few details that suggested that Doña Amparo was Black. This ambiguous characterization was not unusual. The Costumbrista writer José Victoriano Betancourt, in his article "El médico pedante y las viejas curanderas" [The traveling doctor and old medicine women], mocked the services of women herbalists, whose race was not clearly disclosed (37–48). Doña Amparo's Spanish is within the mainstream popular usage of the language, but her pronunciation of certain consonants, such as transference of the r for the l, was a feature of Black speech and often a point of mockery by Costumbrista writers.

Doña Amparo's clients' race is not described either. Their speech reflects a more popular and relaxed use of the language, including a greater number of mispronunciation patterns than Doña Amparo's. This language provokes humor, and it supports her clients' being described as "gullible, so ignorant, so poor in spirit" (471). Although this article is not an indictment of Black religious practices, it draws heavily on well-known herbalist traditions commonly associated with Black women.

Another element of popular Black culture was Doña Amparo's apparent knowledge of Black popular potions, which she called "the healing secret." Her knowledge seems to be endless. Although the narrator cites several of her potions as examples of the vulnerability of desperate people, several remedies are the results of authentic research or they are based on effective home remedies. For example, according to Doña Amparo, ginger cures rheumatism.

The medicine woman had become regarded as a repository of popular knowledge from multiple ethnic sources. The Black *curandera* had strong connections with practices of various forms, mainly religious matters and issues about women's health and their bodily functions. In literary treatments of the type, there are echoes of Celestina. The main character of the medieval play *Tragicomedia de Calisto y Melibea* (1499) by Fernando de Rojas, Celestina is an old, retired prostitute, now a medicine woman, often sought out by women in need of help with their reproductive functions. For example, she performed abortions, repaired broken hymens and cured all kinds of sexual diseases. Women also sought these "witch doctors" in order to buy unusual love potions to attract uninterested men or to make men engaged to other women lose interest in them and favor the paying client.

The dynamic of real versus imaginary effects of Doña Amparo's potions is present throughout the text. Her clients did not doubt that she would cure their illnesses. Each of Doña Amparo's clients is presented as "a tangible example of this terrible backwardness in the lower classes" (472). The remedies recorded as examples of Doña Amparo's medical skills, and the reasons for her large clientele, are rooted in Black medical folklore with connection to the spiritual. For example, for a client whose horse suffered from ticks, Doña Amparo prescribes a powder "made from the skull of a spotted dog who after having suffered from infestation of worms and having been cured by a collar of corncobs, has died from something or other" (473). The horse's owner does not hesitate to follow her advice. He is a peasant whose faith leads him to describe her as "that hand of a saint that you have, may God let you enjoy it for many years" (473). His determination to find a dead dog reflects the Blacks' readiness to procure ingredients for Doña Amparo's unusual cures: "In truth, señora Amparo, you know more than the witches; right now I am going to order Black José Rafé to get me the skull of the spotted dog" (473). Belief in witches, described extensively by the runaway slave Esteban Montejo, was widespread among Blacks and among some Whites. The case of a peasant client illustrates that the traditional belief in witchcraft was deeply rooted among the Galician population of the *guajiros*.

Doña Amparo's remedies are presented in a highly negative light, despite the large number of her apparently satisfied clients. Mockery of her practice is evident in one case of sickness. A desperate mother comes to Doña Amparo because her child has fallen from a tree and, having lost consciousness for two hours, keeps bleeding from his mouth. Doña Amparo's prescription, meant to calm the desperate mother, requires unusually complex preparation:

> You just have to find yourself a wild gourd, split it up into two pieces, take out all the *vicissitudes*, or what is the same, the husks; you search for a vessel never used, put it with a little water over a flame; add a real [coin] worth of sugar candy, a real [coin] of powdered rubber and two spoonfuls of bee honey, and into this infusion add the husks that you drew from the wild gourd; stir it all up and leave it until it is consumed and reduced to a cupful. At once you pray to the syrup seven Our Fathers and seven Hail Marys and have it blessed by a girl of unblemished character, because without this circumstance it would have no effect on the boy; and from this time I promise that Manuel Canuto, having thus taken the miraculous medicine, will remain cured for the rest of his life. (474, emphasis in the original)

Obviously, this prescription mocks well-known homemade brews and sets up for Doña Amparo a way out in case it does not work. There are so many steps in its preparation done by the mother, including finding a virgin girl, that if the prescription did not work, she could blame it on something that was wrong in the preparation, and not on her ability as a healer.

In spite of their absurd ingredients, Doña Amparo's prescriptions may have contained items of Black medicinal folklore, well known by the general population regardless of their ethnic roots. The reference to a *güira cimarrona* [a wild-grown gourd] pointed to Black practices of feeding the orisha Ochún, a powerful deity in Santería practices, with this favorite food item. Ochún also favored honey and sugar-based pastries, a strong reference which is echoed here in *azúcar candi* [candy sugar].

Even having a virgin girl bless the potion had a counterpart in popular medicinal lore. The tradition is known even today as *santigüar* [blessing], a series of prayers said while rubbing the patient's affected body area with assorted oils (mainly of handy natural products of which coconut oil seems to be a favorite). With the rubbing, the medicine woman, often a Black woman, blesses the patient in a combination of Roman Catholic prayers and her self-designed prayers. One way to avoid a dissatisfied client was Doña Amparo's requirement that a virgin girl perform the ritual.

Doña Amparo's downfall, which is at the center of the plot, is a failed prescription. This case is, however, different from that of any of her usual patients. Her client, Clementina, "A married woman, beautiful, rich, without children, and much in love with her husband" (475), a White woman of upper-class background, came to Doña Amparo's hut accompanied by an unnamed woman who knew the medicine woman well. They had high expectations of the *curandera*'s supernatural powers: "able by herself to change the fate, the star, the destiny of the mortal most beset with misfortune" (476). She has no doubt that her friend would find help for her ailment. Clementina's problem is not physical, as were the problems in previously described cases. After eight years of marriage her husband had stopped displaying signs of affection toward her, she explains in a coded reference to the couple's lack of sexual intimacy: "her companion did not feel for her all that enthusiasm, that ardor, that pleasure, which until then he had seemed to experience from her charms and her affectionate and tender embraces" (475). Of course, Doña Amparo, as a confident Celestina, swears that she can help, in spite of Clementina's hesitation.

Unlike in her other cases, Doña Amparo is clearly after Clementina's money. The narrator describes her cold attitude toward the grieving wife: "That was a good capture. The harvest of shining doubloons had to be abundant" (476). Surprisingly, the healer is not prompt in displaying her knowledge of natural remedies. This is clear in her prescribed medicine. She vaguely describes the remedy as of "certain herbs costly and marvelous [ . . . ] with which I am to prepare the marvelous potion" (477). The unusual detail is that Doña Amparo avoids asking Clementina to venture into the Black neighborhood, where her former clients procured ingredients for their prescribed remedies. Intent upon extracting as much money from Clementina as she can, she keeps her client far from the local Black religious community, perhaps fearing that Clementina will meet a former, dissatisfied client. There is also the possibility that Doña Amparo is afraid that Clementina might meet another Black medicine woman equally interested in this naïve client.

Doña Amparo puts a series of rather unlikely questions to Clementina, described as "nonsense questions to Clementina and changing everything into substance, that is, trying to convince her that all she had done or left undone was coming together to justify her misfortune" (477). Thus, it becomes clear to Clementina that her not remembering which foot, right or left, she had put forth upon entering into her home as a newlywed explains what Doña Amparo called her "misfortune." Clementina, convinced that her problem is of a supernatural nature, leaves the house with the first of Doña Amparo's recommendations: to leave a green garter under her husband's pillow. "The garter is the symbol of the narrow bond; it draws, it binds, it reunites" (477).

Upon her departure, the narrator shows Doña Amparo busy at work fixing herbs for Clementina's prescribed remedy. This is the only instance of an indirect description, which is done by asking the reader to look at an untitled "enclosed engraving" (477). The drawing is the work of the artist Landaluze, and the narrator described it as a picture of a woman "standing before her *laboratory* with a characteristic piece of tobacco in her mouth, surrounded by all her utensils and accessories and handling the usual *medicine herbs*" (477–78, emphasis in the original). The narrator seems hesitant to comment on Doña Amparo's race, but a closer look at Landaluze's picture reveals that she was an unattractive, rather evil-looking mulatta. There is no comment on the dark, spooky background (also present in Landaluze's drawing), to which the narrator refers indirectly in passing when he describes Clementina's first reaction upon entering Doña Amparo's hut: "Clementina felt daunted and her first impulse was to go away; but her friend, holding her arm, detained her and murmuring several words into her ear, succeeded in calming her" (476).

In typical Costumbrista style, the end of the story is a lesson for all the gullible readers that still might believe in Doña Amparo's skills, magical or medicinal. Of course, everything goes wrong in a comical way. Following Doña Amparo's instructions, Clementina gives her husband the "medicinal" tea one night after he arrives home complaining of a stomachache. She follows the medicine woman's recommendation that "if your husband took it when he had a fever, for example, or any other illness, it would produce not only the desired moral effect, but also he would remain free of fevers and be cured of all other ailments that he might suffer" (478). Unknown to Clementina, her husband had eaten a dozen oysters, and his pain is just a case of indigestion. Following the basic pattern of psychological dependency, Doña Amparo upholds the premise that a sick husband cured by a loving wife would return her love.

But Doña Amparo's plan backfires. When the husband fails to feel better and even feels worse, desperate Clementina begins screaming that she has poisoned him. The husband, "as his conscience was accusing him of something," also starts to yell for help (478). Upon the doctor's arrival it is confirmed that Clementina has given her husband an unknown potion, as Doña Amparo had directed. Arrested, Doña Amparo confesses that, indeed, she had provided the potion, declaring that "it was all just a tall tale. That there was no such poison, nor was there such a specific, but a simple potion made of innocent herbs" (479). Her job as a medicine woman, like that of a medical doctor, had its ups and downs: "at times she was right in her remedies and at other times not; therefore the case was legal" (479). The husband is cured by means of "help from medical science." The "medical" woman is found innocent after it "was duly proved that the specific of Doña Amparo was only a syrup of insignificant herbs" (479).

The closing of the article indicates that, despite public revelations of the fraud, Doña Amparo might use the case to her advantage. As the narrator mockingly states, the couple stayed together "as a consequence of the fright that both had suffered, the spouses were reconciled; he swearing not to neglect his wife and she never again to resort to consulting any old healer" (479). The message centers on the condition that Clementina would stay away from the healer. She had been previously characterized as "fanatic, superstitious; she believed in witches, in ghosts, in miracles, in I don't know how much nonsense" (477). It seems plausible, therefore, that she would not keep her promise to her husband. An ultimate lesson may have been that not only would Clementina go back to Doña Amparo but that, as long as there were gullible, superstitious White women, Black *curanderas* would exist. Like the original literary character Celestina, Doña Amparo used knowledge of women's psychology in gaining clients. This street-wise knowledge was shared by other urban female Black characters as a way to survive financially at the expense of innocent White people.

Gelabert's interest in exploring Black traditions was not meant, however, solely to produce negative comments. His Costumbrista article "El puesto de frutas" [The fruit stand] introduced a number of urban Black figures, and one female Black character was viewed positively.

Following the style of his previous article, Gelabert, in "El puesto de frutas," set out to describe and provide a plot for an untitled engraving by the graphic artist Landaluze "which used to be offered very often for the passersby's contemplation not even twenty years ago" (Gelabert 453). One character, a fruit vendor, ña Tula, "a Black Ganga woman, no longer young," becomes the main character. Ña Tula sold tropical fruits (*zapotes*, *anones*, and *mameyes*), her only way to collect "scanty means in order to be able to rest when she became old and cranky" (453). Around her other Black characters congregate, seeking each other's company—a motif that leads to minor plots of inconsequential significance.

There is Rosalía, a mulatta, who, in spite of having finished her shopping, is still chatting with ña Tula and Torcuato, the Black calesero [coachman]. Both Rosalía and Torcuato are jokingly remembering "all that happens in their masters' houses" (453). These anecdotes include a story that involves a fruit bought at ña Tula's stand. This particular episode is written in the style of an *entremés*, a short comic theatrical piece that focuses on the interaction of characters who face a rather absurd situation, and the way that they come out of it. As in most *entreméses*, the wealthy White character is mocked, a reflection of the strong sociopolitical background of this genre, which catered to the lower classes.

The funny anecdote in "El puesto de frutas" is Rosalía's retelling the story about ña Tula's *mamoncillos*, also known as *queneps*, a small fruit that is sucked carefully, because it is slimy and people sometimes choked on its pit, often with tragic consequences. The story, like an *entremés*, is short and to the point. Rosalía's mistress, Miss Merse, loves the fruit and often sends her slave-maid to buy them at ña Tula's stand. The mistress is careless, according to Rosalía, speaking in a pretended high-class Spanish that the narrator mocks: "She starts sucking and sucking and talking and talking with her daughters, and through the *circumference* of the fruit the seed slipped out and then came shouts to bring the house down" (453, emphasis in the original). The humor of the situation is increased by Torcuato's constant interruptions of Rosalía. In one of them, "showing great amazement," he puzzles, "And she shouts that way with a seed in her windpipe . . . that is what is called having a throat of iron" (453). Another strong comic device is the use of many words of bozal, African-based Creole elements, in the Spanish language, by all the characters, as they mockingly tell or comment on the story.

The end of Rosalía's story brings in a new character, a young man, a neighbor and a medical student, who "with the greatest ease took out of Miss Merse's throat the damned fruit seed" (454). In an indirect characterization the calesero praises highly the intelligence of the White medical student. This heroic deed is celebrated, as Torcuato indicates, saying, "Now you see, my friend, that the student knows more than a jutía" (454). His comparison of the medical student with the *jutía*, a native rodent known for its cleverness, is meant to be a positive remark and also a reflection of the calesero's sympathetic alliance with their White customers or masters. Rosalía ends the story with another anecdote. La niña Lola, one of Miss Merse's daughters, falls in love with the unnamed young medical student. Jokingly, however, Rosalía suspects that he had taken advantage of the situation, "and as this man is tender-hearted and he likes blondes very much, according to what he says, after one week they were engaged and I believe that they are even going to get married, all because of her mama's having swallowed a mamoncillo's seed" (454).

The remainder of the article centers on the interpersonal relationships among the Black characters. Rosalía, a mulata fina, as implied in her White-like behavior, openly flirts with Torcuato, and flaunts her beauty as a light-skinned woman. She brags that White men flirt with her everywhere she goes: "My God! Is it my fault, ña Tula? No matter what I do, I can't avoid their calling me cinnamon, heavenly mulatta, sugar candy, divine dark one, and I don't know what other things that they say to me wherever I go" (454). Even the son of her master, in spite of having a girlfriend, "his blonde, Miss Lola, that he says he likes so much," often makes open sexual advances toward Rosalía (455). Rosalía's recollection seems to be directed toward Torcuato, who had openly displayed admiration for the behavior of White men: "I say, for me, that instead of having a pink face like his fiancée, I am brown like washed wheat, and that instead of my hair's being like hers, it is very curly" (455).

By boasting about her straight hair and her fair skin, attributes of a mulata fina, Rosalía is hoping, unlike other Black women, to land the love of Torcuato, presumably a mulatto, judging from his ability to speak standard Spanish. Torcuato has not shown any sexual interest toward Rosalía, perhaps because she is a slave, or because she is not as light-skinned as she perceives herself to be. Rosalía's flirtatious conversation is abruptly interrupted by intrusion of a new character, María Justa, a Black *curra* woman.

The *curro*, an urban Black of the marginal neighborhood of Manglar (a swampy area) in Havana, was a well-known type frequently used by Costumbrista writers in articles protesting their involvement in criminal activities. María Justa is not condemned here, however, for her possibly criminal background, but for her intention to commit a criminal act, inspired by her unfaithful husband. She appears as a counter figure to the mulatta Rosalía, who disrespectfully refers to her in Creole argot as "slutty, hussy, bad blood; Don't you see her with her cheap shawl hanging and the bit of tobacco in her hand, taking up the whole curb. I can't stomach her" (456). Torcuato, in spite of his earlier flirting with Rosalía, openly prefers the raw beauty of a Black woman to the tamed, pretentious behavior of a mulata fina.

To his surprise, Torcuato's daring sexual advances and proud self-boasting of his status as a calesero do not interest María Justa. She is too busy to pay attention to Torcuato's nonsensical flirting. María Justa is on her way to catch her lover red-handed with "a mulatta bitch, *whitish, and husband thief,*" in an open reference to Rosalía's early obsession with her biethnic background (456, emphasis in the original). On another level, María Justa's rejection of Torcuato addresses the economic differences at play among these three characters: "You carriage drivers, because you wear green and red livery, you put a hat on your head and carry a whip with a silver handle in your hand, you figure that you are worth more than the entire people of color. But you are wrong, Torcuato, because we women born in el Manglar have blood boiling in our body, we don't let anybody abuse us, even if he is the king of coach drivers" (456).

The strong sexual dynamics of "El puesto de frutas" remain unresolved. The conclusion of the article is, unlike what one might have expected, a positive comment in praise of an urban tradition. Nostalgically, the narrator pauses to document the existence of such fruit stands. Between 1850 and 1860, "they were everywhere in Havana, housed and mobile, the latter consisting of boards that Black women carried on their heads, loaded with pineapples, *chirimoyas*, papayas, avocados, mameyes (pink and from Santo Domingo), *anones, zapotes,* bananas from Guinea and from India" (457). At the time of the writing, those stands were things of the past, hence the purpose of the article. The reasons for their extinction were modernity and the strong influence of foreign products. Unlike previous generations, who had enjoyed eating the extensive variety of Cuban tropical fruits, the new middle class had different tastes: "employees in the present epoch have replaced fruits with lager beer, with absinthe, with vermouth cocktails" (457). When "one of the most unusual fruit stands that I recall" went out of business, it became the inspiration of this Costumbrista article (457). As part of the lesson of the story, different from that of any of the previous articles, the narrator not only mourns the disappearance of this typical urban tradition, but also claims it as representative of a native Cuban tradition. This popular custom was one dominated by Black women, as were the makers of the tortillas of San Rafael.

Although it may appear that the mulata fina's behavior was static, that she was a tame character in her White-like demure actions, contrasted with the raw, sexual appearance of the Black woman, there are characters in others of Gelabert's articles that contradict these patterns. In "Lucha con las criadas" [Struggles with maids] a male narrator reproduces his conversations with White women in Havana who remember the worst of their experiences with Black female *criadas de mano* [house servants]. One of them details her interview with a mulatta, described as "a flirty mulatta, with a big ass and much bouncy flesh," a trait that appears close to that of the sexy María Justa (42). In another article, "Hoy que no tengo asunto" [No subject today], Gelabert, narrating as his alter ego Aben-Omar, attempts to answer letters from his fans. One of them comes from a woman puzzled by her husband's insistence that they take in a "mulatica," a young mulatta, not a Black woman, as a house servant. "Una mujer escamada" [A suspicious woman], quoting her husband indirectly, says that he is adamant about hiring a mulatta: "He says, of course, that for serving meals, making beds, preparing a drink, carrying a message in the neighborhood, and for anything else that might occur, *cinnamon* is better, being more respectable, more elegant and even *better smelling* than the *living jet*, who, unlike the *mineral*, smells . . . and not of amber, as Don Quijote used to say. My husband's insistence *smells foul to me*" (Gelabert 142, emphasis in the original). Perhaps because of the obvious, oversexualized characterizations of Black women, Aben-Omar leaves this letter unanswered.

Costumbrista writers did not, however, consider Black women characters to be representatives of Cuban identity. That should not be surprising. As late as 1872, a publication entitled *Las mujeres españolas, portuguesas y americanas* [Spanish, Portuguese and American women] attempted to provide, as its title implies, a record of the regional differences of these territories and the types of women who inhabited each. Even though the articles devoted to the island stressed regional differences, they did not explore the impact of Black women in the countryside, some of them still under the restrictions of slavery. In the case of Cuba, the only mention of Black women is not even a sentence, but a slight reference to them in an article about the role of rural *guajiras*, White peasant women: "Black women destined for hard labor in the fields" (Guerrero 15).

A print of a peasant woman, appropriately entitled "La guajira" [The peasant woman], accompanied the article. This woman, although dressed for tropical weather, is still overdressed. She stands against a highly romanticized landscape, which includes an equally exaggerated straw hut, not an accurate depiction of the hardships of country life detailed in the narrative. Neither is there any documentation that this countryside (the province of Havana) is heavily inhabited by Black and slave women.

Further evidence that the author deemed White women to be true representatives of Cubanness is the beautiful color print of two such types: a wealthy "Dama de la Habana" [Lady of Havana], seated in a luxurious living room, looking more like a fanciful parlor in a Madrid townhouse, and a "Señora de la Habana" [Married Lady of Havana], a richly dressed mistress in a house that is perhaps meant to represent a master's house on a plantation in the province of Havana, as the outline of an exotic countryside suggests. Although the images seem to be positive, the narrator deems these ladies conceited: "In Spain the Cuban woman is recognizable only with a fan, when it isn't exaggerated to the point of being ridiculous, placing beside the lady a Black woman whose only occupation during the day is to fan cool air to the niña, as Ethiopians call their masters, no matter what their age" (Guerrero 9). In spite of the statement that the mistress was always accompanied by a Black woman, there is no Black figure in the print.

The obvious absent image, one carefully ignored by most Costumbrista graphic artists and essay writers, is the mulata fina, who often served as "lady in waiting" for upper-class White Cuban women. As a sexual playmate of wealthy White men, the oversexualized figure of the mulata was too contentious to clear the moralized censorship operating in Cuba. Her eroticized characterization could only serve as a political symbol of the Cuban colonial status in unpublished abolitionist novels, such as *Francisco* and *Cecilia Valdés*.

# 4

. . . . . . .

# The Costumbristas' Views
# of Manly Black Males

## Uppity Blacks and Thugs

Blacks on the island of Cuba are our poetry, and one must not think otherwise, but not just the Blacks, but Blacks with Whites, all mingled, and to form then the pictures, the scenes, which have to be infernal and diabolic, but exact and evident.

Félix Tanco Bosmeniel, qtd. in Salvador Bueno, *El negro en la novela hispanoamericana*

Slavery is unsustainable from the point of view of all aspects of morality, reason and law, and, consequently, nobody of upright conscience can defend it.

Antonio de las Barras y Prado, *La Habana a mediados del siglo XIX: Memorias de Antonio de las Barras y Prado*

By the eighteenth century freed Blacks and mulattoes controlled most of the manual trades in Cuba (Castellanos, 1:85). The rules of *coartación*, the self-purchasing of one's freedom, historian José Luciano Franco stated, provided slaves the opportunity to enter in large numbers into the work force in Cuban cities (*La diáspora* 198; Knight, "Slave" 114). José Ferrer de Couto, in his *Los negros en sus diversos estados y condiciones, tales como son, como se suponen que son, y como deben ser* [Blacks in their diverse stages and conditions, as they are, how they are supposed to be, and how they must be] (1864), indicated that male slaves often hired themselves out as drivers of coaches, as workers on piers and in custom houses, as stevedores, or as errand runners, available to anyone without the means to own a slave. These activities were so profitable that "anybody who has practiced them for two or three years and is still not free, has not wanted to be free until then because of more attractive objectives" (qtd. in Ortiz, *Los negros esclavos* 289). Many of those who gained their liberty, known as *coartados*, Ferrer de Couto continued, also raised enough money to buy a dwelling, "afterward without much work required; which they almost always obtain" (qtd. in Ortiz 289). The booming economic activities of Cuban cities, said Ferrer de Couto, provided plenty of opportunities to gain one's liberty: "Those who practice productive jobs and industries, such as tailors, shoemakers, tobacco growers, and others similar, who are numerous, and those who dedicate themselves to music and manage to learn to play an instrument, also acquire maximum ease in becoming free" (qtd. in Ortiz 289).

The Spaniard Antonio de las Barras y Prado in his memoirs, *La Habana a mediados del siglo XIX* [Mid-nineteenth-century Havana], remembering his experiences in Cuba as an office clerk for a Spanish-owned grocery store, claimed that in the mid-nineteenth century one-third of the Cuban population was constituted of *gente de color* [colored people]. His definition of that group encompassed "Blacks and people of mixed race who abound on the Island.... They are free, slaves or freed, and in these conditions they live at the service of Whites, in all kinds of tasks, domestic, agricultural and industrial" (107). These lucrative occupations provided the funds necessary for *coartación*, sometimes within two to three years (Franco, *La diáspora* 198). The process of *coartación*, according to de las Barras y Prado, was relatively easy, including the possibility of payment in installments of fifty pesos on a monthly basis until a previously agreed upon price had been reached (110).

The Spaniard José María de Andueza, describing his arrival in Cuba in 1825, in his *Isla de Cuba pintoresca* [The picturesque island of Cuba] (1841), had a similar view of the impact of the Black community on the city of Havana. His impression of the city's population was that of an "immense town of Whites and Blacks" (40). His first experience upon arriving in Havana was in the active market scene at the pier of San Francisco, where Black vendors dominated:

I trod then upon the wharf of the capital of Cuba, that Pier of San Francisco, so long, so heated, so crowded with barrels of flour, of casks of wine, of boxes of sugar, the latter destined for loading, the first and the second for consumption in the city. It was truly a new world that drew my eyes, with its endless noise of carts and wheelbarrows, that came and went without interruption; it was a continued jubilation of sea chants in different languages; it was a heartfelt prayer sung in unison by two hundred African voices, that rose from the mercantile great opera that was being staged beneath the Platform. (6)

The Blacks' presence in the markets, as Jacobo de la Pezuela documented in his *Ensayo histórico de la Isla de Cuba* [Historical essay of the island of Cuba] (1842), was at the center of the active commerce trade in Havana: "The gangs of

Blacks who received and weighed the boxes of sugar and other products, as they put them into and drew them from the shops, they announced the weight with shrieks and noisy racket, causing thus notable nuisance for all the inhabitants of the city" (577).

Not only the heavy manual trades were in the hands of Blacks. José Martín Félix de Arrate's historical account of the city of Havana, *La Habana Descripta* [Havana Described] (1830), placed *pardos y negros* [mulattoes and Blacks] in charge of a large array of jobs, within a highly flattering racial description of this group:

> they are very suitable and sufficient for manual jobs to which they commonly apply themselves and in which they become opportunistic masters, I do not say of the lowest quality, as are shoemakers, tailors, bricklayers, and carpenters, but even of those that need and demand more skill, polish, and genius, as in silverwork, sculpture, painting and carving, as evident in their exquisite products. (105)

According to the Spanish governor Francisco Dionisio Vives in 1832, the "artes mecánicas" [mechanical arts] were in the hands of "colored people" (qtd. in Riverend Brusone 309). Such control of the job market did not go unnoticed. Gaspar Betancourt y Cisneros, in an 1837 Costumbrista article for the newspaper *La Gaceta de Puerto Príncipe*, wrote harshly against what he considered the laziness of the White population:

> In earlier days the powerful landowners assigned one slave to each job. Mr. D. N. had a carpenter slave, another as bricklayer, another as shoemaker, etc. With this uneconomic system the rich degraded arts and mechanics in violation of the most honorable royal orders pronounced in order to restore public opinion to its true center: honor. The crafts facilitated for those that performed them access to becoming free, and lo and behold almost all are in the hands of freed Blacks. (82)

This notion extended to the poor White population, according to Betancourt y Cisneros, who described in another article how widespread this belief had become. He had witnessed it among the youth of his native city of Camagüey:

> our poor Whites are imbued with the same principles and ideas as the rich. My son to serve! My son to work for another! These exclamations horrify a citizen of Camagüey, who does not consider that the son of his heart runs the risk of finding himself in a prison or on the gallows if he does not learn to live from his labor and his property. (101)

Pedro Deschamps Chapeaux made a comprehensive list of the occupations held by freed Blacks in urban Cuban cities (*Contribución*). They were diverse, and, in their interaction with the upper-level White class, some of these Black men gained considerable wealth. Their names, as Deschamps Chapeaux demonstrated, were widely known throughout Havana. Many freed Black men had reputations of being accomplished musicians. This fame was so well accepted that, in spite of prohibitions mentioned by the Cuban scholar Julio J. Le Riverend Brusone, freed Blacks were hired as musicians for churches in Havana because of their "fame as good performers" (310). According to the testimony of the Spaniard de las Barras y Prado, there were no restrictions since there was no racial separation in Havana churches: "to show to Whites that before God all are equal" (112).

In seeming contradiction, de las Barras y Prado spoke of governmental prohibitions on the freed Blacks: "Free Blacks enjoy the same freedom as all the rest of the citizens; they can hold property and even slaves, and many live on proceeds from sales of products; but always the Black, free or slave, is obliged to respect the White, the law conceding to the latter a superiority that has the object of conserving moral force, in order to keep the Black race submitted" (111–12).

Freed Black men often found themselves involved in the delicate national political arena. One case was that of the mortician Félix José María Barbosa, who, as a second lieutenant of the Batallón de Negros Pardos [Battalion of Mulattoes] of Havana, was accused of participating in the Black revolt of 1844, known as La Escalera (7). Another notable freed Black was the tailor Francisco Uribe, who also held a position in the Batallón de Negros Pardos, and was also investigated as a contributor to La Escalera (62). Evidence of his importance was his presence in the abolitionist novel *Cecilia Valdés* by the Costumbrista writer Cirilo Villaverde, as one of the historically based characters.

One scarcely explored source of information about the activities of urban freed Blacks is their wills. These data displayed proof that many of them had been baptized and had entered into religious marriages. There was a common trait among those who created wills: they had had profitable careers that had produced enough money to warrant the legal costs of producing a will and leaving money to individuals or institutions (Deschamps Chapeaux, "Testamentaria" 97). Among other personal information in wills were details about the individual's or the parents' ethnic background, or their African nation. Information about ethnicity appeared often, perhaps as a marker of ethnic pride, which defied the mainstream generic grouping of freed Blacks as a *pardo* or a *moreno* [colored], terms often used interchangeably by White historians and slave owners.

The thriving Black community was a center of attention of nineteenth-century Cuba, as public institutions struggled to cope with changing regulations after the halt of the slave trade, followed by internal violations of international treaties in order to continue to allow the entrance into Cuba of large numbers of slaves. Documentation of Black activities, other than in historical sources, was through public knowledge, and it appeared in several forms. For example, *Diario de La Habana* [Havana Daily], a daily newspaper, throughout the 1840s published news related to crimes and punishments applied within the city limits of Havana. In disproportionate numbers, slaves and freed Blacks were accused of crimes, making up most of the 15 percent of the population involved in illegal activities (Gómez del Valle y Ramírez 170). These numbers were inflated, however, as Gómez del Valle y Ramírez indicated; slave owners often filed false accusations of crimes allegedly committed by their slaves (170). Publication of final judgment of Blacks, mainly news about their execution, appeared commonly in the pages of *Diario de La Habana*: "At the customary hour the Black Evaristo Seco suffered the punishment of death, because of the wound inflicted on Obispo Street on March 3, 1840, with premeditation upon architect Don Pedro Nevoroni, a Swiss national, dead as the result of that wound" (qtd. in Gómez del Valle y Ramírez 17). Such strong negative journalistic reportage would be reflected in the plethora of criminal Blacks in Costumbrista essays.

Another source of information about Black life in the cities was reports about the activities of arrested runaway slaves. Documentation of efforts to determine their whereabouts was carefully recorded in various formats, including, for example, publication of physical descriptions of the escapees with the obvious intention of procuring recognition of them among the readership. Another source of glimpses of physical details about Black slaves was the careful descriptions of runaway slaves in *depósitos de cimarrones* [jails for holding runaway slaves]. In existence in Havana from 1796 until 1855, the *depósito* was a central location for runaway slaves, some taken there by local police authorities but many others by professional slave catchers, who received a payment for their services (La Rosa Corzo, *Los cimarrones* 40, 45). One example of an entry into the *depósito* is the following, dated 1842, of runaway "number 705, José Criollo: . . . age about 24, good stature, chocolate colored, left ear pierced, teeth complete and those of the upper gum sharpened, one scar on the forehead and another in the left eyebrow and some signs of burns on the left side of the neck and on the collarbone on the same side. Said to belong to Don D. Jacinto Azousa. Sent by Captain de Bainoa" (qtd. in *Los cimarrones* 70). Runaway slaves, as the City of Havana's Minutes recorded, often found refuge among the neighborhoods of freed Blacks.

The most common source of information about Blacks was the news published about slaves available for sale. The information was succinct and to the point, with emphasis on their physical traits and their manual abilities. José María de la Torre, in his historical accounts of the city of Havana, *Lo que fuimos y lo somos o La Habana Antigua y moderna* [What we were and what we are or Havana old and modern] (1857), deemed the content of such information important. He summarized some of the information contained in an advertisement for sale of a slave: "One Black female, 17 years old, good laundress, no blemishes, for 250 pesos. One mulatto male, about 30 years old, good cook, healthy, with some defects, except stealing; also for exchange with Black, mules, horses or a carriage" (128). A sign of the low condition of slaves in the eyes of de la Torre is the fact that he quoted the above sales advertisements among examples of other items widely available in Havana, such as "a horse with a very smooth, fast gait," "a harpsichord with two keyboards," and "books of various works in Spanish, English, and French" (128). The last items were evidence of the high degree of learning reached in Havana by the middle of the nineteenth century.

Havana, a city that began to develop into a progressive urban area after 1841, had a colonial and modern charm that impressed international writers (Gómez del Valle y Ramírez 93). It was those colorful sights, not the Black areas, that caught the interest of eyewitnesses, such as Ildefonso Vivanco, author of the travelogue *Paseo pintoresco por la Isla de Cuba* [A picturesque stroll through the Island of Cuba] (1841). The following was his highly romanticized description of the Plaza de Armas, in the heart of historic colonial downtown: "The enchanting music so dear to the children of the torrid zone draws to the Plaza de Armas a pretty and elegant audience that among the whisper of the breeze of the trees and the flowers, the murmur of the fountains and the sounds of music, flows sweetly and peacefully through its streets, conversing, either of love, or of commercial enterprises" (qtd. in Gómez del Valle y Ramírez 122).

Urban civility contrasted with the handful of descriptions of some of the underground Black neighborhoods. Thriving freed Black communities were in existence in major Cuban cities, and particularly evident in Havana's *extramuros*. The modern neighborhoods that grew outside the city walls, or *extramuros*, became in the nineteenth century targets of rather impressive public works. These included the building of plazas, paving of streets, and the creation of promenades, designed in the European fashion. The Costumbrista writers presented a rather cleaned-up version of this new Havana. According to José María de la Torre, in his 1857 historical account of the city of Havana, some of these newly developed neighborhoods had two names: the official governmental one and the one given to them by their marginal Black inhabitants (48). With few exceptions, the Costumbrista articles did not describe Black neighborhoods, but only the fancy, fashionable areas of the White *extramuros*, which developed as the result of the sugar boom.

The *extramuros'* multiethnic background was the subject of an article by a Costumbrista writer signing with the pseudonym E. E. called "La Misa de Gallo en Jesús del Monte" [Midnight mass in Jesús del Monte]. Intending to "study the customs of peoples, to discover their character, to know their nature, and when history does not submit sufficient events, or if those that it bears are incomplete and ill supposed, we judge it necessary to see the people with our own eyes in order to form an exact and complete idea of them," E. E. set out to witness the celebrations during midnight mass in the Jesús del Monte neighborhood (qtd. in Gómez del Valle y Ramírez 419). This area was set in lush natural surroundings, and its background was the overcrowded city of Havana:

> The Church of Jesús del Monte is situated on a hill high enough to dominate a great expanse of land. At its foot there stretches a handsome countryside, whose picturesque landscape well deserved transfer to a picture, and in a north-south direction there is marked the tortuous road, so to speak, amid infinite palms and tropical fruits. Beyond, in the background of this gigantic picture, Havana unfolds, with its castles that surround it, its towers that crown it, its slums that expand it and its peaceful bay that dies at the skirt of Atarés, forming the peninsula that rises over its hill; an overview that offers perhaps the most affective perspective found in the whole island. (421–22)

Of ethnographic interest is the writer's recording of the various social types that attended the mass:

> In one instant the surroundings of the Church were covered with people not of social categories, because a town young and lacking elements of prosperity does not enclose proud aristocrats, affluent businessmen, rich landowners nor military dignitaries, but of men and women in one, same line with little difference if castes were excepted. Let's speak about the generality. It was a pleasure to see the women White and Black, young and old, blond and brunette, all gathered around the temple. (420)

Although it may seem that the article intends to examine the impact of such a multiethnic population on the traditional Roman Catholic celebration of the midnight mass, it takes a different approach. There was no participation of the people in the organization of the mass, which, besides beginning very late at night, appealed to few, as indicated by many people's leaving the church even before the service began. This was in contrast to other popular, religious celebrations also of Roman Catholic origin but with a strong Black component, such as the carnival, Kings' Day or Corpus Christi. These festivities, as portrayed in Costumbrista essays, were rowdy and very popular among the Black community.

Cirilio Villaverde, a well-known Costumbrista writer and novelist, in his article "La Habana en 1841" [Havana in 1841], writing about the urban *extramuros*, also praised the lavish components of this area, as a "new, healthy city," but he also ignored the Black quarters (Bueno, *Costumbristas* 167). The absence of references to the Black neighborhoods was due perhaps to Villaverde's intention to praise the highly European character of the city. One trait that made Havana different from other cities (presumably Paris, London, Rome, and Venice—cities frequently contrasted with Havana in the text), according to Villaverde, was Black music and dances. The scene presents slave carriage drivers, known as caleseros, waiting for their masters on their parked *calesas*, the coaches that roved the city in large numbers over the recently designed elegant boulevards of Havana. To make their wait pleasant, the drivers "sing and dance to the sound of their little, melancholy instruments: songs, dances and instruments that probably don't have, if you will, the poetry that Byron found in the barcaroles of the lazzaroni of Venice, but that don't lack novelty and expression, above all for the foreigner who hears them or sees them for the first time" (169). Villaverde's positive rendition of the calesero was, however, an exception. Most Costumbrista writers scorned these men as either conceited drivers dangerous to helpless passersby, or as lover boys engaged in sexual liaisons with mulatas finas.

In historical accounts the expanding urban settings of an economically booming Havana demonstrated the aspiration to become an image of civility. Discussions of parallels between Havana and other European cities were common. For example, the Spaniard José María de Andueza's travelogue compared Havana with a Parisian street scene (not a Spanish one):

The streets of Havana are handsome, rather wide, straight, badly paved and bright. Among all of them the street that deserves preference is La Muralla, famed for its multitude of commercial establishments that have their site on it, and for the taste and elegance that distinguishes them: to Muralla Street come women of Havana at night and on foot with the intention to stock up with rich fabrics, with the purpose also of rummaging through shops and of trying the patience of the elegant clerks, more indulgent, refined and obsequious than in any other capital of the world, without excepting Paris. (12)

The flourishing capital city was often equated with fashionable European cities considered models of urban modernity. This tendency to praise Eurocentric urban patterns may explain the relatively few episodes describing in detail the Black neighborhoods that survived the *extramuros*' modernization of Havana. For the most part, these areas were viewed as mere backgrounds to a handful of Black criminal types, the *curro*, who resisted social pressures to abandon a rather peculiar lifestyle.

The rise of the Cuban cities coincided with the development of a Cuban identity. Jesús Guanche, labeling it a national "ethnic entity," placed the beginning at around the middle of the nineteenth century (135). Some of the traits involved in the process included recognition of common components, such as language, national character, and "self-consciousness of belonging to this people . . . outwardly expressed as Cuban" (Guanche 128). Two Black types explored by Elías Entralgo, the *mulatos campesinos* [peasant mulattoes] and the urban slaves, "are the first types in the transition from working castes to national classes" (*La Liberación* 13).

Rogelio Martínez Furé, speaking about popular folklore, stated that one of its functions had been to become a "form of cultural resistance and manifestation of class struggle" ("Imaginary" 110). This struggle, which in the nineteenth century in Cuba included a national policy to resist recognition of Black traditions, promoted, according to Martínez Furé, a conflict, in which Black and White cultures became adversaries (111). Costumbrista writers made targets of specific Black male types, whose highly individualized behavior, as Martínez Furé pointed out, indicated their willingness to resist conformity to mainstream culture in favor of their own Black traditions. Portraits of these Black types focused on their preferred fashions, mainly absurd pieces of clothing worn by the *curros* or their personal accessories, or on the writers' notions that certain Black males engaged in unlawful behavior, including readiness to become assassins. Few Black females, and even fewer Black men, were depicted as acceptable figures of Cuban identity.

In prints and in other art forms there were exceptions to the common, stereotypical physical depictions of Blacks. De las Barras y Prado had high praise for the physical appearance of both male and female Blacks: "Black Creole men usually have regular features, as do Black women, among whom there are some, when they are young, who are very attractive, and both because of this circumstance and because of the scarcity of white women in Havana and in other large towns, mulattos abound. This product of both races is in general rather perfect in features and usually is of sharp wit" (114). He himself was a Spaniard. In popular jokes and in the popular *teatro bufo* [comic opera], Spaniards were in constant pursuit of the mulata fina.

Costumbrista literature stressed the strange behavior of selected types of Black males, often the center of a plot whose main purpose was criticism of what the writers perceived as barbaric, popular traditions, some of which retained a not very obscure connection with urban slavery practices.

The Costumbrista writer's self-imposed role as defender of mainstream Cuban traditions, a common topic of discussion among historians throughout the nineteenth century in Cuba, may explain his lack of interest in denigration of the physical traits of Black male types. His interest in the Black male did not lead to a physical portrait, but to a systemic campaign against certain urban Black traditions. Juan M. Villergas, in his introduction to Francisco de Paula Gelabert's collection of articles, *Cuadros de costumbres cubanas* [Pictures of Cuban customs] (1875), offered his view of the importance of Gelabert's articles: "the reader takes pleasure in the animated painting of human types, one enters into the housings of various social classes that, not because some may be one of those that generally writers choose to ignore, fail to deserve a privileged study if one pays attention to whether in them is included what is characteristic of each people" (Paula Gelabert 5).

Villergas's indirect reference to racial backgrounds in his "various social classes" would seem to indicate that Gelabert treated Black characters as participants in these emerging Cuban customs, but none of the articles (all of which highlighted urban traditions) included a Black protagonist. In the pattern of other Costumbrista writers, Gelabert included Blacks in his articles as mere shadows, peripheral figures without much impact on the fabric of social life in Cuban cities. They were "negritos," or house servants ("Caer en gracia a los vecinos" [To take a liking to the neighbors] 26); voluptuous Black maids, who, overhearing a neighbor's music for a birthday party, stopped their tasks to listen to "a dance so provocative that all the female servants of color in the neighborhood danced it in the street, with the greatest frenzy and passion" ("Un baile en casa de Periquín" [A dance at Periquín's House] 32).

In spite of the dominance of Black males in manual trades, images of Black males in Gelabert's articles are highly negative. He was either a lowly street vendor, a *pregonero*, known for his loud, original announcements of his merchandise ("El día que hay dinero en casa de Ramalazo" [The day when there is money in Ramalazo's house]) or a crazy coach driver, a calesero, whose vehicles congested the Havana streets ("De sorpresa en sorpresa" [From surprise to surprise] 125). There was even a mention in passing of a Chinese worker, an indentured worker, whose services were preferred over those of a Black slave: "How can you compare a Congo Black to a Chinaman who can read and write?" ("De sorpresa en sorpresa" 118).

The Black male figure most common in Costumbrista articles was the criminal. In an article by Gelabert, White women in cities had to learn to defend themselves with household weapons against Blacks. In one article a female was attacked by "a huge mulatto, who came to rob me, and from whom I defended myself with some tongs" ("Las descaradas" [The shameless ones] 68). In Gelabert's essay "Las que andan como locas" [Those going-around-like-crazy women], a minor Black male character was a criminal because of his consumption of alcohol in a worthless existence in a bodega.

One striking characteristic of "Las que andan como locas" is Gelabert's reproduction of urban Black speech, as exemplified in the following translation.

Without ruckus or malice,
I declare with great delight
that I know beyond question
that even if the man gets addicted,
There is nothing like rum. (124)

The Black speaker, known as el capitán Araña [Captain Spider], had been known since his youth to be a *cheche*, a classification that a narrator left untreated. The word *cheche*, according to the Cuban anthropologist Fernando Ortiz, frequently served as a synonym of *negro curro*, among the toughest of the Black criminal underground groups in urban centers in Havana (*Nuevo catauro* 194). The *curro* became the central theme of several Costumbrista articles, which focused on this group's peculiar way of dressing, their use of strange clothing accessories, and their ways of speaking Spanish, in a slang that opposed the overcorrected use of Spanish by some other Blacks, such as the Black coachmen's or the mulato fino's refined speech and the sweetness of the tone of his voice. The *curro* was not, in short, the effeminate version of a White gentleman.

Another piece of evidence that Gelabert did not intend to accept representation of a Black in his catalogue of Cuban customs can be found in his epilogue. "Resumen y punto final" [Conclusion and a final point], written from the autobiographical perspective of a writer who was constantly questioned, and sometimes confronted, by unhappy real people who claimed to have been used as models for some of his articles. None of these people were, however, models for some of his minor Black characters. Those disgruntled readers were White people. Gelabert's total marginalization of the Black from being an active member of Cuban society was further evident in his statement about how he came across models for his articles: "I copy a little from what I observe outside, even when I find myself seated in the very parlor of my house; I copy another little bit from memory, and the rest I imagine, I divine it, by means of intuition" (310).

José Victoriano Betancourt took up the Costumbrista task of serving as an eyewitness of representative Cuban traditions. In his article "Velar un mondongo" [The wake of a tripe], about an odd rural custom performed by *guajiros* [peasants], Betancourt wrote as an introduction the following statement about his aim:

> Customs form, so to speak, the moral features of peoples, being a very exact type for service as a base for observations by those who dedicate themselves to that task, useful under all aspects. Human habits are subject to infinite modifications, and they come to erasure in such a way that they leave only some imperceptible imprint, on whose affiliation the meditations of some antiquarian are exercised. (17)

Like Gelabert, Betancourt rejected Black types as protagonists of a custom deemed to be part of a developing Cubanía. In his listing of the national ethnic origins, however, Betancourt named "el indígeno" [the natives] and the "extinct reflection of those that reigned in Europe many centuries ago," as roots of current Cuban traditions (17). Without much of an explanation, in two pieces— "Los curros del Manglar," a Costumbrista article, and "El negro José del Rosario (Décimas)," a poem to a *curro*—Betancourt made the Black thug a protagonist in a plot that stressed the violence surrounding this controversial Black figure. Costumbrista essays constantly contained strong images of criminality, perhaps fueled by numerous newspapers' accounts of male Blacks' alleged involvement in criminal activities. The criminal Black male was not, however, a protagonist of any Costumbrista piece.

Collectively, a surprising omission from most Costumbrista articles is in-depth exploration of religious practices associated with Black men. Those references were limited to cataloguing the public display of Black cults, mainly in parades. One example was the so-called *diablitos*, who, according to Fernando Ortiz, were male Blacks dressed in the traditional garb of their African nation or in a grotesque costume. They exhibited themselves in the streets during religious feasts, particularly at Epiphany, to beg for money from the passersby (*Nuevo* 223–24). The *diablitos* appeared in Gelabert's article "Vanidad y pobreza, todo en una pieza" [Vanity and poverty, all in one piece], along with references to the *ñáñigos*, members of one of the all-Black secret societies, in "Niños precoces y desarrollados" [Precocious and well-developed children]. Another Black religious parade associated with the Roman Catholic Church was that of the feast of John the Baptist. Gaspar Betancourt y Cisneros, although he did not mention specifically the Black community, called for governmental control of "horses . . . masks and musical groups," elements of notable importance in Black parades ("San Juan de 1839" 210).

More puzzling is the omission of references to the dances performed on the premises of *cabildos*, all-Black associations that served throughout the nineteenth century as centers of mutual help for slaves and freed Black populations. These Black dances were mockingly depicted in the graphic arts of the time, a testimony to their influence among urban Black communities. The development of Cuban Creole dance rhythms had its roots in the sensual *cabildo* Black dances. The indecency of the so-called *danza cubana* [Cuban dance] was a subject of Costumbristas. For example, Valerio's "La danza cubana" [Cuban dance] attacked the immoral character of some of these Creole dances, such as the *guaracha*, in "¡¡¡Danza!!!"; [Dance!!!]. The article declared that this sensual rhythm was responsible for the corruption of the White Cuban youth. That message would appear almost verbatim in references in passing in many Costumbrista articles.

The obvious negative opinions of Costumbrista writers encompassed all Blacks, even those who attempted to incorporate mainstream values into their lives. Other more positive types, such as the mulato fino, were absent from Costumbrista essays. They would appear later as the *negrito catedrático*, the Black wannabe professor of the *teatro bufo*, but as a buffoon that characterized this blackface-like theater. The preferred Costumbrista image of the Black male would be the *curro* [thug], a scapegoat for the inherently racist slave Cuban society of the nineteenth century.

## The Uppity Blacks and the Black Thugs in Urban Cuban Life

Cuban society, like other slave communities in the Caribbean, exhibited highly structured social divisions in a "complex interplay of race, colour, gender, occupation, caste and class" (Heuman 138). Julio J. Le Riverend Brusone described the Cuban social fabric as part of a "hierarchical society," in which a complex division based on racial background determined not only the individual's position, but also the occupations available to him (310). At the peak of social and economic prominence was the "aristocracy in landholding and in politics," which was followed by merchants, landowners, judges, and civil servants. A third category encompassed craftsmen, employees, and salary earners. The lowest group was that of the marginal, the poor (138). Blacks belonged to Groups 3 and 4, and a few gained acceptance into Group 2. Costumbrista articles drew images of representative Black members of the last two social groups.

Social divisions among urban Blacks reflected racial subclassifications among them, often determined by their degree of Whiteness in appearance and in manner, and, therefore, visual proof of their willingness to assimilate into mainstream social structures. Although color was at the center of the colonial social status, acceptable behavior in line with urban civic patterns became the ultimate determinant of the success of individual male Blacks in Cuban slave society of the nineteenth century.

The ultimate male Black expression in imitating a mainstream gentleman was the figure of the calesero, the driver of the fashionable *volantas* or *quitrines*, or coaches. The calesero, as depicted in Costumbrista articles, was always a Black man, often handsome (or, at least, he viewed himself as such), of an imposing physical constitution, whose acceptance into the fancy city mainstream life, particularly in Havana, came about because of his historically close relationship with plantation owners (Heuman 142). Other examples of the caleseros' willingness to perform within the parameters of a privileged urban White society were their attempts to speak Spanish correctly and their overly proper, fancy uniforms. There were several kinds of caleseros, indicative of the degree of their willingness to take advantage of a racist social system. Their uniforms, some of them rich, would become also a focus of attention of graphic artists, such as Landaluze.

*Quitrines, volantas* or *calesas*, as different types of carriages and calashes were known in Havana, caught the attention of Cuban and international writers throughout the nineteenth century. According to Riverend Brusone, there was a fever of *calesas* [calashes] in Havana by 1740, simple vehicles in design: "two wheels sustained by strips of leather, it had two or four seats, and was covered by a collapsible top of leather" (196).

Of Spanish origin, the *quitrín* seemed to have been redesigned for Cuban urban settings and for rural landscapes. It was inspired by the style of such Madrid street vehicles (Pérez de la Riva, *La habitación* 6) or of similar vehicles in southern Spain (Riverend Brusone 196). The Spaniard José María de Andueza, upon his arrival in Havana, described the *quitrín* (the word was new to him):

> A quitrín is an elegant carriage, comfortable, within which one can sleep or make oneself visible. They have assured me that in Madrid there are some quitrines, but up to now I have seen none, so I can't possibly compare those of Havana to our prosaic, and fast calesines, in which, if it rains, one gets wet to the skin. The quitrín is the temple where Cuban beauties receive the sighs and adoration of the men who see them pass by, like the passing of flashes of light that strike from one pole to the other the tropical atmosphere in the hot September afternoons. (7)

Not clear within the text is the type of Spanish *calesín*, or coach, de Andueza compared in this artistic description of the Cuban *quitrín*, of which there were several versions. He briefly made an allusion to a *quitrín* with a collapsible top, the favorite vehicle of the beautiful Habanera, the White woman of Havana, for travel around the city. The image of the *quitrín* with the Creole woman is given in poetic language. It also echoes popular artistic renditions: "a Habanera goes seated in it; she reveals to those who admire her the mystery of the mythological birth of Venus, rising from a shell in the surf of the sea" (7). The Habanera's preference to travel in a *quitrín* was also an inspiration for several print artists.

The *quitrín* was lavishly decorated and comfortably provided with cushions by the many dealerships available in the city for their purchase and maintenance. De Andueza's description of the *quitrín* reflects the wealth of booming commercial Havana. Other eyewitness accounts and Costumbrista writings about them boasted about their demonstration of the wealth of the city: "Rich stirrups and springs adorn it; many of these are of silver; there are also some gilded in fired gold: drawing them is a lively horse covered with handsome and brilliant trappings" (7). Depending on the length of the ride, up to three horses could be used.

The elegance of the *quitrín* completed the magnificence of the newly created boulevards of Havana's fancy *extramuros* neighborhoods, a favorite playground of a wealthy upper class. Captivated by the scenery of the area, where the city had started growing into the countryside of the Province of Havana, de Andueza wrote the following romantic paean to the *quitrín* in the urban landscape:

> It was a beautiful afternoon in May. The rays of the sun, veiled by a transparent blue and white gauze, weakly colored the outlines of the capital of Cuba, reflected with shades stronger and brighter on the hill above which rises the Castle of the Prince. The breeze from the fields refreshed the environment, heated a few hours earlier by the burnings of that same mysterious bonfire, whose flame was dying among floating clouds, precursors of the night, and a multitude of carriages, that like triumphant chariots showed off with pride the opulence and the attractions of the charming women of Havana, came and went along San Lázaro road; raising mountains of dust, into which all the women had to vanish sooner or later. (25)

The driver of the *quitrín* was the calesero, whose description here was free from the racial undertone that dominated de Andueza's memoirs: "the calesero, always dressed in amusing livery with braids of gold or silver" (7). On the back of the *quitrín* was a helper, known as a *paje* [page], whose chores were those of an understudy: "The back is kept for the page, who in any case is a Black boy of ten or twelve years, prettily dressed" (7).

The slave Juan Francisco Manzano served as *paje* for several masters. Consistent with the elaborate uniform of the calesero, the *paje* also wore elegant costumes: "For special occasions I wore an outfit with wide, scarlet pants trimmed in gold braid; a short jacket without a collar, made of navy-blue satin adorned the same way; a black velvet cap with a black tip embellished with braid and red feathers; two gold French-style rings; and a diamond pin" (54; trans. 55). According to Manzano, the *paje's* tasks, other than assisting the calesero and the passengers, included holding up a lantern for the night rides through the particularly treacherous countryside's dirt roads on trips from the cities to the big plantation houses. There are no Costumbrista essays in which *pajes* had a significant role in the plot. They are merely mentioned in passing.

*Quitrines* were infamous sources of news because they were often involved in accidents. De Andueza spoke about the bad conditions of rural roads that caused the "many" mishaps (7). These accidents were also attributed to the poor driving skills of the calesero, who was often described as an abusive and poorly trained driver. According to Jacobo de la Pezuela's *Ensayo histórico de la isla de Cuba* [Historical essay on the island of Cuba] (1842), although the traffic into the cities was chaotic, the calesero was primarily responsible for accidents, including the *quitrines* that hit passersby on foot: "The carts in the traffic, carriages for hire, and the horses were driven in town to the road, maliciously or involuntarily they knocked down people who were walking" (577). Stricken passerby accidents must have been common, as suggested in American traveler Samuel Hazard's *Cuba with Pen and Pencil* (1871), whose travelogue included his drawing of a pedestrian hit by a *quitrín*.[1]

De Andueza spoke of a second kind of quitrín business, which he labeled "de alquiler" (7). This *quitrín*, available to anyone for hire, lacked the luxury of private vehicles and did not have a *paje*. A major difference was replacement of horses by "short, fat, fast mules, which currently are fashionable for carriages" (7). De Andueza did not dwell on the racial nature of the caleseros for hire, nor did he describe the clientele for this humble version, presumably catering to a lower, mixed social class of poor Whites and up-and-coming Blacks.

The earliest Costumbrista publication featuring a calesero as a main subject is an untitled article published in *El Substituto del Regañón*, dated May 26, 1801. The article, by an unsigned author, presented as part of "my scoldings," his nagging observations about the calesero in the city of Havana (qtd. in Lezama Lima, El *Regañón* 216). In the style of future Costumbrista articles, the voyeur writer (which the author stresses by entitling the series of articles "Vistas de la ciudad" [Views of the city]) finds himself at Christo Square. As an omniscient narrator, he transcribes a conversation among "four or five caleseros at a stop"

(216). These were freelance coach drivers, freed Blacks, available for hire, the lowliest of the caleseros, without a paid post in a well-to-do household. Their conversation, not transcribed in the bozal language in which it supposedly took place, is interrupted by the arrival of a "good-looking young Black man" (216).

A recently freed slave, the nameless young Black man is jobless. He claims that he had no useful manual skill with which to support himself, "because having been a servant in his master's house, he managed to buy his freedom with the money that he had saved in the store on the Plaza, and he did not know what was the best way to earn a living, because pushing a wheelbarrow is rather hard work and labor on a farm is even more so" (216). The caleseros' advice is, of course, to become a calesero, a recommendation that the recently freed Black finds ludicrous: "the advice seemed good to him, but he had the difficulty of not knowing anything about this work, and, therefore, he would be put at risk at each step" (216). The drivers laugh at his ignorance, and in the remainder of the article they ridicule their so-called training. This lack of skill became a subject of strong criticism in Costumbrista essays arguing against the activities of the calesero.

The article's overwhelmingly critical tone does not imply, however, that the calesero's unprofessional behavior is due to his ethnicity. This point is clear from the beginning—his commercial dealings are similar to those of other (unmentioned) workers:

> Man is suitable for anything to which he dedicates himself, and it doesn't consist of anything except going out for your ideas, whatever they may be, and no matter how ill reflected they may be, but to set a slow pace, to have an air of self-satisfaction, enough daring to venture, and charm to persuade people that he knows this or that, although he may be ignorant of the principles of the simplest thing: furthermore, that the job or employment of each one is the one that gives knowledge, as we observe all the time in a thousand persons, who without understanding one word of all that they hear and see, because some are more stupid than we, they get a job and carry out its assignments like an expert. (217)

The generic nature of the comment seems to be directed at the state of manual professions in Cuba, of which most were practiced after the granting of official licenses or permits. Many of these manual trades were performed by Black males—a fact that may prove that, indeed, the article was meant to be an attack against them.

The remainder of the essay explains that the calesero was successful, not so much because he was clever, but because the structures of a highly hierarchical society allowed him to manipulate and deceive the system. Unlike in other articles, examples of the calesero's manipulation were not meant to be comical, but social criticism of inefficiency in the performance of his job.

The street scenes in the article are amazingly funny. After telling the young Black man not to worry about not knowing how to ride a horse or mule, because "these animals know naturally how to turn into the various streets," the drivers explain that the calesero's task is of another kind (217). Not really busy maneuvering the horse, the seasoned caleseros continue to offer advice: he was to shout at the passersby, forcing them to step away from the moving carriage. This crazy behavior was the result of the slave mentality, in which money provided individuals a cover to act foolishly: "many of those that ride in it have a privilege, that fills them with pride and bad manners, in order to go ahead of all the rest who don't go in the same way" (217). The *quitrín*, or, rather, the money to hire a ride, provided the means of a social equilibrium in which the gentleman walking on foot had to move away (or faced the physical consequences of an accident), even when "in the carriage that we control may go a Black or a Chinaman, with fuller lips than those of the very horse that we are driving" (217). The reference to *belfos*, the horse's lips, was an obvious reference to artistic renditions of blubber-lipped Black men, popular throughout the nineteenth century. The absence of a sympathetic portrait of the caleseros in this article intimates that the author intended to demean the Black characters with this indirect portrait.

Even the calesero's option to become a paid member of the staff of a wealthy White man (there was no indication that a woman could own her own driver) suggests social criticism of Havana society. The man who hired a private calesero sought to "make other men uncomfortable, and to set up his prerogatives to be defended from insults hurled upon the rest" (218). Simply put, those men must "take extraordinary pleasure in seeming to be what they are not, this is: daring and ill bred" (218). Protected by a convoluted legal system (an indirect reference to the existence in Havana of lawyers who took care of slave-related businesses), accidents often went undeclared by the victims, or "we usually have such benign masters that they defend us with cape and sword" (218).

There is no formal ending to this article. The young freed Black seemingly followed the old caleseros' advice to the letter. One month after that meeting, "he is dispatched more than all those who advised him" (219). The reference to his success indicates the ease of climbing up the economic ladder in Havana, but not to overcome the strict racial observance of "Whiteness." It also addresses the presumably large number of White men, "daring and ill-bred," willing to pay a calesero for their terrifying rides around the city.

The newspaper *Noticioso y Lucero* [News bulletin and bright star], on January 1, 1842, published a strong admonition against caleseros. Signed with a pseudonym, "El compadre" [The Buddy], the article, "El calesero," explored more in detail the two kinds of coach drivers, the *calesero de alquiler* [rental driver] and the *calesero particular* [the privately contracted driver] (Gómez del Valle y Ramírez 425). The article established two clearly different profiles of these types of drivers. The differences between the two caleseros were evident at various levels, both physical and behavioral. The best-developed figure was the calesero de alquiler. This examination is the core of the article, which, unlike other Costumbrista essays, does not display a clear-cut message, perhaps because the piece was intended to reflect indirectly the state of colonial Cuba, still struggling with legal issues about slavery and its impact on the developing bourgeois social class.

The calesero became a reflection of the Cuban urban social structure, as a mirror-like glimpse into households that the calesero served. His physical appearance varied according to the type of master or boss he served or worked for. He was "an essential part of a man of good taste," presumably the upper-class White man who could afford his services as part of his household's servant staff (198). In the lavish life of the plantation owner, the master's slave calesero became the top man among the slave workers. The description hints at dislike, however, toward a figure that attempted to imitate the White master:

> Look at that other guy like a gentleman on an arrogant steed, driving with skill, dressed neatly and elegantly, showing off the handsome forms of his body, the cute jacket of Andalusian origin, decorated at his neck and sleeves with a ribbon of a coat of arms, black braided hat, shiny boots, cuffs and spurs of silver, an earring of gold hanging from one ear, because it is a token from his beloved. (Qtd. in Gómez del Valle y Ramírez 427)

The private calesero's physical appearance would also reflect that of his boss in traits clearly drawn in different types of descriptions: "Does he have three or four sweethearts, is he elegant in dress, happy and expert?" If so, he "belongs to a gentleman" (427). Another kind of calesero had a less attractive appearance: "[he] is nearly forty years old or slightly older, if he dresses severely, wears a tie, almost always white, is married, has a sad face," these were visual signs that he belonged to "devout or elderly ladies" (427). Variations in the uniform, as detailed in the article, directly reflected the financial means of the calesero's boss and indirectly indicated the various kinds of professionals who could afford a private calesero:

Is he slovenly, does he go to sleep on the horse, a taciturn countenance, a simple jacket and does not always wear boots?: he belongs to a physician or to a notary public, or to a lawyer; if you see him a little bit dirty, without boots, with the air of a man who is going to business and a bit bored, he works for a traveling salesman. If his jacket has a thousand ornaments, if it is over-laden with silver, if good taste has not determined his toilette, if he goes along as stiffly erect as a spindle, but without charm, that one belongs to a shopkeeper. If he always wears holiday clothes, luxurious, with an air of protection and his carriage very clean, that one belongs to some authority, judge or boss. (427)

On the other hand, there was the calesero de alquiler, a much cheaper version of the private calesero and, thus, less elegant. Here and in earlier articles, his portrait is negative. He was the most hated presence in snarled Havana traffic, solely responsible for many accidents in the city. This type of calesero was described as superstitious, a drunkard, and a partygoer.

In spite of these negative traits, his figure is far more prominent in literature than the private calesero. In a more literary approach to the subject, the writer "El Compadre" made the coachman-for-hire into a "symbol of motion," a trait seemingly positive, in contrast to the alignment of the private calesero with the White status quo that he blindly served. Thus, the coachman-for-hire and his negative traits (behavioral and physical) became related to the society at large that he knew so well from his fares around the city: "the symbol of motion: now ready in one place, now in another, he is a harlequin whose dress varies infinitely, if today we see him in new shoes, tomorrow be sure that he will wear old ones, his boots are never made-to-measure; if he puts on spurs, they have to be old and unmatched; his hat is different from any other hat in the world" (425). As a barometer of Cuban society and, more specifically, as a marginal member of mainstream society, the calesero de alquiler took on a strong, romantic character: "Finally, he is the exclusive man, independent, enemy of the yoke; he lives like the Arab of the desert, astute, brave, and if you will a Tartar, [ . . . ] he is the soul of the Wandering Jew" (426–27).

The closing argument about the types of caleseros was that all of them were one, "And all these varieties are recast into just one, in which it constitutes, so to speak, the true calesero, distinct and pure" (199). That honor fell to the calesero for a plantation owner, derogatorily presented as "the gossipy calesero" (427). The slave calesero had, according to the article, a close relationship with the master he served, revealed in his careful treatment of the *quitrín* and in the many attentions he lavished upon the master: "he is the one who visits the saddler in order to give his opinion about the tackle of the carriage; it is he who drives to the farm, and goes equipped with his machete, ready to defend it if necessary, because he displays his worth and faithfulness" (427). Although it may seem that this was a positive portrait, the article concluded with a description of a rather demeaning, self-imposed role of the calesero: "it is he who informs the master about disagreements and gossip of the machine operators and he does it almost always with impartiality and dropping hints, because he knows how precarious his position is" (427).

The reference to the machine operators remains without explanation. Perhaps it was an allusion to the calesero's secondary role as a spy on the workers at a sugarmill, whether they were slaves running the plantation's machinery or they were the White workers in charge of the supervision of the operation of the machinery.

The runaway slave Esteban Montejo offered a similar negative description of the slave calesero, whose privileged position in the favor of the plantation owner he belittled as that of a "señorito de color" ["colored dandy"] (16; trans. 20). Montejo recalls one master's driver: "I remember he had an elegant black, a first-rate driver, with an earring and all. All those coachmen were ass-kissers and snitches" (16; trans. 20). As in the case of the mulato fino, the reference to "señorito de color" may also point to effeminate behavior in imitation of the Blacks' perception of the White masters' manners. This negative portrait was absent, however, in Suárez y Romero's overwhelmingly positive characterization of a calesero in his "El cementerio del ingenio."

"El Compadre" presented further evidence that the slave calesero had an unsympathetic role among other slaves. The plantation driver vied with the *mayoral* [the overseer] in charge of supervision of the slaves, in an adversarial relationship described thus: "they treat each other as friends that sooner or later are to be enemies; they are two rival powers that fear each other, that respect each other; they present courtesies to each other and damned if they can stand each other!" (428). Whether their animosity was rooted in their competing for the master's favor is not fully described; however, the writer presents the slave calesero at the same level of trust as an important White manager.

An indication that the slave calesero was not willing to incorporate himself fully into the mainstream patterns of acceptable social behavior might be seen in the previous reference to an earring, often of gold. El Compadre's article noted that this piece of jewelry was part of the calesero's traditional outfit. It would appear to be associated with Black marginal male characters, a rare connection between the calesero as an uppity Black, and criminal male Blacks wanting to remove themselves from any association with White mainstream culture. Wearing jewelry became the trademark of Black thugs, the *curros*, whose outlandish outfits caught the attention of Costumbrista writers.

A striking element in the characterization of urban Black men, particularly evident in the calesero, was the Costumbristas' hesitation to award them a whole set of White, mainstream traits, even if they were behaving mostly like mulatos finos. The calesero, whether private or for hire, retained certain negative traits more akin to those of the *curros*, who were associated with criminal activities. Like the *curros*, thugs of urban slums in Havana, the calesero was restricted to a specific territory within an area of action. White Costumbrista writers barely dared to explore *curros*, however, perhaps because of their strong sociopolitical connotations as a visually negative byproduct of slavery.

Prior to the development of the *curro* as a literary character, Cuban Costumbristas showed interest in documenting other figures related to criminal activities in urban areas. One group was the *mataperros* [dog killers], street boys and teenagers whose terrorist behavior, such as attacking street dogs, gave them a bad reputation as individuals in training for more serious crimes as adults. The *mataperros* seem not to have been limited to Black males; Esteban Pichardo defined them in his *Diccionario provincial casi razonado de voces cubanas* [Almost reasoned provincial dictionary of Cuban words] (1836) as "vagabonds or street roving boys, disposed to pranks and evil deeds, that abound everywhere" (470). But an untitled article published in *El Regañón de la Habana* in 1800 did present the *mataperros* as predominantly Black. According to that article, they were infamous for interrupting religious ceremonies such as baptisms and funerals, demanding money from the participants, who, if they refused, were severely attacked verbally and physically.

*El Regañón's* article denounced a *mataperros'* terrorist attack at the conclusion of a baptism, when the godfather attempted to leave the church: "when he went out to the street and got into his carriage, about twenty-five or thirty of these boys called mataperros, young Blacks and mulattoes and even Whites, that kept importuning him very loudly to throw a handful of monies as was their custom, it seems, on these occasions" (qtd. in Lezama Lima, *El Regañón* 87–88). Although the *mataperros* were described as predominantly of Black background, the presence of White children indicated that the lack of economic resources extended to the White community. It also revealed the incorporation of White children into marginal Black groups. The Costumbrista writer José Victoriano Betancourt's article "El juego de mates" [The game of marbles] (1849) described this in detail, the *mataperros'* favorite diversion, played in the streets, that brought together White and Black children. This street connection would have an impact on all-Black religious associations, such as the *ñáñigos*, so that some of them eventually would allow admission of White men into their groups.

The *mataperros* in *El Regañón*'s article became more aggressive after the godfather managed to get into the carriage, fleeing the scene without having given money to the roaring group. They followed the *volanta* in large numbers, while singing, "a sort of a song in which one said: 'Figs.' And all of them repeated, shouting several times, 'Figs I want'; and others 'Figs I am called'; with such rhythm that it seemed that they had all learned the music, since they didn't stray from it at all" (88). The godfather, ignoring them, continued unmoved, in spite of "so great a commotion that everybody went out to doors and windows to see what was happening" (88). Then the *mataperros* started chanting a more menacing song: "One said, 'Carabalí, papá.' All responded, 'Jejele.' One, 'Out with the lard, no more.' All, 'Jejele'" (88). After this chanting, the *mataperros* started throwing stones, aiming at the godfather, who still refused to stop the *volanta*. Consequently, the carriage suffered an accident and derailed. The godfather, still under stone attacks, had to seek refuge with a nearby neighbor, where he remained for many hours, because the *mataperros* continued surveillance of the house.

*El Regañón* again criticized the vagabond children in another untitled article published in 1831. The theme, as in the 1800 article, led the reader to consider their unruly behavior, "the boys' scandalous noise in baptisms" (qtd. in Lezama Lima, *El Regañón* 471). The term *mataperros* is not used; instead there is a description of a "mob of vagabonds, who, abandoned by their parents and masters, and without the slightest instruction or sense of shame spend their days in the outskirts of parish churches in order to use the occasion to earn money by their instigations and impertinences" (471–72). The article details the *mataperros'* unruly means to force the godfather to give them money, including, as the previous article detailed, the chanting of songs and the physical aggression of throwing stones while pursuing the carriage.

In both of these articles there are veiled references to other marginal criminal groups that associated themselves with the *mataperros*. In the 1800 article, indirect references indicated the presence of others of "perverse habits" (89), while the 1831 article pointed out that the *mataperros* were often joined by "other persons from the dregs of the town" (472). The background of those groups remains unexplored, in spite of the fact that a solution to ending the evil practices of the *mataperros* is the essence of the article's message. Only education of Havana youth and, by extension, Cubans in general, would stop the practices of the *mataperros*:

I do not fail to recognize that education is the principal cause of this and other degrading practices of our civilization and customs: I consider that the remedy is in the hands of masters and fathers that ought never to neglect the conduct of their slaves and children, or to lose sight of their actions, and to scold them severely when sweetness and good advice are not enough to restrain them, their first actions, which are the first steps on the road to crimes, that trouble or damage the honorable and peaceful resident and disturb the tranquility and good order of society. (473)

Education at home (by parents or masters) seems to have been the only solution, according to the article, since other official methods had failed or had not been applied. Although it was against the law to do so, godparents had continued to give money to the *mataperros*, perhaps following the example of tipping practices for slaves, observed by masters, particularly in the countryside.

A striking detail about the *mataperros* is the fact that they appeared in the Costumbrista essay collection *Los cubanos pintados por sí mismos* [Cubans' self portraits] (1852) as the only racially bound type representative of a Cuban "tradition." The article, entitled "El Mataperros," by José Joaquín Hernández, defined the racial constitution of the *mataperros* as mainly White, as a product of neglect: "The fatal preoccupation that exists among us that Whites not dedicate themselves to a job, causes idlers to abound, and when the *mataperros* grows up, to find himself in its dark sphere, surrounded by beings that pervert him and enroll him in their detrimental and disgusting sects" (317). There was no explanation that slavery was a cause of conditions that gave rise to a large unemployed White male community, as previous Cuban and Spanish historians had commented. Also unexplored were the "detrimental and disgusting sects," presumably better-organized underground criminal groups in existence in the Cuban urban areas.

"El Mataperros" is today, however, a useful article to explain the development of criminal gangs in the streets of Havana. An analysis of the components of a "mataperros culture," clearly defined in Hernández's article, reveals thematic connections among the *curros*. The "curro culture," the Costumbrista writers Carlos Noreña and José Victoriano Betancourt wrote in their respective articles, would become a signature of urban Black culture. Like the *mataperros*, however, the *curro* appeared as a highly negative and hated character.

According to "El mataperros," this group formed a cohesive street-based gang of children between the ages of eight and sixteen years old. At the latter age, they "change direction" (314). The type of new direction was not discussed, but it is plausible that the boys eventually joined other organized criminal groups, such as those of the *curros*. Deprived of a formal education for different reasons (such as indifferent parents, death of a parent, or overworked parents), the *mataperros* took to the street, which was his locus, as stated in all the previous Costumbrista articles. Wandering around the city (there was no mention of whether this was Havana), the *mataperros* spent time targeting weak passersby, such as "the blind man who begs for alms, the little Black who goes quietly on his errands or the devout women slowly leaving the novena" (315). As previous articles indicated, the *mataperros* disrupted processions associated with the religious ceremonies of baptisms and funerals. His favorite diversion was to torment street animals, from which dogs "surely bear a severe beating" (315).

The *mataperros* was against the establishment, and he openly dared to disobey the law: "he is an offender against all the orders emanating from the government in regard to the police" (315). The article clearly indicates that there was a demarcated *mataperros* crime culture, a fact that was not evident in earlier Costumbrista articles. *Mataperros* were grouped in gangs known as *partidas*. The meetings were held in certain unmentioned city neighborhoods. The pride of belonging to certain groups was evident: "I am of the Canteras gang, and another man boasts of belonging to the Joyos gang" (315). There was little information given about the activities of these groups; they seem to spend most of their time fighting against rival factions or playing together.

Some of the *mataperros* group activities involved gambling, which official sources of the time indicate was a source of criminal activities in the city of Havana. The *mataperros* played dice and cards: "When scarcely into puberty the mataperros already knows very well which are the gatherings of gamblers, these being his only companions. He well knows how to load the dice, and he knows perfectly the handling of the trick cards and marked cards" (316). The expression "loading the dice" appeared written in italics in the original, perhaps to express *mataperros* jargon. The *mataperros* was a professional cheater: "None of the shady mysteries of cardsharps is hidden from him: he appropriates all their habits" (316). The gambling money and the sale (a *poncala*) of merchandise that "someone unwary sells him on credit" were his only sources of income (316). Again, the use of a specific term, *poncala*, underlined in the text, may reflect the fact that some of the *mataperros* jargon was already known to or even used by the mainstream community.

The *mataperros* groups were extremely well organized, inspired by techniques that they frequently observed in public actions of the military. The narrator of the article finds puzzling the *mataperros*'s attraction to a restrictive military lifestyle, which seemed to go against their natural, romantic-like spirit of lovers of a life free of legal obstacles: "The mataperros's character is most independent and most opposed to subjection [to the law], and at the same time most decidedly keen on all things military for which the most rigorous discipline is the first motive. This liking leads them to the extreme of organizing their gangs in a military manner" (315–16).

The *mataperros* groups often engaged in fights against adversarial factions, just to "maintain the honor of the neighborhood to which they belong" (316). The dangerous fights took place in the streets: "in pitched battle they decide their competitions with blows with rocks and clubs, creating havoc until the arrival of the police, which were unable to do much to stop these encounters" (316). These encounters were well organized and reflected a military type of planning. There were two kinds of encounters: group and individual. The individual fight seems to have been more appealing to the article's narrator, who describes it in detail:

> At other times the combat is between individuals and it is carried out between those of the most renown and fame from the gangs, to whom the name cocky guy is given, perhaps because of their constant disposition to fight: good taste or failure in these encounters results in respect for the winners, but in no humiliation for the losers, who again try their luck when they *refresh their blow*. (316, emphasis in the original)

Although the use of italics for the phrase "refresh their blow" appeared to dismiss the gravity of these fights, it may also have reflected a street-criminal jargon used by the *mataperros*, which the narrator carefully records throughout the text.

Another notable element of the *mataperro* culture was their liking of music, which the writer presents as a positive trait: "It's a regular thing for him to have a good ear, and on first hearing a counter dance, a paso doble, a waltz, he catches them and whistles them perfectly: from this they draw a great resource in their youth in order to spend happily the nights of raids" (316). Whether the assumption here is that they incorporated their own composing into mainstream White music is not explored further. The *mataperros* could play musical instruments (there was no mention of what kind), providing the possibility that they created their own music: "there are few who do not learn to play some instrument, even if it is by ear" (316).

Earlier Costumbrista articles had mentioned in passing this group's involvement in major criminal activities, such as the "dirty brothels," in association with the *negro curro del Manglar* [the criminal Black thug of the swamps] (317). Fernando Ortiz, the noted Cuban historian and anthropologist, placed the *curro* within a booming underworld community in existence in Havana throughout the nineteenth century. According to Ortiz, *curros* were "some Blacks and mulattoes originally from Seville and with traits specific to the city of Havana" (*Los negros curros* 3). They were culturally bound figures at the center of a transatlantic trade. Their origins reflected specific geographical coordinates, as well as peculiarities about ways in which they dealt with racial issues. For Ortiz, who since 1909 studied the *negro curro*, the fact that the *curro* exhibited common characteristics with Spanish counterparts was an important element in his concept of "Afro-American transculturation" (1) as a way to understand the hybrid elements of Cuban Creole culture. Today this concept could be considered a precursor of Transatlantic Studies.

The *negro curro*, Ortiz asserts, was a product of urban life, particularly of the pier areas of Havana and Regla, Guanabacoa and Marianao (*Los negros curros* 13). He also points to the wealthy sugar-supported societies of Matanzas and Cárdenas (in the province of Matanzas), which the *curros* might have inhabited. These areas often imitated the sophisticated lifestyle of the capital city of Havana (*Los negros curros* 13). They had access to ocean ports, which became a "corrupt and criminal environment" (*Los negros curros* 13). Although Ortiz traces the origin of the *curro* to similar marginal, urban Black male groups in Seville, he describes the type of the Cuban curro as "the most common and historical Havana expression" (*Los negros curros* 1).

Like the *mataperros*, the *curro* developed within the urban marginal areas on the outskirts of *extramuros*. There were significant differences, however, between the *mataperros* and the *curros*, particularly evident in the peculiar dress code that the *curro* observed. Ortiz, like nineteenth-century Cuban Costumbrista writers, was interested in the *curros'* physical appearance, which produced crude figures. While Costumbrista writers often described the *mataperros* as a pauper ("he is always dirty and ill clad and at times without shoes and hat"), the *curro* appeared as a dandy, but with an exaggerated use of mainstream clothing ("El Mataperros" 315). According to Ortiz, the *curros* "were distinguished by their language, their dress and their accessories (shirts, trousers, footwear, hat, handkerchief, earrings, rings), by their gaits and by their evil life of crime and of courage, always armed with knife at hand: challengers, boasters and daring" (*Los negros curros* 3). This definition appeared in other, similar statements in Costumbrista writings of the nineteenth century—texts that offered Ortiz data of primary importance. Costumbristas also remarked about the *curros'* peculiar use of the Spanish language, not unlike the *mataperros'* criminal codes, but different from the slaves' and the freed Blacks' use of bozal.

According to Ortiz, the *curros*, like other Black groups, displayed a series of defining characteristics. These traits revealed, however, a desire to remove themselves from Black-related groups. Unlike the *mataperros* and the all-male religious associations known as ñáñigos, the *curro* did not form groups; "he operated on his own initiative and individual goals" (*Los negros curros* 6). Ortiz vaguely refers to individuals who did get together to perform "some undertaking" (7), but those instances did not lead to a permanent "fraternity" (*Los negros curros* 7). There were fights with knives among individual *curros* using knives, but unlike other groups they did not display a stabbing, marking style (7).

In their social entertainment, again they differed from other groups that developed musical rhythms, songs or dances, as the *ñáñigos* did mainly for their well-organized religious ceremonies (Ortiz, *Los negros curros* 7). The earlier *curros* did not play musical instruments—also a trait different from that of other Black groups, particularly those associated with religious groups, who used specific instruments for rituals.

At a later stage, the *curro* did play the *bandurria*, a stringed, guitarlike musical instrument of Andalusian origin (Ortiz, *Los negros curros* 7). Ortiz presents this as proof that the *curros* attempted to remove themselves from African cultural boundaries, as they avoided "calling to mind ancestral institutions of the Black continent" (*Los negros curros* 7).

Further proof of the *curros'* desire to remain untainted by African musical traditions, so closely related to religious performances, may illustrate a reason why the *curros* did not develop a syncretic belief system, as did the *ñáñigos* and the practitioners of the Yoruba Regla Ocha and the Congo *mayomberos* (Ortiz, *Los negros curros* 12). The *curros'* religious belief system was the trait least explored in Costumbrista writings. Even Ortiz makes only vague references to what could have been the *curros'* religious observances. Categorically, Ortiz denies that in *curros'* gatherings there would be "witchcraft and conjures, as the ñáñigos still use professionally to a greater or lesser degree in their spells" (*Los negros curros* 12). The *curros'* religious practices would have been, according to Ortiz, a reflection of a mixture of popular devotions in the urban pier areas of the mid-nineteenth century in Cuba:

> The curros doubtless would go from time to time, like the rest of Cuba's inhabitants, to consult with some Black practitioner of witchcraft, a brujero, for him to work the spells and incantations from the Congo, just as they would go to a gypsy for her to read the cards or to an island woman for her to pray for them and to sell them the prayer of the Just Judge, famous among the mafia of Seville for protection of thugs against prosecution by justice. (*Los negros curros* 12)

Whether the negro *curro del Manglar* projected an urban image inspired by transatlantic fashions other than the African is not easily ascertained. It is evident, however, that the *curros'* birthplace was the Black neighborhoods of Havana. El Manglar, a swampy area, was a neighborhood on the outskirts of Havana, along the coast of the Havana harbor. Ortiz writes about a bodega called Del Cangrejo, located in the Manglar, as one of the operating centers of the *curros* (*Los negros curros* 15). El Manglar, located in nearby *mangles*, or mangroves, was the name of this area, which was also known as Del Cangrejo [Crab]. Its location in the vicinity of the drainage canal, source of an abundance of crabs at least until 1857, inspired the name of the bodega (Gómez del Valle y Ramírez 114). Other *curros*-related areas in Havana, according to Ortiz, were the suburbs of del Horcón and Jesús María (*Los negros curros* 15). These geographical referents appeared often in Costumbrista writings of the time as places identified with political uprisings of 1826 in "secret meetings of colored men" (Riverend Brusone 373).

Citing the historian José María de la Torre's memoir of the city of Havana, Ortiz establishes the peak of *curros* activities as the middle of the nineteenth century. According to de la Torre, the *negros curros del Manglar* "sometimes upon orders to kill crabs, killed a passerby" (qtd. in *Los negros curros* 4). The demise of the *curro*, according to Cuban historian José Luciano Franco, took place at the end of the century. He did not disappear completely, however; Franco places him as a figure in the processions of the Havana carnival in the first decade of the twentieth century (*La diáspora* 200). Ortiz does not offer a concrete time span for *curro* culture, which "disappeared for no obvious reasons," but he points out that it became incorporated into "theatres of customs, in carnival masquerades of musical groups of poor people, and in our folklore" (*Los negros curros* 1).

Costumbrista writers exhibited interest in documentation of the *curro* lifestyle, often in depictions of a secondary or shadow character. Other Cuban or Spanish historians or international travelers to Cuba did not report the existence of the *curro*, perhaps because of that group's isolation to specific geographical coordinates within the city limits (the pier) and the marginal outskirts areas (*extramuros*), which were not tourist attractions. *Curro* culture, according to Ortiz, caught the attention of the Costumbrista writer because it had the appeal of a character associated with a "picturesque literature of customs" (*Los negros curros* 1). In spite of the strong eyewitness elements used, however, the Costumbrista writers, according to Ortiz, had no interest in profiling the *curro* from a sociological angle, "of the various aspects of his life, nor as a scientific theme of ethnography" (*Los negros curros* 1).

Contrary to Ortiz's statement, Costumbrista writers did not view the *curro* as a prospective picaresque literary figure. *Curros* continued to be perceived as criminals. Neither were the antisocial negative symbols of their behavior explained as a result of the negative impact of slavery on the developing national culture.

One Costumbrista author whom Ortiz often quoted was José Victoriano Betancourt (1813–1875). His article "Los curros del Manglar" made the *curro* not only become a central figure, but a protagonist of a detailed plotline, a sort of barometer that traced changes in national customs. Betancourt, whom Ortiz referred to as "perhaps the Cuban Costumbrista who dedicated the most attention to the Black curro" (*Los negros curros* 4), was also the author of a complementary poem entitled "El negro José del Rosario (Décimas)." Betancourt's narrator, like those of previous articles on *mataperros*, served as an eyewitness reporter, a characteristic that explains Ortiz's interest as an anthropologist. As an inquiring traveler in his own land, describing exotic elements associated with the *curro*, Betancourt's article displays the obsessive quality of a voyeuristic observer. This is particularly evident in the numerous scenes involving descriptions of the *curro*'s person and behavior.

Betancourt, hailed as "among the first Costumbrista writers in Cuba" (Santovenia 9), published prolifically in various literary genres. The critic Emilio Roig de Leuchsenring identified Betancourt's first Costumbrista essay, "El enamorado" [Man in love], published in 1838, as a study of national "types" (*Los escritores* 143). A writer of poetry and one of the first Cuban editorial writers (Suárez-Murias 377), Betancourt's literary career started early, and it led him to co-found several serial publications. His reputation was solidly established as a Costumbrista writer who was "among the four or five greatest Cuban local color writers" (Day Corbitt 42).

Like other Costumbrista writers, Betancourt often signed his articles using a pseudonym, such as in "Velar un mondongo" [Wake for Tripe] (Roig de Leuchsenring, *Los escritores* 145), his piece about an unusual, fast disappearing rural custom. He often expressed strong opinions. Roig de Leuchsenring summarized Betancourt's Costumbrista production as his "declaration of a moralizing eagerness, the ardent desire to infiltrate into all his fellow citizens the ideals of mobility, purity and civic-mindedness" (*Los escritores* 147).

As a practicing lawyer, Betancourt was involved in local politics. He was also a member of the writers' group of the abolitionist Domingo del Monte (*Diccionario* 116), although there is no recorded correspondence between the two in del Monte's *Centón*. He found himself involved in political incidents pertaining to the slave revolt of 1844, but he was not legally prosecuted, unlike the famous novelist and Costumbrista writer Cirilo Villaverde. Betancourt continued to support leftist political ideas, and eventually, during the War of 1868, his revolutionary spirit forced him into exile. In 1870 he left Cuba for Mexico, where he served as a lawyer and later as a judge. He never returned to Cuba.

Betancourt's article "Los negros del Manglar, El triple velorio" [The three-part wake] and the poem "Décimas El Negro José del Rosario" were published on December 31, 1848, in the magazine *El Artista*, of which Betancourt was often a contributor. That Costumbrista article must have retained a strong historical value, since it appeared in the publication *El Liceo de la Habana* in 1860 and in *La Discusión* in 1882 (Santovenia 37). The critic Salvador Bueno spoke about Betancourt's ability to offer "dissection of the society of his time" (*Bosquejo* 26), a trait that must have been debated among the contemporary readers of Betancourt's Costumbrista essays.

Betancourt's essay "Los curros del Manglar," as the title announces, openly dealt with the *curro*, a controversial Black male figure in the highly structured society of Havana in the nineteenth century. As Ortiz pointed out, Betancourt was "the Costumbrista who dedicated the most attention to the Black thug" (*Los negros curros* 4). He, unlike other Costumbrista writers who presumably preferred to ignore the existence of this marginal Black type, openly explored a Black figure with a negative profile. His view was limited, however, centered on certain traits. These were: clothing style, demeanor, walk, and speech patterns. Clearly absent was a sociopolitical analysis leading to a sympathetic psychological profile.

Betancourt describes the existence of a male *curro* fashion at greater length than any other physical characteristic:

> The curros had a distinctive appearance, and it was enough just to see them to classify them as such: their long locks of braided hair, falling down on the face and the neck like big reptiles, their short teeth filed in the carabalí fashion, the shirt of embroidered gauze, their trousers almost always white, or carefully striped, tight at the waist and extremely wide at the legs, the canvas shoe, cut low with a silver buckle, the jacket with a little flounce of short, sharp-pointed tails, the flashy straw hat, with long, hanging, black silk pompoms, and the thick gold rings that they wear in the ears, from which they hang hearts and padlocks of the same metal. (131)

Dressing against the status quo, as Betancourt indicates, this *curro* attire was unique: "the gear that only they wear" (131). The demeanor included a confrontational attitude, reflected in the way that the male walked. The male *curro* observed a walking pattern that Betancourt offered as a negative trait: "They are known, too, by their gait, wiggling their hips as if they were hinged and swinging their arms forward and backward" (131).

*Curros* spoke Spanish, not bozal, but Betancourt qualifies their speech as "tan físico y disparatado" (loosely translated as "so rhetorical and nonsensical") "that at times one didn't understand them" (131). Along with that particular use of the language, they had a peculiar voice inflection, which Betancourt mentions as "the special inflection that they give to their speech" (131). Although this trait would remain understudied, the reference may point to a developing Cuban "accent," a Creole form different from the acceptable Spanish peninsular use of the language, reflected in the personal letters of the upper-class intelligentsia of the time.

A final characteristic of the *curros* was their main location. They inhabited the Manglar, in the *extramuros* of Havana. Their field of action may have been restricted to the neighborhood of Jesús María. They were "famous in the annals of Jesús María for their relaxed code of behavior and for their murders, which more than once have caused trembling among the peaceful dwellers of the suburban neighborhoods" (131). Betancourt does not define any of those "relaxed [types of] behavior."

Betancourt's characterization of the *curro*, with emphasis on that character's flamboyant physical appearance, led Ortiz to explore what he labels a trademark of marginal behavior: "As one sees, he was a totally bizarre type, all smugness and show, in dress, in courage and way of life, in defiance" (*Los negros curros* 36). Living at the edge of society, both in terms of geographical location and acceptance by proper mainstream Cubans, the *curro* was the center of Betancourt's "Los curros del Manglar." His intention to explore such dark sides of marginal customs may be responsible for his reputation for exploring "urban scenes so suggestive as those referring to the curros del Manglar" (Portuondo 25–26).

In spite of what appears to be intended as a study of a character, "Los curros del Manglar" is not a highly descriptive analysis of *curro* culture. Other than the previously quoted passage about the male *curro*'s clothing fashion, which seemed to have gone against the acceptable dandy-like preferences of the White Cuban gentleman, or even the elegant uniforms of the Black caleseros, Betancourt offers no physical details about this peculiar urban culture. Peppered throughout the text there appear reproductions of dialogues meant to illustrate Betancourt's prior description of the *curro*'s language as "rhetorical and nonsensical." Even that attempt at an extended characterization failed, because his reproduction of such unusual linguistic patterns did not differ much from the stilted dialogues in the fashion of bozal speech by other Costumbristas. Few critics have spoken about this use of the *curro* speech, but the Cuban Emeterio S. Santovenia in an early monograph on Betancourt does praise his reproduction of the *curro* jargon: "he imitated faithfully the speech of the Black curros" (38).

Betancourt heavily depended on the use of dialogue in developing a plot that is implied in the subtitle, "El triple velorio" [A three-part wake]. As in other essays on customs, the plot is uncomplicated. A narrator, perhaps Betancourt himself, as indicated in his nickname, Pepe, sets out to stroll the streets of the city of Havana in search of a theme for a Costumbrista article. Prior to that moment, which also marks the beginning of the action, he had expressed strong opinions about the current state of Cuba's racial relations. Referring to Cuba as a melting pot of sorts, "a compound of races, which are original types, whose combination can be compared only to a cloak of many colors mixed by chance," he communicates the purpose of the article at hand (130). Cuban society was struggling with social changes, evident in the inclusion of Black popular components, still designated as part of "the African race," which he defines: "The African race, considered as a group, offers information sufficient for writing, either for analysis of their national character, or for the infinite modifications that they receive in this environment by being crossed with the rest of the castes" (130). He does not focus on the "Africans," a veiled reference to slaves still arriving in Cuba, but on the Black Creoles: "The Creole species, whose types scarcely show analogy with the primitive, presents a multitude of diverse traits" (130).

The example chosen to illustrate that "Creole species" is "the negro curro del Manglar," to be examined "by one of its faces . . . painting an original custom, if one wishes to be extravagant" (130). Although that one activity is not related to the *curro*'s reputation as a criminal, the tradition at hand, the "velorio de un parvulito" [the wake for an infant], would eventually illustrate the *curro*'s marginal position as a cold-blooded criminal, even at a religious activity such as a wake for an infant.

Following a basic literary pattern in which a local character finds himself touring the city of Havana, the narrator runs into a friend, Esteban, who enthusiastically invites him to join him to witness "a wake for an infant, the son of the mulatto Timoteo Pereyra, alias Bilongo; now you know that he is a curro from the Manglar; there you will observe the customs of this swine" (132–33). Although at first Pepe is hesitant to embark upon an exploration of el Manglar ("that is a neighborhood of devils, and we can lose our skin"), Esteban eventually calms him down (133). Esteban was Timoteo's lawyer, and Timoteo feels indebted to him for having released him from jail for a crime that Esteban cleverly did not disclose to Pepe. With a reluctance unusual in a willing observer of Cuban customs, Pepe agrees to go into the Manglar, "not without grave danger to our ribs because of the rough twistings of its streets, and to our lives because of the multitude of flying knives, which at that time were placed in an honorable man's shoulder blade, without knowing how" (133). This would be the stage for the article, "the theater where we were going to fish for observations," equated in literary significance to those of Victor Hugo—"as worthy of being described for its crimes and nocturnal mysteries as that painted in masterly strokes by Victor Hugo in his immortal: *Notre Dame de Paris*" (133).

In spite of his apparent willingness to report the activities surrounding the wake, the narrator says little about the wake, presumably a religious service, but Esteban summarizes for Pepe in one short paragraph the *curros'* customs for the occasion:

> when some infant boy of this race dies, they send for the godfather, who pays for the wake of the godson; after the necessary preparations, the body is laid out with all possible luxury, they hold a wake for him, they eat and drink without remorse the whole night; and at dawn, they hide the body, which they place in a well, in order to preserve it by the coolness of the water; they remove it again, lay it out and they have a second wake; but they never celebrate the second wake in the same street; for the third wake they use the same measures until, when the body is corrupt, they take it to be buried. Each night is a bacchanal, or better expressed, the representation of the horrible pandemonium that Milton paints for us with his divine brush. (136–37)

As if following a literary cue, Pepe's description emphasizes a "bacchanal," which he witnessed on this third day of the wake, as he nervously awaits the arrival of the corpse.

The plot does not dwell on the religious activities of the wake for a *curro* child but on the interaction of the attendees: "some twenty persons of both sexes, among Blacks, mulattoes and *dirty* Whites, all assassins; most of them wanted men, and the rest having completed their sentences" (134–35, emphasis in the original). The reference to dirty Whites contradicts Ortiz's statement that the *curro* remained marginal to the lower classes of White society. This also explains that earlier in the text Betancourt had explicitly restricted his study to the "negro curro" community, implying that there were White *curro* men. All these characters are at ease together, keeping each other company, playing physical games allusive to a bullfight: "they played at donkey, and between games, they threw a little bull, that at times charged as if it were a beast, leaving some of them sorry for having made passages at him" (135). There was plenty of alcohol. Everyone shared the bottle, referred to as a "little Black girl of rum": "from to time one of those rascals put a glove to a little Black girl of rum, that rose in the center of the table (almost emptied by the rough time she was having among so many rogues), and giving her a loving kiss, he handed her to his nearest companion, with the expression, *Go the conga*, that received in response the saying, *Come to me the conga!*" (135, emphasis in the original).

There is no improvement in the article's revolting tone after the corpse finally arrives at the home. The portrait continues to offer numerous references to "hellish scenes" (135). The attraction of the party is the exposed corpse, at whose center stood the body that emitted "a disagreeable odor, produced by the decomposition of the cadaver that they were carrying to the living room" (137). Any reference to a religious observance is limited to a quick view of the corpse: "They placed the body in a box lined with sky-blue fabric, and they put this box on the tomb lined with the same cloth, scattering later on the ironwork and the pavement funeral flowers, French roses and various other kinds" (137). After the windows of the house were open to dissipate the stench of the corpse, the wake officially got under way: "now the curros could spend the night getting drunk with the doors open, without the local authorities being able to prevent their meeting, since by this means they evaded their zeal, and they could indulge in such abominable desecration" (137). This loose mention of legal restrictions upon meetings remains unexplained; perhaps the wake, as a religious gathering, was excepted from the regulation. The secular celebration, not the activities of the wake, constitute the remainder of the article, which the narrator concludes with a denunciation: "it seemed to me that I saw reproduced, before my very eyes, the horrible Saturdays that (according to the author of a lovely little book entitled An auto-da-Fe in Logroño) took place in Zarramagurbi" (139).

In spite of what might have been expected from the indirect reference to a witches' Sabbath, the narrator places no emphasis on the religious activities. Whether or not the *curros* were known in Havana for their peculiar way of celebrating the wake for an infant, presumably the subject of the article, after a long wait for the arrival of the corpse at the house, the narrator chooses to document only the rough interactions of those he has joined to participate in the wake. They were, after all, cold-blooded criminals, a fact that Pepe, the fearful narrator, stresses throughout the text.

According to Fernando Ortiz, Cuban Blacks in the city observed complex funeral practices, which were restricted by law. One of such restrictions may illustrate some of the activities that Betancourt failed to document in his article. An Edict of Good Government and Police of 1843 ordered the following dispensation for funeral parades: "Mourners in the burial of people of color, if they do it on foot, will have to go two by two and not in any other way, dressed in their ordinary clothes and not with the costume of a little devil or any other, and they will not be able to stop in the bars either going to or returning from the cemetery, under a fine of eight pesos for the violator" (qtd. in *Los negros* 55). The costumes of the *diablito* appeared often as background to urban Black parades in Costumbrista articles. Ortiz displays a similarly negative view of the Black wake, which he illustrates as an example of his theory of transcultural-ism: "African survival, adopted by even the lower social levels of the White race, were doubtless the wakes, fiestas (to use the most appropriate word), that took place in the home of the deceased on the occasion of a wake for the dead. The fiesta consisted of satisfying gluttony sumptuously and eroticism and the noise-making typical of Africans, with dances, chants, and music, all sprinkled with swallows of African alcohol and of Cuban rum" (*Los negros* 54).

Various post-emancipation Black groups developed funeral practices. For example, practitioners of Santería or Regla Ocha believe that "death is only to be feared when it occurs prematurely, especially in unborn or very young children" (Neimark 47). A high priest, a *babalawo*, is consulted in order to keep the dead children's spirits, known as *abiku*, from becoming mischievous. They can turn against their former parents, or come back to claim the lives of any other babies born within a year after their death (47).

There are in Betancourt's article, however, faint indications that a Black re-ligious funeral ceremony may have taken place. An "oración" [a prayer] (136), which was not transcribed or commented upon, was part of the preparations prior to the arrival of the child's corpse. A song followed as the body entered the house, part of the activities of a parade in which participants were "singing in chorus a vulgar song typically used by them" (137). Pepe's only comment about it is a dismissal of the song as part of the gross behavior until then ob-served: "A sort of psalmody half melancholy, that at that hour, in that place, and sung by those monsters, pierced the heart with terror, and seemed like the chant of a conjurer invoking the Demon" (137).

In lieu of a full description of the religious activities, the narrator focuses on the festivities, which included plenty of food and alcohol. He describes only those Black partygoers whose traits support the narrator's negative accounts of the events. As figures of aggression, his male *curros*, in particular, are presented as subhuman. One was a "mulatto . . . whose face was almost hidden among some enormous braids that like serpents hung from his head" (125).

The presentation of Black women is not positive either. Of serious sociologi-cal interest is Pepe's statement that *curras* from different neighborhoods, like the male *curros*, display animosity against each other. This information is pre-sented as part of a conversation reproduced in the so-called "private language" of the *curro*. As two Black women wonder which of the *curras* is the mother of the dead child, they offer an indirect description of the *curra* woman. Having seen no one crying, one of them concludes that the mother of the child is not present. The other Black woman denies such an allegation, allegedly because, "these curras don't cry" (138).

The Black women's conversation is overhead by a third *curra* whose physical description reflects a common popular saying: "a mulata larger than the hope of a poor man" (138). The offended *curra* addresses the women: "Listen, Mrs. Unknown, take it easy talking about the *curras*, who have not eaten your dessert and have more sense of shame than you" (138). They respond with an undue display of animosity. The answer does not reflect neighborhood animosity, but their personal notion of social status: "'More sense of shame than I,' answers one of the three, 'you cannot have, who probably were some common slave'" (138).

There is no physical altercation, perhaps because another *curra* woman comes to warn the two women to leave at once. This dialogue continues in the line of the *curro* "figurative language": "'Snail, you and your house leave'" (138). The two women obey the warning and leave, but first they too express their sense of social superiority over the other two Black women: "'Petronila, let's go, we are not trashy, nor have we come to make a scene'" (138).

This scene serves as a preamble for an ending rather to be expected. Inside the house, a group of male *curros* has continued to drink ("all the heads were changed into stills"), turning the scene into a crude display of male *curro* behavior (139). Worried that the men have started to behave in an erratic fashion, Pepe asks his friend to leave at once. It was too late. As they are leaving the house, they witness a fight that results in murder. A short passage ends the article: "the assassin ran away in front of us, with the speed of a bird, carrying the knife in his infamous right hand, still dripping blood, his countenance filled with fright and ferocity" (140).

Betancourt's article differs from the traditional Costumbrista essay in that the ending does not contain a concrete moral message. The last sentence replaces the usual lesson. It simply points out the narrator's remorse about having been in the Manglar, among criminal *curros*: "Esteban and I took by chance the first street turning that we found, filled with fear by the tremendous consequences to what we saw exposed, for the sake of observing the customs of the curros of the Manglar and the triple wake" (140).

Betancourt's narrator's escape from the Manglar indicates his notion of the danger in this criminal neighborhood, where he had been until then presumably protected by a "friendly" but nonetheless criminal *curro*. Critics have pointed out that White male voyeurs while observing Black males often draw "a line of exclusion demarcating imagined danger" (Perkinson 187). This element is strongly evident throughout this article, which maintains as its primary focus the fights of the male *curros* and not the traditional religious wake. Symbolically, the *curro* remains restricted to the Manglar neighborhood, where, as the introduction of the article indicates, Betancourt hopes it will stay hidden away: "The public and private life of our society presents a fund of customs opposed to each other, that, because of their special nature makes more shocking the political mixture [*sic*] of such heterogeneous elements and affords at each step abundant material for observation and study" (130).

Judging by the handful of representations in Cuban Costumbrista literature, *curros* were restricted to the coordinates of the evil Manglar neighborhood, and within those margins they seemed more likely to appear as insignificant thugs without much influence on the thriving suburban areas of the city of Havana. Jill Lane pointed out that this type of "portraits of street life" (28) was the crudest material of Costumbrista essays and, therefore, most likely to avoid the stringent literary censorship imposed in Cuba upon Black themes with a political slant. As part of a "street" scene, *curros* served as a component of a political strategy, or a "black male demonization," that the African American critic Mark Anthony Neal traced in the construction of similar (evil) Black figures in the United States. According to Neal, the media has promoted the belief that "a significant number of young black men engage in 'sexually perverse, predatory behavior (towards) unsuspecting and defenseless victims'" (7). Fear of strong Black males, particularly of the male body, is at the center of "historic fears among white Americans about black male sexuality, interracial relationships, and sexually transmitted diseases" (Neal 4).

As Neal and other African American theorists, such as bell hooks, have indicated, Black males have traditionally struggled against these constrictive limits in the expression of their perceived role of gender: "In patriarchal culture, all males learn a role that restricts and confines. When race and class enter the picture, along with patriarchy, then black males endure the worst impositions of gendered masculine patriarchal identity" (hooks xii). Betancourt's Costumbrista essay was a unique document, not only because it explored the *curros* within their marginal neighborhoods, but also because it provided a negative example against which to compare his perceived positive view of acceptable male behavior. What strikes a reader today is the *curros'* resilient opposition to incorporating themselves into acceptable Black behavioral patterns, of which the mulato fino was the epitome in literary representation. *Curros* opposed the cultured attitudes of which mulatos finos publicly boasted.

Perhaps a similar challenge is obvious today in the so-called "hip-hop thugsta" in the African American music scene. Highly controversial in their public iconoclasm, in their open chauvinism, and in their homophobia, as the critic Neal stated, their "behavior might have been influenced by their perceptions of how black male privilege operates in our communities" (153).

*Curros* set themselves out to be targets of the wrath of either the local police authorities or of the sympathetic abolitionist. Arguably, unlike the hip-hop thugsta's marginality as a tool of political contention, the *curros'* efforts remained carefully neutralized by the Cuban media. This sanitized image was central to the graphic art by Landaluze, which presented *curros* pictured as rather exotic beings, of unique dress and hairstyles. Detached from the marginality that the Black slum of El Manglar afforded them, *curros* lost their negative image as violent byproducts of slavery practices. They became mere caricatures of opponents of the various "white-supremacist patriarchal norm" (hooks 5), whether it was the equally neutralized mulato fino or the emerging "Cuban" male, who, like the *curro*, continued to struggle with the legacy of slavery in the development of the so-called Cubanía.

# 5

. . . . . . .

# Depictions of the Horrific "Unseen"

## Cuban Creole Religious Practices

The arrival in Cuba of large numbers of slaves during the booming period of sugarcane plantations in the nineteenth century fueled the ongoing development of a strong Black culture. There was a special increase of Creole religious practices and belief systems with the arrival of hundreds of thousands of slaves belonging to distinctive ethnic groups. Changes in the formation of Black traditions in Cuba have been ascribed to differences in the organization of a premodern plantation era encompassing the sixteenth, seventeenth, and most of the eighteenth centuries, before the arrival of a technology that would require larger, more efficient sugarcane plantations (Pérez de la Riva, *El barracón* 83). Illegal shipments of slaves were substantial. According to Moreno Fraginals, the last recorded arrival of an illegal shipment was in April 1873 ("Aportes" 13). Difference between the newly arrived slaves, bozales, and the Cuban-born criollos would be an important element in the development of Afro-Cuban traditions.

The new, improved plantation culture created specific jobs for certain types of slaves; that, in turn, developed certain cultural practices. An aspect of plantation slave life that remained unexplored, however, was African religious belief systems, adapted to the specific restrictions on slaves. Costumbristas chose to explore urban Black religions. As an ultimate symbol of marginality, religious public street celebrations became the most common source of visual icons for Costumbrista essays.

As great numbers of African bozales arrived unaffected by European culture, they began to fine-tune Black religious traditions, some of which have survived in Cuba through today (Castellanos 1:61). Although the estimated number of slaves that arrived in Cuba throughout the nineteenth century continues to be a matter of controversy, historians have suggested several figures: between 1853 and 1880 more than 200,000 (Arredondo 29); and from 1820 until the abolition of slavery, some 520,000 (Pérez de la Riva, *Para la historia* 118). The impact of the newly arrived Africans was great. For example, 46.7 percent of the 370,000 slaves in 1861 were concentrated in sugarmills, and two-thirds of them were bozales (Pérez de la Riva, *El barracón* 88).

Today scholars' interest lies in exploration of the types of ethnicities that came to comprise the so-called Cuban slave culture. It has been estimated that slaves brought from Africa belonged to some three hundred groups (López Valdés, *Africanos* 30). Those peoples were from five distinctive African ethnicities: the Yoruba, the Congos, the Arara, the Bantu and the Abakua, (also known as the Carabali in Cuba because of their geographic origin in the Calabar) (Fernández Robaina 6; Guanche 49–59; León 123).

The large concentration of specific ethnic types and the circumstances provided for their acclimation to mainstream life may have accounted for the ways in which a multifaceted Creole Black culture took root in Cuba. Differences in religious practices present among the slave population were in keeping with their ethnicity.

According to Cuban anthropologist Fernando Ortiz, writing in his encyclopedic work *Historia de una pelea cubana contra los demonios* [History of the Cuban struggle against demons] (1959), the impact of Black religious systems in Cuba was extensive and evident in the earliest stages of colonial history. His research also revealed an early participation in and acceptance of Black religious practices by White people. Ortiz comments on a legal case against a Catholic priest, Father José González de la Cruz, who in 1682 attempted to force religious and civil authorities to bend to his wishes to move the village of San Juan de los Remedios to a better location. He claimed that in a new location (on a parcel of land that belonged to him), the village would be free from attacks by pirates. His other reason for the change of location was, however, rather strange. According to his testimony, the devil had warned him during the trances of a possessed Black woman, Leonarda, while he attempted to exorcise her demons. Father González de la Cruz heard through Leonarda's stomach that terrible physical consequences would fall upon the inhabitants of San Juan if they stayed in the current location. Although, Ortiz stresses, the priest's ulterior motive seemed to be to make use of his own lands, he openly exploited local religious beliefs, some of which exhibited elements of European and African religious folklores that in Cuba came together in a process that Ortiz describes as "religious transculturation" (*Historia* 410).

The occurrence with Father González was not unique. Ortiz documents bizarre cases of demonic possession that were taking place throughout Europe as indicated in records of the autos-da-fé, the trials that the Inquisition held against those accused of witchcraft, sorcery or performance of pagan religious ceremonies. Ortiz's interest in Father González's case is due to the fact that there was in existence in Cuba a syncretic religious system that linked particularities of Roman Catholic practices with those of various Black groups, such as belief in the possession of a Black woman *adivina* [soothsayer].

Father González de la Cruz, a delegate of the Holy Inquisition, merely followed their complex procedures in dealing with the documentation and the handling of witches, in a trial with legal procedures similar to those observed in Europe. In this way, as Ortiz's *Historia* documents, the rise of an emerging Black Creole religious system would not only have a correspondence with European practices, but also indicates an early example of Cuban syncreticism of White and Black religions. Ortiz theorizes that Father González de la Cruz's acceptance of the possession of a Black woman was an indication of active Black and Creole religious practices in Cuba.

Ortiz's assertions of the widespread presence of complex Black religious beliefs continue in his extensive exploration of the *brujos*, as he labeled the high priests of various Black groups. He also refers to them as "tata nganga," "mayombero" or "babalao." Ortiz accepted that the Black high priests conveyed proof of the transculturation of the functions of Catholic priests with practices of the "medicine men" of various African ethnic groups. The term *brujos*, as Ortiz used it, implied the presence among Blacks of individuals with a higher status among practitioners of various Black Creole religious practices, an equivalent to Catholic priests in the sense that only those individuals could perform certain prescribed rituals. The Black *brujos*, as in the incident with Father González de la Cruz, could also make prophecies and have visions of future occurrences (316).

In his *Los negros brujos*, Ortiz provides a more inclusive definition of the *brujo*, whose functions in Africa he labels as those of a fetishist. Subjugated by slavery, the *brujo* in Cuba linked his roles as a medicine man and as a high priest of religious rituals (66). It is this second role, that of high priest, that Ortiz explores more in detail. Some of those functions, such as the *brujo's* "ability to conjure evil" caused the character to be dreaded by both Whites and Blacks (65). Ortiz also documents, however, the *brujo's* ability as a fetishist, which created some popular practices still observed in Cuba. For example, prediction of stormy or rainy weather using mounds of salt, known in Cuba today as *caba ñuela*, was a function that Black *brujos* brought to local religious folklore (111).

Performers of syncretic Black rituals were often prosecuted to the extent of the law. For example, in a 1619 letter the bishop of Cuba, Fray Alonso Enríquez, complained about the abundance of Black "brujas," women practitioners, "witches," who often stole items from churches to use in their rituals (qtd. in Ortiz, *Historia* 409). The development of dreaded African-based religious practices in Cuba, which Bishop Alonso Enríquez kept quiet about, was closely related to evangelical methods used by the Catholic Church for the conversion of slaves. The inefficacy of methods used in the forced, legislated conversion of slaves would be an essential cause of the formation of Cuban Black religious systems. In spite of the evidence of Black religious practices, according to Ortiz, there were no autos-da-fé in Cuba (*Historia* 414).

White religious institutions imposed control upon urban slave communities and freed Black communities by restricting their belief systems and also by acting as civic organisms with specific restrictions upon their social and economic mobility. The Cofradía, associated with Catholicism, provided tighter control on slaves' activities and particularly on those of freed Blacks. It grouped together Africans of the same national origin and promoted activities that were intended to be recreational, educational and of mutual help (Urfé 216). As in Latin America, the Cofradía's function was originally intended as a means of religious evangelization, explained in numerous statements by missionary orders: "in order to enlighten the understanding of the said natives, that they may come to know our Catholic faith" (qtd. in Bayle 579).

Their connection with Catholic rituals, and particularly the use of hagiography as a basic tool of evangelization, led to the rise of syncretic belief systems, of which the Yoruba Regla Ocha, better known as Santería, is perhaps the most widely known today. A strong cultural-ethnic, "recreational" body, the Cofradía also encouraged the flowering of Black Creole musical folklore, often associated with religious ceremonies, including the preservation of musical instruments often used in Creole religious ceremonies (Carbonell 105–6; Urfé 220–24).

References to urban Black music and dance as part of public ceremonies sanctioned by the Catholic Church and by civil institutions were a principal subject of Costumbrista writers. One figure, the so-called *diablito* [little devil], a dressed-up member of the *comparsas* [musical groups from Cofradías], appeared as a literary character of minor importance, mainly a shadow figure, in Costumbrista essays and as a subject for graphic artists.

Costumbrista writers seemed to imply, however, that they were completely ignorant of Black religious traditions, particularly of rural practices. Their claim of ignorance about knowledge of these rites may have been another way to avoid censorship of a taboo religious matter.

## Iconic Representations in Rural Religious Practices: *Biografía de un cimarrón*

> There are things in life I do not understand. Everything about Nature seems obscure to me, and the gods even more. They're the ones who are supposed to give birth to all those things that a person sees, that I see, and that do exist for sure. The gods are willful and ornery.
>
> Esteban Montejo, *Biografía de un cimarrón*

> To seek one's ancestors is to search for oneself. You seek an ancestor because you want to know yourself. Any literature is a search and an expression of self that always implies the knowledge of one's ancestors. Any literature is an attempt to portray yourself, to situate yourself in the world, to define yourself in relationship to others and to yourself. People don't write for any other reason. . . . Whether it is written by Whites or Blacks, English or Chinese, literature is a search for self, an effort to elucidate oneself.
>
> Maryse Condé in Françoise Pfaff's *Conversations with Maryse Condé*

The influence of plantation landowners, hinted at in Anselmo Suárez y Romero's Costumbrista essays on sugarmills, was rarely explored in Cuban literature produced in the nineteenth century. Historians have argued that the Cuban economy was dominated by the production of sugar; therefore, the plantation owners directly influenced laws and regulations pertaining to the management of sugarmills, including the treatment of slaves (Pérez de la Riva, *El barracón* 87). They formed a tight "landowning and slaveholding oligarchy" (Knight, *Slave* 133), with influence extending from their ability to exercise censorship of publications dealing with details about slavery to their power to affect legislation in favor of their maintenance of slaves.

Their power to affect censorship was summarized by the abolitionist Rafael M. Labra. In 1870, in his activist historical account of slavery in Cuba, *La brutalidad de los negros* [Brutality against blacks], Labra wrote: "Anybody would say, upon observing the profound silence kept today in Spain about the problem of emancipation of Blacks, that there are no longer Blacks in Cuba" (5). Speaking up in favor of slaves' rights, according to Labra, brought an implication that the speaker also had a pro-independence posture.

The strong relationship of slavery to the Cuban status quo may explain slave owners' influence on legislation in their favor, in spite of international abolitionist resistance. Tightening of the slave laws was evident in the slave code of 1842, which reflected a "stronger emphasis upon the obedience of slaves to white persons" (Knight, *Slave* 131). These laws, which historian Pérez de la Riva considered a late legislation on issues pertaining to slavery, seem to have been addressed in order to appease plantation owners' restlessness during the Spanish crown's international negotiations on the slave trade and on prospects of abolition (*El barracón* 18).

It was a comprehensive body of laws, ranging from specific regulations on religious instruction to the prescribed allowances of food and clothing. The laws were highly restrictive on slaves. The laws determined their field of action, whether in plantations or in the cities. They limited the types of business slaves could embark upon (with the permission of their owners) and they restricted their celebrations in public ceremonies or social activities, mainly those related to musical performances and dances. They also contained specific regulations on the capture of runaway slaves.

Although religious indoctrination seems to have been a major legal concern, in practice it was not a pressing issue for any of the parties involved—the Church, the slave owners, or the governmental organisms in charge of the application of the laws. Article 5 of the 1842 slave code specifically mandated religious instruction of the catechism for slaves, or slave owners might face a fine (*Slave* 127). In regard to plantation slaves, it also restricted work on Sundays (*Slave* 127). The existence of these laws would lead to demands by Spanish authorities for kinder treatment of slaves in Cuba. In the words of Spanish governor José de la Concha, in his report on *El estado politico, gobierno y administración de la Isla de Cuba* [The political state, government and administration of the island of Cuba] (1835), the slaves' religious education explained their relationship as equals to Whites observed by Cubans:

> On the Island of Cuba, at least in the greater number of slaves involved in domestic service and in various jobs and work of the towns, there do not exist that discipline and those habits of blind obedience that slavery implies and that originates in the moral and religious education of the slave and in respectful circumspection in the owners. (22)

Governor de la Concha was speaking about rural slaves who had avenues to access mainstream religious and civil indoctrination. He lamented the poor state of religious life found in the countryside, particularly the low number of priests available to serve a community of slaves and Whites:

> The abandonment in which the education of the clergy themselves has been for long years, and the ruin threatening many churches, chapels and oratories make even more deplorable the picture offered by clergy and worship, to such a point that it can be said, no longer about just the slave population that, crowded in the sugarmills, lack spiritual instruction and

nourishment, but also about free people, White and of color, that a good number of them are born, live, marry and die without having anyone to baptize, marry and bury them. (114)

This state of abandonment of both slaves and freed Blacks, as well as of the White populations in rural areas, that the runaway slave Montejo spoke about, gave rise to shared religious practices, mainly of Black origin, in which Whites and Blacks participated as equals.

A visual symbol of the plantation owners' power to impose restrictions upon the management of slaves was the creation, officially sanctioned, of the *barracón* [locked living quarters for slaves]. A wave of slave revolts throughout the 1830s had led in 1844 to a major political upheaval, known as La Escalera, in which White and Black activists became involved, including some Costumbrista writers. After La Escalera, plantation owners developed the concept of the *barracón* (Pérez de la Riva, *El barracón* 29), which the American traveler Samuel Hazard, on a trip to Cuba in 1866, described: "On the larger places, these are generally what are called barracoons, or quarters for the slaves. They are large buildings, constructed of stone, in the form of a quadrangle, on the inner side of which are the rooms for the negroes, to which there is only one main entrance; this is shut at night when the hands are all in" (355).

A tight control of plantation slave life led to a distinctive rural slave culture, at the center of which various Creole Black religious practices were prominent, sheltered within the intimacy of living in the *barracón*. Historian Pérez de la Riva attributed to the closeness of these primitive living arrangements the dances and ritual ceremonies that maintained a strong hold on slaves on sugarcane plantations (*Barracón* 37–38).

Life at the *barracón* is a principal topic in Esteban Montejo's account of his life prior to becoming a runaway slave. Published as *Biografía de un cimarrón* [*Biography of a Runaway Slave*] (1966), it includes his descriptions of well-defined slave religious and other sociocultural practices. He indicates that White people working on sugarmills not only knew about Black religions but also often participated in some rituals. Montejo, however, placed emphasis on the slaves' religious life, which he categorized according to specific African ethnicity. Unlike the mulato fino Juan Francisco Manzano, Montejo proudly established his closeness to African culture.

A major difference between Montejo and Manzano is Montejo's detailed personal account of his ethnicity. According to his testimony, Montejo was born on December 2, 1860. Like Manzano, Montejo was a criollo, a slave born in Cuba; however, he proudly disclosed his ethnic origins, recording that his father, Nazario, was a Lucumí from the Oyo region, and his mother, Emilia Montejo, was a *criolla* of French origin (14; trans. 18). Montejo's interest in the documentation of the ethnic origins of his described slave traditions is evident throughout the text. This characteristic can be attributed to the anthropological interview process conducted by trained sociologist Miguel Barnet, which led to the gathering of Montejo's memoirs.

At the estimated age of 103 years, Montejo spoke extensively about his experiences growing up on sugarcane plantations to Miguel Barnet, a professor of folklore at the School for Instructors of Art and researcher at the Institute of Ethnology of the Cuban Academy of Sciences (14; trans. 18). Barnet, under the auspices of the revolutionary Cuban government, started in 1963 a series of interviews with Montejo, who at that time was "a very serious man, healthy and completely white-haired" (5). Montejo had clear memories of his childhood and of his experiences as a runaway slave in his youth (5). His unusual background of having been a runaway slave eventually led Barnet to interview Montejo extensively and exclusively (5). From his conversations with Montejo, Barnet compiled the text of *Biografía*.

The purpose of Barnet's initial project was to explore "general aspects of religions of African origin still preserved in Cuba" (5). Information from an old woman practitioner of Santería would have better fulfilled that objective, but Barnet chose Montejo, whose stories did not refer directly to religious topics, but whose words, according to Barnet, "reflected an inclination to superstitions and to popular beliefs" (5). Eventually, although Barnet explored Montejo's memories in his eyewitness accounts of Creole Black religious practices, the conversations expanded to include subjects related to "slavery, life in the barracones and life of a runaway slave in the wilds" (6).

Work routines, including specific tasks, recreational activities, and life in the *barracón*, make up most of Montejo's recollections of his life on a sugarcane plantation. Details of specific steps in the production of sugar resemble similar scenes in Anselmo Suárez y Romero's literary descriptions of the mill, the heart of the mechanical facilities in the sugar-making process. Also as in Suárez y Romero's Costumbrista articles, Montejo remembered important characters that worked on the plantations, divided not only by racial origins but also by their roles in the production of sugar. Unlike Suárez y Romero, Montejo in his memoirs gave preference to slaves who resisted the status quo, beginning with himself, in a self-characterization as a born runaway, and to slaves involved in forbidden activities, particularly in Black Creole religions.

Like Suárez y Romero, Montejo indicated key slave and White figures in terms of their tasks performed on the plantation. Unlike Suárez y Romero,

Montejo emphasized in his examination of these social types the means by which extremely controlled slaves managed to develop a life closer to their African ethnicity or to Creole versions adapted to the circumstances of slavery. These divisions explain the specific traditions observed at the sugarmill, in which religious activities had an important role.

On the plantation there were clear social divisions, of which the primary figure was the master, presented by Montejo as "a million bad things, a blockhead, grouchy, stuffy" (16; trans. 20). Among the slaves there were other, highly developed social structures. This was due, perhaps, Montejo suggested, to the master's preference to live in the capital cities of the provinces where the plantations were located. Even so, *la casa grande*, as the master's plantation house was known, became an image of civility and an attraction to those slaves who wanted to escape the harshness of field work. Unlike Juan Francisco Manzano, Montejo avoided contact with the master's house. Montejo's fear was that, if he caught the attention of the master, he could become the slave houseboy.

Montejo characterized this type of slave: "the little black boy . . . was pretty and lively," and he was "sold out" to the White culture of the master. He described the house slave as marginal to most aspects of Black plantation culture and, specifically, of Creole religious practices. Montejo proudly claimed that he kept away from contamination by the master's influence, because "I was a cimarrón from birth" (18; trans. 22). Negative views of house slaves contained effeminate images of them throughout the nineteenth century, especially evident in visual art forms.

Montejo's memoirs are framed within his self-professed early rebellious nature. As a potential runaway slave, he kept away from individuals (slaves or not) closely associated with the status quo. He began, instead, to learn means of survival from slaves skilled in such practices. They were the *negros de nación* [slaves born in Africa], also known as bozales, who remained marginal despite efforts to incorporate them into plantation culture under White dominance. They were Montejo's protective shield against a second type of White character, the priest, who attempted to incorporate slaves into the White status quo through the evangelization of Catholic practices as required by law.

Montejo's documentation of the influence of *negros de nación* indicates that their control over life at the plantation was overpowering. One reason for that power was the fact that some masters became involved in Creole religious practices. It was the *negros de nación* who became symbols of authority, replacing the master or the *mayoral*, the supervisors of sugarmill activities, both of whom became secondary characters in Montejo's portrait of the slaves' lives on a plantation. The positive image of active, powerful *negros de nación* is contrary to Suárez y Romero's portraits of them as simply aloof hard workers.

At the time that Montejo befriended *negros de nación*—Africans who had chosen to remain uncontaminated by White cultural patterns—those men were old; and, although they fulfilled specific tasks for the slave community, they had also begun to lose significance as sources of cultural information. For Montejo, however, an apprentice in the art of survival in the wild as a prospective runaway, the *negros de nación*, "the African, from over there, from the other side of the big puddle" (38; trans. 41), served him well. From them, Montejo learned about the power of herbs, evident in the longevity of these men and their strong constitution in spite of their advanced age: "Because the problem is not in poking you or pinching your tongue. What you have to do is have confidence in herbs, which are the mother of medicines" (38; trans. 41). The Black practitioners were more effective than the medical doctors, or even the well-appreciated "Chinese doctor," who came among the thousands of *culíes*, as the coolie workers became known in Cuba.

Critics have suggested that the development of Creole Black religious practices was closely related to the inefficacy of the methods of evangelization; however, Montejo insists throughout his memoirs that the Spanish Catholic practices, as brought to Cuba, merged easily with Black religions because "Catholicism always falls into spiritism. That has to be taken for granted" (126; trans. 130). The assimilation of Catholic practices into distinctive Black religious observances, particularly the incorporation of certain liturgical Catholic elements, did reflect the relaxed ways in which the Catholic Church observed legal requirements to provide study of the catechism for slaves. For example, as late as 1883, Ernest de L'Epine, in his travelogue *Un Parisien dans les Antilles* [A Parisian in the Antilles], observed the informal ways in which Catholic ceremonies were celebrated in a group mass by a priest who barely had contact with the slaves: "A drop of water, a grain of salt, a prayer, a blessing sufficed to sanctify the whole bunch" (qtd. in Pérez de la Riva, *El barracón* 42).

Montejo briefly documented the presence of priests, who are the last type of White characters that he placed on the plantation. The priest, like previous White characters, had a minor role in the slave's life, so most Blacks were impervious to a conventional religious life. Montejo described the priests as prissy, stating that they would not go into the *barracón* "no way, no how" (32; my translation).

In a similar statement, María de la Cruz Sentmanat, a former slave, in her testimony recorded by historian Pérez de la Riva, said that the slave "always mistrusted priests" (qtd. in *El barracón* 41). Her explanation of this mistrust reveals the well-defined power structure observed on plantations: "During slavery, the clergyman was always an unconditional ally of the landowners, from whom he collected a fee for periodically visiting his mills, and at times for not visiting them. They tried to get from the Blacks by means of the confession secrets about offenses that they had committed, and then they went to denounce them to the masters so that they were punished" (42). Such animosity against the priest and the fact that the Church seemed to have made no real efforts to promote a heartfelt religious conversion prompted historian Pérez de la Riva to come to the following resounding conclusion: "the Catholic religion had little place in the barracón; in the many descriptions that we have studied there is no evidence of a monument or image representative of the official religion, nor traces of daily practice of any Catholic rite" (*El barracón* 42).

Montejo recorded, however, specific functions that the priest performed on the plantation beginning with the version of the catechism designed specifically for slaves. According to Montejo, this task was done lightly because priests often avoided contact with slaves. In their place, they delegated the actual evangelization to house slaves, who became "the priests' messengers" (33; trans. 36) and probably informants of the slaves' whereabouts. Montejo's description of the slave catechist continued his previous negative profile of this type of Black, whom he considered a traitor to Black Creole values. Some were so conceited in their belief that they were different from the field slaves that they took up Catholicism as proof of their new identity: "they were so refined and so well treated, they became Christians" (33; trans. 36).

In reality, Montejo claimed, none of the slaves, either the "houseboy" or the field worker, understood the catechism: "Truth is, I never learned that doctrine because I did not understand it at all" (33; trans. 36). Such types of accusations were widespread. They led Cuban ecclesiastical authorities to publish in 1797 the first manual of catechism for recently arrived slaves (bozales), *Explicación de la doctrina cristiana acomodada a la capacidad de los negros bozales* [Explanation of Christian doctrine adjusted to the capacity of black bozales]. Written by Nicolás Duque de Estrada, a priest presumably born in Cuba, this manual, in a style reminiscent of the catechism for young learners of the Catholic faith, also incorporated advice about the correct treatment of slaves, material found in popular handbooks on management of plantations and of slaves (Fernández de Castro 25).

The impact of Duque de Estrada's manual is not well known today; however, the abolitionist and slave owner Domingo del Monte spoke about it in *Biblioteca cubana* [Cuban library] (1846), his bibliographic compilation of books published about Cuba (Fernández de Castro 26). He summarized his opinion about

Duque de Estrada's text: "The author's aims, his correct performance, and the air of simple and ardent Christian charity he breathes do the utmost honor to that remote era when priests were posted in the sugarmills—priests capable of producing such books, masters who hired and paid them, and theology professors who applauded and encouraged their perseverance in so saintly a mission" (qtd. in Moreno Fraginals, *The Sugarmill* 54). Suárez y Romero made no reference to the presence of a priest in his Costumbrista articles. When he wrote to del Monte, he did not even mention seeking the company of a priest during his period of cultural isolation on a plantation.

Despite the documented absenteeism of priests, Duque de Estrada's text suggests that the priest actively participated in the slaves' religious life. Among his strongest suggestions is his statement that recently arrived slaves should not be forced into learning quickly the complex Catholic theology. A 1789 Spanish law required that slaves be evangelized "in the principles of the Catholic religion and in necessary truths," leading to their baptism within a year of their arrival at the plantations (qtd. in Ortiz, *Los negros esclavos* 409). The regulation also stipulated days set aside for such religious instruction. In reaction to these regulations, Cuban plantation owners declared their concerns that this type of prescribed instruction severely limited the slaves' hours of labor on the plantations. They also argued that the slaves' religious instruction was already fulfilled in two ways. First, old slaves were to serve as godparents of the recently arrived slaves, in a relationship that "stimulated" both parties (qtd. in Laviña 48). Second, although slaves were evangelized (there was no mention of the means), not all of them learned at the same rate. Thus, a one-year term would not be sufficient for all slaves (qtd. in Laviña 48).

At any rate, some slaves devoutly observed Catholic practices. For example, they prayed the rosary on a daily basis (qtd. in Laviña 48). There is no comment about who was in charge of conducting the prayers of the rosary, whether it was the old slaves or the lady of the house when she visited the plantation. The presence of the White lady in the luxurious *casa grande* was a theme often depicted by artists of the time. She was depicted in an engraving that served as an illustration for an article in *Las mujeres españolas, portuguesas y americanas*; [Spanish, Portuguese, and American women] (1872). Montejo ignored the presence of White women on the plantations. They are not characters in his memoirs, presumably because they had no influence upon the slaves' lives. There is no mention of slaves' praying the rosary either; their only evangelization occurred through teaching by the hated mulato fino house slave.

The most impressive feature of Duque de Estrada's catechist manual is his in-depth approach to teaching Blacks the theology of the Roman Catholic Church.

Breaking away from the biased view that judged slaves to be ignorant and savage, he considered Blacks to have the ability to reason and a soul, elements essential for their understanding the so-called mysteries of the faith: "each Black has a rational soul, that is to say, a precious Vessel in which is deposited the sacred Blood of Jesus Christ Our Lord, who died for them" (67). He recommended that the lessons, organized in terms of subject matter, take place on a daily basis. They were to be short, in order not to overwhelm the slave students, and during the day, not at the end of a long workday (73).

In a formidable text, Duque de Estrada did not water down Catholic theology. In fact, there seemed to be a leap of faith that a non-native speaker of Spanish could indeed comprehend the complexities of the terms involved. He gave no major explanations about how to teach Spanish to the recently arrived slaves, but he warned about the necessary qualifications for the catechist (presumably a priest): "But it is necessary, first of all that he who teaches must understand what he says, and know how to say it perfectly, in order to say it with meaning and not teach them to say nonsense" (66). One of his techniques included a warning that the teacher must "speak slowly, distinguishing the syllables, taking much care that they not begin to repeat before he completely finishes the word, and not say another word until all finish repeating what he said" (66). Repetition of the prayers, leading to perfect memorization of the words and absorbing their meaning, was a central pedagogical device. In order to facilitate perfect utterance of the prayers, Duque de Estrada stressed that slaves could be taught to read the lips of the catechist. For this reason, he insisted that the lessons should not take place at night or in dark rooms (73).

Slaves with a more advanced knowledge of the Spanish language were asked to establish analogies between Catholic theological concepts and elements of their rural settings. His point was that the slave should say the prayers correctly in order to fully understand the doctrines. Duque de Estrada stresses throughout the text that the role of the catechist is to teach understanding of Catholic theology, "not for them to know only the words; but for them to recognize what the words mean," but certain abstractions remained distorted in the minds of slaves (72).

His example is the comprehension of the meaning of the virginal conception of Jesus Christ. He warned that slaves should not be allowed to make any alterations in the wording of a prayer. "[A slave] prays, for example, the Credo and he says: the Virgin Saint Mary was born, suffered under the power of Pontius Pilate, etc. One corrects this for him, making him say it correctly and trying to make him understand that 'Virgin Saint Mary was born' is not the same as 'He was born of Virgin Saint Mary'" (67). The solution for the correction of this mistake is puzzling, merely addressing a grammatical inaccuracy, distorting the meaning of the miracle of a virginal birth: "with this simile: You don't know agua [water]? You don't know yagua [palm thatch]? He will answer, yes. Well, tell me, are water and palm thatch the same thing? No, one thing is the water to drink, the other thing is palm thatch for a hut, well that is the way this is too: it's one thing that the Virgin Saint Mary was born and another thing to be born of the Virgin Saint Mary" (67).

This emphasis on the presence of Mary, the virginal mother of all Catholics, was evident in Montejo's earliest memories of his life on a plantation. Commenting on the power of nature, which would become a leitmotif throughout his memoirs, Montejo states that, "Jesus Christ is the most talked about. Jesus Christ was not born in Africa. He came direct from Nature herself because Mary was a virgin" (13; trans. 17). One interesting point in the paragraphs dealing with the virginal birth in Duque de Estrada's text was the addition of noncanonical facts. For example, he categorically indicated that another of the wonders in Mary's pregnancy was evident in the following fact: "God also made another miracle, because the bodies of men are made in forty days and those of females in eighty days; but God made the body of Our Lord Jesus Christ quickly, quickly, in one instant, as in the opening of one's eyes" (83).

An outstanding feature of Duque de Estrada's text is his handling of a popular belief system that strayed away from traditional Catholic theology. For example, in order to explain the seriousness of Adam's sin of disobeying God's order not to eat the fruit of the tree of knowledge, Duque de Estrada states that the slave should be taught that Adam "made penance for nine hundred years" (84). Punishment for breaking divine rules is a central theme of Duque de Estrada's exposition, and he drew many parallels to good and bad behavior on a plantation. Sins were equated to disobeying a father (91). Good behavior was rewarded with the prospect of eternal life in heaven, and bad behavior led to confinement in hell. That place to suffer eternal damnation, "los Infiernos" [hells], was described as not unlike restraining facilities on the plantation, where rebellious slaves often received physical punishments: "Hell has four cells, which are deep, deep down in the earth. Most deeply in the middle of the earth, underneath all the other hells, is the hell where the devils are, and the souls of those who die in mortal sin" (86). The second hell is called purgatory, "where the souls go of those who die without mortal sin," but they are denied entrance into heaven because "one does not enter heaven with even a trace of sin" (86). The remaining hellish accommodations are the "Purgatory of souls of those who die with tiny sins, called venal sins" (86), and a "prison called Limbo for little children who die without having been baptized" (87).

The insistence on good behavior and threats of eternal damnation to hell-ish jail cells were presented as overwhelmingly important. The physical torture that Jesus Christ endured under Pontius Pilate was equated to the slaves' hard work on the plantation (85). Such a comparison may be attributed to Duque de Estrada's siding with the plantation landowners in a process that has been described as a "paternalistic terrorism" (Laviña 37). It is also patent, however, that because of the extremely harsh physical labor on the plantations, Duque de Estrada placed slaves at a high level of theological estimation. This is evident in his parallel between the hard-laboring slave and the suffering Christ.

Although rewarding good behavior was illustrated with the theological con-cept of the final judgment, the simile used to illustrate this point allowed for a rather strong image. As the slave was accustomed to report and to pay conse-quences for a job badly performed, "as the manager punishes the slave who does not fulfill his task" (88), the final judgment also became the moment when the slave would finally receive payment for good behavior:

> But look, God does not act like the manager or the master, but a Father. Here when the slave fulfilled his task they don't punish him, but neither do they pay him anything, because the manager says in his heart, what am I going to pay him for? For that he is a slave, for serving his master, that is his obligation, and if he fails to do it, there is the punishing board and the stick. But God does not do that. To him who fulfills his task, to him who keeps his commandments, God does not close his mouth, but says, Come here, So-and-so, you have completed your task, not as a bad slave, but as a good son: come now to heaven to be with me, your Lord and your Father, to rest forever and forever. (88–89)

While the good master was defined with the same expectations as a loving fa-ther who provides for his children, he too must endure punishment for viola-tions of that family covenant. Punishment would come to both—to the master if he failed to provide for the slaves' well-being and to the slaves if they failed to complete the tasks expected of them.

As expected in a catechist manual, the major emphasis is on the presenta-tion of the Catholic Church's theology. Of particular interest in the develop-ment of the so-called syncretic Black Creole religions was the exploration of individual concepts, the "mysteries" of the faith, central elements of Roman Catholicism. The mention of specific African groups (Carabalí, Congo, Mina, Mandinga, Lucumí, Ganga, Chambá, Malagás) seems to indicate that Duque de Estrada was addressing them specifically (116). Another interesting refer-ence was his setting in opposition the Congos and the Carabalís, whom he saw as rivals on the plantations (118). Duque de Estrada explicitly commanded these groups:

> Learn what they teach you, since that is good for you, do not harden your heart, don't act like people in Guinea, who do not know God, nor do they know God's orders. Guinea is finished, you will never return there, now you are Christians, now you are sons of God, now you know the commandments of God's law, now you know that those who keep those commandments go to heaven, and those who don't keep them go to hell. (118–19)

An in-depth knowledge of Catholic theology, according to Duque de Estrada, would make the slaves "sons of God," and presumably equal (at least in the eyes of the Catholic God) to their masters.

Duque de Estrada's objective was to convert the Africans quickly from their native belief systems, in which several divine entities played central roles. There was, therefore, in his manual a careful approach to the explanation of the divine mystery of the Holy Trinity. As his definition made clear, "they are not three gods, but only one true God because although in God there are three persons, all are one and the same God, because they have one and the same being and divine nature" (63). The explanation for the concept must have been difficult to grasp, so it was presented in several illustrations, such as: "Just as one finger has three really different bones, and all three bones are only one finger" (71). That Trinity was responsible for the creation of mankind and nature, in a process that contains echoes of the book of Genesis:

> This unique God of three Persons: Father, Son, and Holy Spirit, created or made out of nothing (since that is to create) everything that we see, and also all that we don't see. Heaven with all that is in Heaven: angels, sun, moon, stars; the earth with all that there is on earth, men, women, all animals large and small, trees, plants, flowers, fruits, water with all there is in it; wind with all there is in it; fire . . . (71–72)

It is curious, however, that in spite of the emphasis on the powerful creation of the world, a supernatural event stressed in "he created or made out of nothing," reverence to this three-in-one divinity is not clearly indicated. In fact, there is no emphasis on how to pay tribute to any one of them, other than obedience to the Church's commands, as a sign of good behavior leading to eternal life, and reverence for the ultimate sacrifice of Jesus Christ through his death. Duque de Estrada did not indicate means of devotion other than observance of the Church's sacraments. Even those sacraments were carefully catalogued and their importance limited to specific tasks that made up the highly restricted life of the slaves on the plantation.

The sacraments allowed to slaves were three: baptism, the Eucharist, and confession, perhaps because these allowed limits on the field of action of slaves, making them submissive to the status quo as voiceless, forced workers. Those three sacraments and the commandments, which Duque de Estrada emphasized as "Commandments of God's law and of the Holy Mother Church," were mandated as obligatory of all Catholics, presumably including slaves, as "obligations of our state" (65). Those mandated tasks were described in terms of the slave's conditions as a forced worker:

> To keep the Commandments is to do what is ordered. He who does what his Father commands him, keeps the Commandments of his Father; he who does something that his master orders him keeps the commandment of his master; he who does something that God orders him keeps the Commandment of God; he who does something that the Church orders him keeps the commandments of the Holy Church. (90–91)

Observing the Church's commandments, suspiciously close to the working requirements on the plantations, would be rewarded with eternal life in heavens, and, as a fringe benefit, the slave would be in good standing with the feared *mayoral*, the slaves' administrator.

In spite of Duque de Estrada's care to limit his catechism to his interpretation of Roman Catholic canonical laws (as they applied to converted slaves), there were instances in which his interpretation may have included a reflection of native African practices. One such instance appeared in his definition of the Church's sacraments, which he labeled "the seven remedies made by our Lord Jesus Christ of his own blood in order to cure the sickness of the soul, which are sins" (65). This literal concept of *remedio*, a prescribed medicine for the soul's ailment, the slave would understand as an equivalent to the *trabajos*, spells or prepared religious remedies, which often included offerings of animal blood as a central part of prescribed rituals. Duque de Estrada made a literal interpretation of the sacraments as remedies: "so that they will be beneficial, so that the soul may be cured of its sins and get well, it is necessary to take these remedies, as ordered by our Lord Jesus Christ, who is the doctor" (95). The concept could find an echo in those of the plantations' *brujos* as religious and medicinal practitioners.

As a whole, in spite of Duque de Estrada's obvious, self-imposed limitations in introducing elements of Catholic devotion, at times his teachings of the catechism transferred into syncretic Creole religious beliefs. When he revealed that the sacraments totaled seven, he did not name them all. That specific numerical reference appears today in the Yoruba practice of Santería or Regla Ocha. The "siete potencias" [the Seven African Powers] are an "awesome septet formed by Elegguá, Orúnla, Obatalá, Oggún, Changó, Yemayá, and Oshún" (González-Wippler 268), almighty orishas, deities related to natural forces (Cabrera, *Koeko* 154; Cáñizares 48–54; Cros Sandoval 84–85, 181–85; Wedel 81–88). Devotion to them includes specific regulations for their feeding, as part of their highly stylized rituals. Elements associated with the Roman Catholic sacraments, such as the holy water, also have found a place in Santería practices. Duque de Estrada stressed the importance of baptism: "through baptism, his soul remains clean, without any sin, any sign, any stain of sin" (113). The equivalent in Santería practices is the use of holy water in various types of ritual cleansing baths (González-Wippler 268; Cabrera, *Koeko* 196; Cabrera, *Reglas* 23; Cros Sandoval 67–68).

A salient element in Duque de Estrada's manual of the catechism is his silence concerning saints, although he explained that slaves must be taught to understand the concepts behind the Credo of the Apostles (67). Even in that case, an important prayer in the understanding of key theological concepts of the Roman Catholic Church, the explanation concentrated on a partial interpretation of the devotion of the Virgin Mary.

Mary, named throughout the text as the Virgen Santísima Señora or as Santa María Virgen, was the only divine entity, other than the Holy Trinity, that appeared in Duque de Estrada's catechism as an example of a saint. Mary was to be called upon for help in times of need through the well-memorized Hail Mary. It is a prayer that, as Duque de Estrada stressed, had a particular divine power, evidenced in the verse: "Saint Mary Mother of God, pray for us sinners now and in the hour of our death" (112). That covenant established between the slave and Mary, through careful and daily repetition of Hail Marys, implied a close relationship such as that of "our godmother" (112). With this image Duque de Estrada may have intended to debunk the practices of Santería that promoted the cult of one pre-selected orisha as a guide for each individual. It is clear that he wanted to make central devotion to Mary as essential as observance of the commandments and the sacraments. As a promise to devout followers of Mary, that is, those who prayed Hail Marys morning, afternoon, and evening on a daily basis, Duque de Estrada indicated that Mary had for them a special reward: "If we pray the Hail Mary with a good heart, the Virgin looks kindly upon us and speaks to God for us, she is our godmother, she asks God to pardon our sins, to give us a good death, and to carry us to heaven" (112). At the end, it might have appeared, as Duque de Estrada set the dynamics of devotion to Mary, that a sincere and constant reverence to Mary would ultimately lead to eternal life: "God does not cover his ears: he always does what his mother tells him, because he loves her greatly. So if you want the Virgin to be your godmother, you must love her very much, greet her always, and ask her with all your heart to pray for us while we are alive, when we are dying, since that is the hour of death" (112).

Duque de Estrada's statement about Mary's divine presence at the death of a slave may have implied the absence of a priest for that moment. This supports Esteban Montejo's poor opinion of the priests who served slaves on plantations. Montejo made specific references to the few functions that the priests performed. None of them corresponded to service as catechist, which Duque de Estrada so carefully prescribed.

According to Montejo, priests attended rituals on a regular basis only if they were paid. Those functions required financial transactions, with threats to report violators to their masters. Under such arrangements, all slave women were obliged to baptize their babies within three days of giving birth. Thus, at least on paper, according to Montejo, "That was why all the children were Christians" (76; trans. 78). Another ecclesiastical function was to give permission for first cousins to marry. This custom, presumably common on plantations with higher numbers of males than females, was allowed and resulted in another financial transaction imposed upon the Black: "Marriage between cousins was looked down upon, and that's why they had to pay, in order not to fall into sin. Of course that arrangement was good for the priests. Right there they had another handout" (129; trans. 133).

In short, Montejo's picture of the priest's character was highly negative. That was particularly evident in depictions of priests' sexual misconduct toward "pretty White women" with whom they had children that were known as their "godchild" or "nephew" (76; trans. 78). This unreligious behavior was in contrast to that of their Black counterparts, the *brujos*, whom Montejo considered to be wise men and repositories of wisdom. Their role, away from the prying eyes of masters and plantation administrators, corresponded to that of judges, keeping an internal order of life in the *barracón*.

In spite of Montejo's negative portrait of the role of priests, he does state that they performed rituals related to the Church's liturgy. Some of these, Montejo recalls, were in observance of the celebration of patron saints, a Roman Catholic tradition that was completely absent from Duque de Estrada's text. Montejo recalled three such fiestas *patronales* [patron saint feasts]: those of Santiago, Saint Ann, and Saint John. Although the priests seem to have had a central role in these ceremonies, since they "prayed for a long time" (76; my translation), Montejo does not offer a text of those prayers nor does he offer any description of the types of ceremonies performed. He claims that participation by the slaves indicated not necessarily Catholic devotion but their maintenance of their native religious beliefs. The process was simple and it seems to have worked. Montejo claims that under the guise of celebrating the patron saint, Blacks in urban settings carried on the rituals in their devotion of the African orishas: "They [White people] passed by and at most asked a question: 'What's going on?' And the blacks answered: 'Here we are, celebrating San Juan.' They said San Juan, but it was Oggún. Oggún is the god of war. In those years he was the best known in the area. He's always found in the countryside, and they dress him in green or purple. Oggún Arere, Oggún Oké, Oggún Aguanillé" (74; trans. 76). These fiestas *de santos* [feasts of the saints] were held in individual *casas de santos* [saints' houses], as the urban African *cabildos* became known.

In the close confines of the *barracón*, *negros de nación* were the religious practitioners, not the Catholic priest, who Montejo claimed never came close to the living quarters. Referring to those Blacks as "brujos" or "brujeros" [witchcraft practitioners or makers of witchcraft], Montejo went to them seeking knowledge of herbal medicine. In spite of his supposed interest in learning about the *brujos'* herbal practices, he kept no records of such lessons. The *yerbas* [herbs] appeared related to two distinctive religious customs: that of the Yoruba, today known as Santería, and that of the Congo, mainly practices that Montejo referred to as Palo mayombe (Cros Sandoval 65). The longest and most complete descriptions of these practices are of rituals of Palo mayombe. In particular, Montejo's descriptions of the Congo's handling of demonic forces, the "preparation" of a cauldron to conjure up strong spirits and the "charging" of amulets were among the longest and the most detailed scenes in his fascinating exploration of the world of the Cuban Palo, often feared even today (Cros Sandoval 66).

Other people on the plantation, regardless of their race, shared Montejo's fascination with the *negros de nación's* religious practices. The slave *brujos* were both feared and sought out for their efficiency in making *resguardos* [talismans or charms], *prenda* [a charged object, often a stone], and offerings to the *cazuela* [cauldron]. According to Montejo's testimony, masters, particularly those initiated as Freemasons, often sought the help of the *brujos*, in Palo mayombe. These White people, "Counts and Marquises [ . . . ], who said they were Christians" (121; trans. 125), learned from the elder Congos how to feed the cauldron for their own personal benefit: "While you work mayombe, you'll be lords of the earth" (121; trans. 125). Another indication that powerful White men knew well and feared the efficacy of those underground Black religious ceremonies, Montejo added, was the fact that the *mayoral*, the plantation manager, feared these practices: "They had their eye on the black witches out of the fear they had for them. They well knew that if the witches wanted to, they could crack you open like a beetle" (126; trans. 130).

Montejo's preference to deal with the *brujo* was evident throughout the text, with the implicit declaration that neither the priest nor the Yoruba practitioner had the power of the *brujos*. Montejo considered the priest a money grabber, but he seemed not to quibble about the *brujo*'s similar practice of charging money for his *trabajos* [spells]. Unlike ceremonies that the priests performed (which seem not to have had any supernatural impact), at the core of Montejo's memories was the powerful magical abilities of the *brujos*, demonstrated in many cases and by means of the most unusual supernatural "formulas." Some of the potions were intended to facilitate a healthy life among slaves, particularly regarding issues of sexual behavior, kept under control by means of *trabajos*.

In contrast to the Black *brujo*'s status as the central figure of the religious life on the plantation, Montejo portrayed the Catholic priest as physically weak and ineffectual in terms of spiritual powers. A notable inclusion of Western religious belief did not come from the priests, but from immigrants from the Canary Islands who settled in large numbers in the countryside near the plantations. They became paid workers on the plantations. As Suárez y Romero indicated in his Costumbrista articles, and as historians at the time confirmed, they became antagonists of slaves. Montejo also displayed a negative attitude toward them. He warned the reader that the *isleños*, as *canarios* were known in Cuba, were to be feared: "You have [to] be careful with the Islanders because they know a lot about witchcraft" (65; trans. 67). Unlike the Catholic priests, the Spanish *brujas* [witches] displayed amazing spiritual powers, including their ability to displace themselves from the Canary Islands to Cuba at will. How this happened, as in almost all other descriptions of supernatural occurrences, Montejo does not fully describe. The influence of witches was, however, long-lasting, as evidenced in the abundance of tales about mischievous witches in the Cuban countryside (Feijóo, *Mitología* 293–322).

In spite of the Roman Catholic priests' distance from the religious life of slaves, there are indications that elements of the popular practice of the Catholic faith influenced slaves. The earliest records showed that the Cuban Roman Catholic Church had expressed an interest in establishing churches in rural areas outside the wealthy provinces of sugarcane producers. Concerned about the lack of rural churches, in 1610 Cuban Bishop Armendariz commanded plantation owners to take their slaves to churches in Havana "for celebration of sacraments and other religious acts" (Riverend Brusone 122). As the number of the slaves on plantations grew, such visits to the capital city proved to be difficult. This resulted in a command in 1680 that called for establishment of a "certain type of missionary work" by calling priests to visit plantations regularly (Riverend Brusone 120). The visits of priests would have brought to the plantations devotion for Catholic saints.

The presence of Catholic saints as patron saints preceded the arrival in the Americas of any religious order. Perhaps the most obvious example is the name of one of Christopher Columbus's ships, the *Santa María*, although the crew never referred to her as such; they preferred *Marigalante* [Sexy Mary], a much more appropriate name for the round-bellied vessel (Sale 8). As if guarding against evil spirits, this cult of the saints, which had been central to the Christianization of western Europe, was an important component of Spanish Catholicism (Reff 23). The saints' roles as negotiators for "protection against drought, plague, locusts" (Reff 23) continued in Cuba, and in the other Latin American countries. Churches were founded with the names of particular patron saints. They became well known for their celebrations of a saint's feast, and on some occasions for the miracles associated with the religious icons housed there. Such was the case of the celebrated Virgen de la Caridad del Cobre [Virgin of Charity of Copper].

Caridad del Cobre is a mulatta icon with origins in the early part of the sixteenth century. Her initial devotees were slave copper miners; however, by the mid-nineteenth century, she had become an element of Cuban national identity (M. González, *Afro-Cuban* 81). By 1760, as indicated in Nicolás Joseph de Ribera's *Descripción de la Isla de Cuba* [Description of the island of Cuba], her following had transcended the geographical limits of Santiago, and she had numerous devotees:

> Santiago del Prado (commonly called the Copper) is a small town of Blacks and mulattoes, some free and some slaves of the King. It is on the slope of a mountain in which there are many open copper mines, on whose peak is a church in which there is veneration of an image of the Most Holy Mary with the title of Charity, where people from everywhere go on pilgrimage, and some miracles have been experienced. (Qtd. in Pichardo Viñals 100)

The establishment of churches in the Americas, particularly in rural areas, has been equated with a religious imperialist practice as part of a "more extensive process of inscribing the American landscape with Christian symbols and meaning, rendering it both intelligible and tractable" (Reff 17). In the province of Havana, rural churches dated from 1640, with the foundation of the Church of Santo Cristo del Buen Viaje [Holy Christ of the Good Voyage] (1640), followed by the Church of the Espíritu Santo [Holy Spirit] (1661), the Iglesia Auxiliar del Santo Angel Custodio [Auxiliary Church of the Guardian Angel] (1679) (Riverend Brusone 121). As elsewhere in Latin America, such a practice implied civilization of the wilderness ["el monte"], which was a negative space where evil forces ruled (Reff 25).

Montejo expressed negative opinions about the Catholic Church. He insisted that slaves freely observed native African religious practices and did not associate themselves with the rituals of the Catholic Church. He himself was opposed to the Congo practices, which he considered evil, and he viewed Creole worship in negative terms, collectively referring to it as *brujería* [witchcraft]. In his memoirs, however, there are frequent contradictions that reveal his awe of the orishas' power, superior to that of the foreign imports of Catholic saints: "The strongest gods are the ones from Africa. I tell you it's a fact they could fly. And they did whatever they wanted with their hexes" (14; trans. 17–18). From his unsubstantiated statement that the plentiful fleas in the barrack huts were the work of witches to his affirmation that Congo witchcraft produced more results than practices associated with Santería, Montejo's *Biografía* contains a compilation of the triumphs of Creole Black religious practices over the mild effects of Catholic saints on the life of slaves.

Montejo used the term *santo* in reference both to the Catholic saint and to the Yoruba orisha. The former slave María de la Cruz Sentmanat indicated that traveling salesmen sold in the barrack huts "engravings of [la Virgen de la] Caridad [del Cobre] and of Santa Barbara (qtd. in Pérez de la Riva, *El barracón* 40), images used in Santería practices. According to Montejo, the Congo religion came to be known as "brujería," perhaps because Santería adopted the iconography of Catholic saints, but the Congo belief system seemed to remain closer to the native pagan forms: "Witchcraft is more common with the Congos than with the Lucumís. The Lucumís are more allied to the Saints and to God" (31; trans. 35).

Montejo does not go into detail about the orishas or their Congo equivalents. He gives only one example of an orisha, the almighty head of all orishas, as observed by the Yoruba, whom Montejo describes: "Obatalá was an ancient, so I heard, who was always dressed in white. They said that Obatalá was the one who created you, and who knows what else. People come from Nature, and so does Obatalá" (32; trans. 35). He had heard this explanation from the *viejos de nación*, who according to him, held the knowledge about religion (33; trans. 37). Thus, the *viejos de nación* were highly sought out, unlike the Catholic priest, who rarely made his presence known among the slaves on the plantations. Those *brujos* were responsible for the true religious life of the slaves, he says (33; trans. 37).

Montejo's numerous anecdotes of unusual events in or around the barrack huts supported his opinion that the slave never truly converted to the Catholic faith. To prove his point, Montejo brought to the forefront the role of the *brujo*, as a preferred equivalent to the Catholic priest, both as a practitioner of religious ceremonies and as an "evangelist." The *brujos* kept alive native mythologies, organized in a complex theology communicated to the rest of the slave population by means of *trabajos* [spells] and by oral literature. That folk tradition included proverbs, moral stories structured as animal fables (Cabrera *Ayapá*), and religion-inspired stories, known as *patakí* or *apatakí* (Cabrera *Koeko*; Feijóo, *El negro*). These became material for research by the earliest Cuban anthropologists (e.g., Fernando Ortiz and Lydia Cabrera), who transcribed the rich religious folklore as expressed to them by former slaves and their descendants.

In an interesting piece of anthropological information, Montejo indicates that, in addition to oral traditions, religious data kept the cult alive through secret marks made on the walls of *brujos'* rooms: "They were long lines and circles. Even though each was a saint, they said that the marks were secret" (32; trans. 36). This statement contradicts Costumbrista Suárez y Romero's description of the slaves' living quarters, which he presented as plain and uniform structures. Placement of the "secret marks" inside the huts served to circumvent regulations that prohibited "putting on the front or inside symbols to differentiate one hut from another, indicating special hierarchy or religious association" (Moreno Fraginals, "Aportes" 27).

Montejo's major contribution to the documentation of Black Creole religions was his observations from a privileged position as an insider, not as a voyeur (as in the case of Suárez y Romero) but as an eyewitness to religious events and also as an unwilling believer in Creole religious practices. His memory may have been affected to some degree by the passage of time since his life as a slave, and by the ideology of the Cuban Revolution of 1959, but as a former slave Montejo offered rare insight into Creole religious life. The only records of the prevalence of active Creole belief systems on Cuban plantations of the nineteenth century are his descriptions and some brief accounts that Cuban anthropologists obtained in their interviews with former slaves in the early decades of the twentieth century.

There were no Costumbrista articles written on the often murky and controversial subject of Black Creole religious belief systems practiced on plantations. This lack of publications may reflect religious and political institutions' hesitation to provide effective ways of suppressing such forbidden acts. At any rate, only a handful of Costumbrista articles attempted to address even urban Blacks' religious activities encoded in public musical displays, in parades in celebration of prescribed Catholic saints' days. Their silence is in contrast to the many witnesses' accounts that documented thriving Afro-Cuban religious practices.

## For Everyone's Pleasure to View: Urban Black Religious Parades

> . . . after many years of residence on the island, [the slaves] were as ignorant in Religion as the day they left the jungles, without knowing how to express the most common ideas in the language of the country. This made me suspect that they had not been baptized, or that they had been baptized without the preventive measures of the canons that the parish priest should have required.
>
> Miguel Estorch, *Apuntes para la historia sobre la administración del Marqués de la Pezuela en la Isla de Cuba*

Information about the required conversion of the African slave in Cuba was often documented throughout the nineteenth century. A historian and member of the Havana City Hall, Miguel Estorch, writing in 1856 about the current living conditions in Havana, expressed doubts about the assumed assimilation of the slaves into the Catholic faith. This subject was rarely discussed in print in Cuba at the time. Striking elements of Estorch's low opinion of the "savage" slaves were his judgment that they appeared not to have been truly converted and his deep concern that they could barely speak Spanish, a fact for which he also made the priest, and by extension the Cuban Roman Catholic Church, fully responsible.

In all laws and regulations concerning the treatment of slaves, there was the assumption that, with conversion to Catholicism, slaves would also learn the Spanish language, as indicated in the catechism by Father Duque de Estrada. Being Catholic and speaking Spanish were signs often explored in Costumbrista articles as proof that slaves or freed Blacks had abandoned their uncivilized customs in favor of Cuban culture.

Slaves and freed Blacks living in cities, with freer mobility than rural slaves, had at their disposal more ways to come together in order to observe native traditions. The urge to group themselves, seeking comfort in social activities, was evident in many entries in the chapter minutes of the meetings of the City Council of Havana, available in two volumes from 1550 to 1574.

City ordinances recorded the earliest images of African slaves and freed Blacks within the city limits of Havana. Most of the records are ordinances or regulations restricting slaves or freed Blacks to a limited range of types of manual work and to specific living arrangements (for slaves and for freed Blacks), with information about the location of and materials to be used in their dwellings (for the freed Blacks). There are also glimpses of the impact of Blacks' cultural traditions upon daily life in Havana, including most prominently their earliest attempts to meet to perform activities forbidden by law, such as their gathering in social settings to enjoy music, dance and alcoholic beverages.

One matter absent from the City of Havana's minutes is any recording of religious observances by slaves or freed Blacks. Other than a request from a church for permission to purchase slaves to work in construction, there are no entries about Blacks' connections with any official religious organization and no reference to the underground practices of native African religions in Havana.

One rather curious entry regarding public religious celebrations concerns a prohibition effective April 1, 1569, "that no woman walk in the procession of Holy Thursday" (2:121). It is reasonable to assume that these women were Spaniards, a code word for White women used throughout previous ordinances. Behavior during the Holy Thursday procession may have been unruly, influenced by Blacks' participation, but that is not stated in the text.

Laws and regulations pertaining to slaves rarely contained major dispositions about their education, other than religious indoctrination. The earliest of the laws on slavery, a "Royal Warrant and Instruction to be Circulated in the Indies on the Education, Treatment and Employment of Slaves" (1789), called specifically for "education suitable for them," but it merely mandated their religious conversion (qtd. in Ortiz, *Los negros esclavos* 408). Half a century later, the education of slaves was still limited to their religious conversion. The Edict on Governing and Policing the Island of Cuba of 1842, by Governor D. Gerónimo Valdés, established that the slave had to be evangelized according to "the capacity and the circumstances of the slave" (qtd. in Ortiz, *Los negros esclavos* 439).

The acceptance of Catholic practices as an indication of civility, as Montejo observed in his comments on slaves' religious practices, would lead to the Blacks' incorporation of certain theological elements into native African traditions. Some of these Creole traditions, mainly public religious parades celebrated as saints' feasts, in which Whites and Blacks participated, became subject matter indirectly addressed in Cuban Costumbrista essays.

In reaction to the Blacks' urge to gather in social events, mainly musical and religious, an institution known as a Cofradía was created in an attempt to control such activities as well as the Blacks' social and economic mobility. Loosely translated as a "brotherhood society," the Cofradía, organized under the jurisdiction of a *cabildo* (council or chapter), was a legal association of Blacks (slaves or freed) belonging to the same nation or ethnicity. The concept was transplanted from Spain. Earlier Cofradías had been organized in Barcelona (1454–1455), in Valencia (1472), and in Seville (1475) (Rout 20). José Saco, the most important nineteenth-century Cuban historiographer on slavery, described the Spanish model of the Cofradía, quoting Ortiz de Zúñiga, a chronicler in Seville, who wrote in 1474 about the condition of African slaves in that city:

In Seville Blacks were treated with great mildness since the time of King Enrique III, permitting them to gather for their dances and feasts on public holidays, as long as they turned up willingly for work, and they were more tolerant of captivity and, as some became outstanding in ability, one was given the title of mayoral (manager) who served the rest of the slaves as a go-between to their masters and settled quarrels about injustices. (Qtd. in Franco, *La presencia* 7–8)

Association of the Cofradías with the church in devotion to a saint was part of laws established under Alfonso X The Wise: "wanting to bring order to civil and ecclesiastical matters of Seville, he divided its inhabitants into guilds and classes and it was his will that among themselves they should establish brotherhoods and Cofradías, each guild taking some Saint for their special patron, whose chapel would serve for their assemblies and their chapters" (qtd. in Ortiz, "Los cabildos" 128).

In Cuba, the first Cofradías were active relatively soon after the initial importation of slaves during the sixteenth century. Members were organized in specific ranks. The rulers were known as *reyes*, kings and queens who presided over activities, particularly dances. A reference to such a dance appeared in the City of Havana's Acts, entered as a complaint from Bartolomé Cepero, attorney of the city of Havana, on January 20, 1568. He reported that "Blacks, male and female, of this city call themselves kings and queens, and they have gatherings and conferences and banquets where they create scandals" (2:54). Although the complaint also asked for a remedy, the board asked for more information. If that information was eventually provided, there are no other entries on the activities of these feasts hosted by Black kings and queens. Missing from the complaint is information about the place where these Black banquets took place, whether it was a private dwelling of a freed slave or the locale of a Black Cofradía. The complaint about the loud banquets by Black kings and queens may have been an oblique recognition that these activities had an unorthodox religious character.

The Cofradías, associated with Catholic churches that served as host institutions, further promoted devotion to patron saints. Related to the evangelization process, in Mexico by 1579, for example, the first Cofradías were founded by the religious orders of the Franciscans, the Augustinians, and the Dominicans (Ayala 207). The importance of the Cofradía as an agent of pacification and religious indoctrination in the Americas was codified in a warrant of 1602, in the earliest legal entry about the functioning of these bodies: "Agreeing that in those held by Indians and by Blacks there should be decency and good order required, and no excess" (qtd. in Ayala 207). Manuel Joseph de Ayala asserted that the Cofradías were governed by laws compiled as Laws of the Indies, of which the oldest entry dates from 1600 (207). In a summary of the four laws pertaining to its functioning, de Ayala stressed that the Cofradía was intended as "an institution of pious purposes and of charity, promoted by and bound to the clergy regular and secular" (207). Among the most legislated of its activities were "processions that in turn were used as one element of Christianization" (207).

In Cuba, among the earliest documentation of data concerning Cofradías, according to de Arrate's history book, *Llave del Nuevo Mundo* [Key to the New World] (1761), were records of the founding in 1598 of Nuestra Señora de los Remedios [Our Lady of the remedies], "upon petition of freed Blacks of the Zape nation" (196). De Arrate documented several other Cofradías functioning in the city of Havana at the time when he was writing. All were composed of freed Blacks, not identified by their nation or ethnicity: the Espíritu Santo [Holy Spirit], San Benito de Palermo (196), and Santa Catalina, mártir (200). In spite of the importance that de Arrate gave to the Cofradía, José María de la Torre failed to mention them in his book on the history of Havana, *Lo que fuimos y lo que somos o La Habana antigua y moderna* [What we were and what we are or Havana ancient and modern] (1857). He did, however, offer a detailed account of the founding of churches in which Cofradías were housed. A comprehensive listing of the various Cuban Cofradías organized by ethnicity is today widely available (Martínez Furé, *Diálogos* 123–24; Deschamps Chapeaux, *El negro* 31–46; López Valdés, *Africanos* 54, 61, 66, 90, 131, 162–64, 188–89; Hall, *Slavery* 115–17, 119–20).

Cuban anthropologist Fernando Ortiz's research on the Cofradía has explored in detail its internal organization. Drawing from Esteban Pichardo y Tapia's *Diccionario provincial, casi razonado de vozes y frases cubanas* [Provincial dictionary, almost reasoned of Cuban words and sayings] (1836), Ortiz equated the Cofradía to a "chapter, council or chamber that showed representation from all the Blacks of the same origin" (*Orbita* 122). In a highly organized internal structure, the Cofradía was managed by its own members, who elected a *rey del cabildo* [king of the *cabildo*], sometimes a character who had held social importance in Africa, or simply the oldest member (122). Also known as *capataz* or *capitán* [overseer or captain], the king of the *cabildo*, according to Ortiz, was elected to a four-year nonrenewable term. He oversaw all social activities (124). Citing a 1903 publication on *cabildos* by

Ramón Meza, Ortiz described the king's colorful attire, inspired by the military fashion of the time: "braided jackets, starched shirts, enormous ties, brilliant peaked hats, wide and loud sashes crossed on the breast, medals, sword at the waist and a great stick with a silver handle, a symbol of his authority" (123). There was also a *rey suplente* [substitute king], known as *isuru*, or *chiquito* [little] (Ortiz 125).

The king also supervised the collection of membership fees and imposed fines on members, mainly in punishment for their violation of civil laws (125). He had full control over the *cabildo*. This was the opinion of Antonio de las Barras, who in his memoirs concisely defined a *cabildo*, which he considered one of the Blacks' "most characteristic customs," and he spoke highly about the role of the king: "Those arriving from Africa, known here by the name of negros de nación, are divided according to the regions from which they come, into groups, and they form Cabildos presided over by a chief elected every year, to whom they give the name of king, and all respect this person, even in their private relationship, as a superior" (119).

Other important ranking positions included a queen, a second-in-command, known as *mayor de plaza*, and an *abanderado* [flag bearer]. Martínez Furé described an extensive organization, "an organization of women, in addition to that of men, composed of a matron, two to six attendants, a steward and six members" (*Diálogos* 124).

The Cofradía had a strong component of a mutual-aid society, as Pichardo indicated in his dictionary. "They gather funds and form a sort of society of pure entertainment and of help, with funds from their treasury" (qtd. in Ortiz, *Orbita* 132). Ortiz stressed that the Cofradía money was used to help members in the following conditions: in sickness and in purchase of liberty of old people or of invalids (131).

For mainstream culture, the most obvious aspect of the Cofradía traditions was the musical celebrations that were held on their premises or in public parades during holy days. Such incorporation of African elements into Catholic ceremonies had taken place relatively early. In 1573, the Havana Town Hall had disposed that freed Blacks "be lent to help" in the parade of the Corpus Christi (qtd. in Ortiz, *Orbita* 131). Innovations in traditions of the Corpus Christi parades in various Latin American countries made these celebrations more "pompous, richer than those in Spain . . . more varied, because of the group of Indians" (Bayle 748).

The Corpus Christi, celebrated sixty days after Easter Sunday, grouped in Cuba all the Cofradías into a festive environment that included "masks, with 'gigantes' [giants], bulls, ponies and tarascas [serpents]" (Riverend Brusone 204).

Another activity associated with these parades included celebration of plays— texts that have not survived. Nothing is known about their authors, whether Spaniards or Cuban criollos (Pichardo Viñals 43). In the nineteenth century, the Cofradías were well known for their participation in the parade on the Día de Reyes [Kings' Day or Day of Epiphany], celebrated on January 6.

The importance of the *cabildo* as an institution that promoted the development of a Black Creole culture has been thoroughly explored. Rolando Mellafe indicated that the Cofradía was intended as "a protective social institution for free time and even for idleness of the Black element through free expression of the cultural objectives expressive of recreation imported from Africa" (126–27). Manuel Moreno Fraginals indicated that the urban *cabildo* allowed "survival, to a high degree of purity, of certain cultural manifestations, including language, which acquired a ritual status" ("Aportes" 16). Julio A. León pointed out that the *cabildos* gave rise to three distinctive African Creole cultures: the Yoruba, the Bantú and the Appapa or the *ñáñigos* (123), adding that their activities preserved in particular "the magic formula, the moralistic proverbs and the fables of educational type" (124).

This emphasis on grouping Blacks of the same ethnicity continued to be observed late into the nineteenth century. For example, the Cabildo Arará Magino, founded in 1890, established the following two requirements of its members: "it is necessary to be honorable and never to have belonged to the extinct association of the ñáñigos. The cabildo will give celebrations on all festive days in use by its nation, or African dance, forbidding interference of drumming not belonging to their nation" (qtd. in Martínez Furé, *Diálogos* 124). The close association implied performing native African music that would retain African "musical instruments, dance steps" (Franco, *La presencia* 24–25).

Tomás Fernández Robaina indicated that the *cabildo* was organized as a way to "avoid unity of slaves and to keep down ethnic and tribal rivalries" (7). Thus, according to Fernández Robaina, the process created prime conditions for the development of Black Creole cultural forms, specifically religious belief systems. Political transformation to western patterns of civilization did happen, but as Fernández Robaina stressed, for the slaves and the freed Blacks only in visual appearance did this conversion take place. The process, which is often referred to as syncretism, promoted Creole religious forms, of which Santería is the best known as a "religion that in its exterior aspects takes the names of the Catholic saints" (7). Numerous witnesses over the years denounced this merging of belief systems. For example, the French chronicler Friar Jean Baptiste Labat stated from Cuba in 1742: "blacks did without scruples what pagans used to do by conserving secretly all of the superstitions of a pagan cult with the practices of the Christian faith" (132).

Today, the concept of syncretism as a merging of a type of African religion with the Catholic devotion of saints has been debated (Cros Sandoval 78–81). Referring specifically to the "imagery syncretism," that is, use of Catholic icons to cover rituals of native African deities, which Friar Labat denounced, Jorge Emilio Gallardo traced the ongoing debate throughout Latin America among practitioners of Creole religious practices. The opinions range from the extremely conservative, as many practitioners "have refused to withdraw the images, although they well know that the foundation of worship does not pass through them" (Gallardo 29) to more liberal observers who understand devotion to the Catholic saints to be an independent component: "We don't want people to stop believing in Santa Bárbara, a lofty spirit, beyond doubt. But we know that Iansan is another energy, she is not Santa Bárbara" (28).

The earliest legal restrictions concerning gatherings of Cofradías indicated authorities' concerns about the power of Creole religious ceremonies. For example, in 1620 the Cuban bishop Enríquez de Armendáriz expressed caution in licensing Black Cofradías in Havana: "particularly one dedicated to Saint Catherine, that two years now two women of color requested license for founding this Cofradía in the convent of Saint Augustine, and in this time I have discovered things worthy of remedy, that removal of the said Cofradía will bring to an end some offenses made against the majesty of Our Lord" (qtd. in Pichardo 1:573).

More specific violations of religious canons appeared summarized in police edicts. In 1794, such Creole religious practices were prohibited: "Even less will the Blacks of Guinea be permitted to raise in the houses of their Cabildos altars of our Saints for the dances that they form according to the custom of their land; whose prohibition the police officials will demand from the foremen without wasting time" (qtd. in Ortiz, "Los cabildos" 19). The practice of setting up altars in which Catholic saints' images were displayed must have been common as the prohibition implied: "taking down before all else the altar, whose image, pieces and furnishings will be handed over to the priest or his deputy in the parish church of the neighborhood, so that he will dispose of them as he sees fit" (19). Violators of this disposition would incur fines.

The influence of religious rituals continued, however, in some of the Cofradía's traditions, such as in the election process of the king, head of the Cofradía. Ortiz, quoting an eyewitness, "un viejo Congo" [an old Congo], describes the selection of the *salí*, the king of a Congo Cofradía. The election took place on the Day of Epiphany, when the names of candidates who displayed *entú* [talent] were placed in a hollow gourd and selected randomly after "three days of vigil and ceremonies to Saint Anthony" (124). St. Anthony, the patron saint of Portugal, according to Ortiz, had had an impact on the Congos. "Comida" [food] was offered to the icon, as part of the election ceremonies (*Orbita* 124).

The constant pressure on Blacks to take part in official religious ceremonies created more syncretic phenomena. Authorities soon realized that a common element among ethnic groups was music, performed during various stages of daily life at liturgical ceremonies, funeral chants, or simply for entertainment. Fully aware of the social cohesiveness of these musical gatherings, colonial authorities allowed the use of music, partly for recreational and pacifying purposes, but also with the intention of making future use of European music for evangelical conversion (Serra 146).

By the nineteenth century, Black Cofradías showed a more highly organized structure. Pedro Antonio Alfonso, in his autobiography, *Memorias de un matancero* [Memoirs of a man from Matanzas] (1854), pointed out the importance of *cabildos* in Matanzas, an important sugarcane producer and an area with a high concentration of slaves: "Freed Blacks and slaves attend and they are permitted from time immemorial to have their flags as insignia of the Cabildo, and here at least the Congo Real nation is allowed to carry one very similar to the national flag itself" (qtd. in Ortiz, *Orbita* 132). Alfonso's view of the *cabildos'* activities was highly complimentary. They were "useful institutions" because "they practice humanitarian and pious acts, tending to manumission of those members whom because of their morality and good behavior they consider worthy of obtaining it at the expense of the funds of the gathering, which are supported by small gifts of charity displayed when they attend the dance, and they are accustomed also to accept the task of curing their sick countrymen" (qtd. in Ortiz, *Orbita* 132–33).

The public came to know the Cofradías because of their musical performances, but their reputation was that of centers of tremendous noise. In Havana a police ordinance of 1792 significantly restricted the celebration of dances within *cabildo* houses: "In the Black Cabildos dances will be allowed only on festival days, from ten in the morning till eight in the evening, at which hour they will have to stop and each go home, without continuation for any reason or pretext" (qtd. in Ortiz, "Cabildos" 20). The ordinance also mandated a prohibition on sales of alcoholic beverages. That same edict moved the *cabildos* outside the center of downtown Havana to the "edges of the city next to the walls" (Ortiz 17, 20). The reason for this disposition was complaints from "honorable neighbors who justly protest the discomfort caused by the harsh and disagreeable sound of their instruments" (qtd. in Ortiz 17).

By 1842, as stated in a police ordinance, *cabildos* were required to limit their musical celebrations to "Sundays and days of obligation" (qtd. in Ortiz, "Los cabildos" 21). Antonio de las Barras y Prado, a Spaniard who worked in Havana in the middle of the nineteenth century, spoke about such weekly Sunday dances on the Calle del Ejido. The allure for the White spectator is evident: "it is impossible to go around there without being dazed," in spite of the strong tone of barbarism that defines that section (119). Those dances were, in short, "composed of natural movements characteristic of a race that finds itself almost in a state of pure nature and whose intellectual activity is still deficient to change their customs" (121). Barras y Prado, a nonparticipatory visitor, probably paid a fee, one of the ways by which *cabildos* increased their funds for their social actions (Ortiz, "Los cabildos" 16).

In spite of de las Barras y Prado's negative reactions, he described the dances in rather close detail and with open admiration for their performance: "These are in form so original and grotesque, that at times they cause admiration and amazement in those who watch, because of the daring and difficulty of their movements" (120). The music of the dances was relegated in importance to a brief passage that stands out for its rather bland and negative observations:

> all of this accompanied by a noisy and monotonous music produced by the marugas, metal pieces and drums, from which they make sound with the palm of their hands, and by a shrill, hellish shouting, with which they finish off their warlike chants. They also have wooden horns that they play from time to time, emitting a mournful sound, similar to that of the conch, with which they increase the noise of that lewd festival. (120)

De las Barras y Prado described such a performance as a war dance, basing his opinion on the dancer's use of a saber, as part of the piece's choreography:

> Generally one Black woman and one Black man step forward to dance, while all the other party-goers form a circle around them. The man usually carries in his hand a saber or scimitar of wood, with which he makes many figures of attacks and parries, but without ceasing movements of his feet and of his whole body, which seems to be agitated by a sort of trembling, just like the woman who dances with him, both making horrible facial grimaces. (120)

The description of the dancers' skillful use of the saber, which may have reflected the *cabildo*'s imitation of Spanish military life (Ortiz, "Los cabildos" 6), also implied an iconic recognition of two Yoruba orishas: Oggún, the ironworker and patron saint of metals (González-Wippler 44) and Changó, the warrior whose double-edged ax is visual proof of his military prowess (González-Wippler 40).

The performance by the pair of dancers was mirrored by others in attendance, referred to as a "corro" [circle]. They too took part in this highly choreographed performance:

> When the dance and the music break out, the ring begins the chants in their own language, on account of which I have never been able to understand them, but it seems to me that they must refer to the deeds of some of their warriors, that the dancers keep imitating with action. There is no way to give any idea of the speed with which they execute the movements of feet and the spins of the body, as well as the agility with which they jump back and forward without missing even one moment the beat of the dance. (120–21)

The *corro*, besides singing in their native language, maintained the rhythm of the music, emphasizing the fast movements of the dancers: "At the same time as this it is obvious that those of the ring and the rest that fill the hall, by involuntary impulse, are following the same beat, now with feet and then with the body, and there is not one person that stops moving and making contorted faces" (121).

Knowledge of the influence of the various ethnic *cabildos* on the development of Black Creole dances was essential to understanding a "wide diversity of expressions in music and in the dancing" (Guanche 69). During the nineteenth century, mainstream culture held strong opinions against Black dances, illustrated in de las Barras y Prado's final statement about the *cabildo* dance that he had witnessed: "In these dances one must not look for refinement of any sort" (121). The Cuban novelist and ethnomusicologist Alejo Carpentier argued, however, that the process of creating Cuban Black music had already taken place by the eighteenth century. In 1776, a Cuban dance, the *chuchumbé*, was introduced in Mexico with immediate success. As described by an observer, the *chuchumbé* was "against any morals," and it was danced only among "mulattoes and other not serious people" (qtd. in Carpentier 53). It was finally prohibited after a complaint reached the Mexican Inquisition. According to Carpentier, the antecedents of the *chuchumbé*, the *paracumbés*, *cachumbas*, *gayumbas* and *zarambeques* were also highly sexual, danced by the female waving her skirt as she pretended to be followed by a male companion. The extreme sensuality was stressed by another eyewitness in 1789:

> The talent of the female dancer resides in her ability to move her hips and the lower part of her kidneys while keeping the rest of the body in a sort

of immobility which does not stop the soft movements of her arms holding a handkerchief or her skirt. A male dancer comes near her and throws
himself onto her, falling to the ground as he is about to touch her. He
moves back and steps forward again, inviting her into a seductive fight.
The dance becomes animated and suddenly it offers a picture whose traits
are so voluptuous that they become lascivious. (Qtd. in Carpentier 54)

Among Caribbean slaves, participation in Black *cabildos* provided both colorful attire of African origin and the introduction of Black beats and rhythms
into mainstream festivities. That is also the case with other Black "inventions"
that contributed African elements to such European celebrations as the carnival
and the *murguilla* [bands of street musicians]. In discussions of these activities,
there is mention of "cabildos, secret societies, Afro-Cuban cults, and the musical groups, or camparsas of the carnaval" (Castellanos 1:57). Scholars have noted
the strong Black substratum of some of today's popular Cuban traditions. For
example, *la tutelar* in Guanabacoa, *las charangas* in Bejucal, *las parrandas de
los Remedios*, *las candeladas de San Juan*, and *las fiestas de los patronos* started
as religious feasts celebrating the observance of Catholic saints' days (Serviat
150–51). One particular character associated with Epiphany celebrations, the
so-called *diablitos* [little devils], would also appear recorded in Costumbrista
writings and in popular graphic art forms of the nineteenth century.

The Edict of 1792 placed severe restrictions on the colorful performances of
Black *cabildos*. They included the type of gathering to be celebrated. For example, funeral wakes at the *cabildo* were prohibited: "for no reason or pretext may
they conduct or allow to conduct to them the cadavers of Blacks in order to perform dances or cries as used in their land" (qtd. in Ortiz, "Los cabildos" 19). It
also established provisions for *cabildos'* street celebrations, which were carefully
curtailed: "In no case shall Blacks go out through the streets in ethnic groups
with a flag or other banner, not even to fetch their kings in their houses, and
even less to have entertainment playing their instruments, nor for any reason
or pretext" (qtd. in Ortiz, "Los cabildos" 21). An exception to this resounding
restriction was entered into an edict of 1842, which established: "Nevertheless,
it will be permissible to celebrate on the Day of the Three Kings the diversion
known by the name of little devils in the same form as that done until this day
and in no other way" (qtd. in Ortiz, "Los cabildos" 21).

The Three Kings' Day Parade had a role within the popular street celebrations in Havana. Referring to the festivities as "el Carnaval de los negros" [the
Carnival of Blacks], de las Barras y Prado offered a strongly negative portrait
of that day, in which "Blacks have ample freedom to abandon their services,

leaving homes deserted" (121). According to de las Barras y Prado, Blacks started to gather at the *cabildos* very early in the morning, where "many decorate themselves with extravagant and strange objects, some appearing also with their body half nude and painted in colors, as in their land, put into big hoops fastened at the waist, which are wrapped in white cords, that reach toward the knees and that make waves in keeping with the rhythm of their movements" (121–22).

The street procession leading to the Palace of the Captain General, the Spanish governor of Cuba, was succinctly described: "The cabildos go out into the street as soon as they get organized, presided over by their respective kings or queens, carrying Spanish flags or banners of other colors, which they wave in the air, and they continue in this way playing music and dancing and asking for aguinaldo [money] from all the Whites they encounter" (122). The begging from passersby for *aguinaldo*, or a monetary gift, was the most common annoyance of these street *comparsas* [musical groups], as some Costumbrista writers indicated. The *cabildo* groups gathered at the Palace of the Captain General, where between eleven and one o'clock, individual groups were allowed to perform "un rato de baile" [for a while, dances] in the interior patio (122).

Again, de las Barras y Prado has a negative description of these events: "One sees there a compacted mass, from which stick out plumes, feathered caps, masks and other bizarre ornaments that move in keeping with the rhythm of their instruments" (122). Each of the groups, which de las Barras y Prado refers to as "tangos," attempted to "make the greatest possible noise," in order to catch the governor's attention: "The Captain General appears from time to time at one of the balconies and throws them tobacco and some coins, to which action they respond with loud 'Long Live Spain!' 'Long live Isabel II!'" (122). In spite of the chaos of this scene, de las Barras y Prado points out that the *cabildos* performed one after the other, with the implicit assumption that each group offered a different and better performance than the previous "tangos": "Thus all the Black African groups go marching: Congos, Ararás, Mandingas, Lucumís, Macuas, Minas, Carabalís and some other one that I don't recall, with Spanish flags on which is written the name of their nation" (122–23).

De las Barras y Prado mentioned an interesting fact that seemed to indicate that not all inhabitants of Havana, including Blacks, enjoyed the Black Cabildos' Epiphany celebrations. This differentiation reflected racial divisions observed in the Black community at large. Those Blacks who did not join *cabildos*, referred to as "the rest of the Blacks and Black Creoles," were classified in terms of their preference to observe mainstream cultural values. As depicted in Juan Francisco Manzano's self-portrait, they rejected *cabildo* activities as barbarian: "The rest of the Blacks and Black Creoles, who, being more refined do not want to get involved in tangos, visit the homes of acquaintances, individually asking for aguinaldo" (124). There was no indication of the kind of *aguinaldo* preferred by these "uppity Blacks," implicit in the description of gifts "more refined," rather than the miserly "tobacco and several coins" that their counterparts were collecting from the Captain General. Black upper-crust society preferred to have their own private fiestas in dance halls known as *cunas*, where they danced to the favorite music of the White upper class, *la danza habanera*, "of course, with great self-confidence, to the sound of an orchestra" (124). The race of the musicians was left unmentioned; however, according to scholars, freed Blacks dominated the musical scene in Havana during the middle of the nineteenth century (Deschamps Chapeaux, *El negro* 105–18). The public Black dances, and particularly the parades of the Cabildo Reyes, were often parodied, as seen in engravings on tobacco-box covers (Kutzinski 55).

Further details about the celebration in Havana of the Feast of Epiphany were included by Antonio Bachiller y Morales (1812–1889) in his historical account *Los negros* [Blacks] (1887). A Cuban-born writer, Bachiller y Morales indicated that the festivities started on the eve of January 6 with a State dinner, which was attended by military chiefs and their dependents (113). The following day, Epiphany belonged to the Black *cabildos*, centered on their march to the Palace of the Captain General.

As de las Barras y Prado had stated, the Black Cabildos marched into the headquarters of the Captain General at an established time. Bachiller y Morales registered the time as ten in the morning (114). Both of their descriptions reflected open distaste for the parades; however, as Bachiller y Morales stated in passing, he witnessed "those scenes several times," suggesting barely disguised voyeurism: "Blacks shouted themselves hoarse singing and they were overcome by fatigue dancing" (114). Like him, others, such as de las Barras y Prado, had also come "drawn by the desire to see Africa in Cuba" (114).

Unlike de las Barras y Prado, Bachiller y Morales wrote a rather brief description of the arrival of the *cabildos* parades to the Captain General's Palace: "the Blacks' Cabildos presented themselves by nations, with their flags, on which usually they painted the saint that they had as patron: their crude drums, marugas, conch horns and fifes produced a hellish jubilation" (114). Of the participants that Bachiller y Morales pointed out, the queens and "capataces de cabildo" [the overseers of the Cabildo], had the most expressive descriptions: "with their plumes and parasols" (114). They represented a "royal" Black type, assuming that Bachiller y Morales meant that they were freed Blacks, mixed with slaves. Although Bachiller y Morales offered no specific visual clue that allowed him to differentiate the freed Black from the slave, he had the kindest thought for the enslaved Black: "that confusion of the unfortunate slaves that were less unfortunate because of protection by law and the presence of others of their kind now free, and the hope of being free some day, offered a picture interesting to consider" (114). Notably absent is an analysis of that "picture interesting to consider" which he quickly put aside in order to present a lament about the slaves' holiday, which seems almost verbatim from de las Barras y Prado's text: "Most of the homes in Havana resigned themselves, as in the times of Ancient Rome, to being their own servants one day in the year" (114).

A common element in de las Barras y Prado and Bachiller y Morales is their descriptions of the secret activities of the *ñáñigos*. This subject had been treated by Costumbrista writer Enrique Fernández Carrillo in his article "El ñáñigo," which was left undated in Salvador Bueno's Costumbrista anthology. In spite of what the title would seem to convey, the ñáñigo is not a protagonist in the article. There is no plot, as in most Costumbrista articles, but a report about their rules, described as *ñáñiguismo*, that the critics Jorge and Isabel Castellanos consider "a mixture of hits and misses" (4:92).

Fernández Carrillo's tone and information were shaped by his highly hostile words: "Idolater is the Black, and his idolatry constitutes his religion" (372). His observations, unlike those of de las Barras and Bachiller y Morales are centered on negative traits of the *ñáñigo* society—a dreaded, all-male society that encouraged delinquent acts against non-initiates, referred to as "profanes" (374). Most of the information in the article seems to be of common public knowledge, including, most prominently, references to the sacrifice of a rooster, which was killed with a stick, not with a metal weapon, in the initiation ceremony: "the ñáñigos do not enter the room with weapons. The death of the cock, which has a place in their ceremonies, is done with a stick. The neophyte must drink cock's blood in the act of initiation" (374).

Perhaps because of the secretive nature of *ñáñigo* societies, de las Barras y Prado's descriptive passage on this dreaded group is significantly shorter than that of Bachiller y Morales, who took a historical approach to this controversial subject. De las Barras y Prado did not place the *ñáñigos* within any religious group; they were merely "a shady association for robbery and pillage" (123). His narrative contradicts even this statement, because he placed the *ñáñigos* within an initiation ritual (he did not explain how he had access to this violent scene): "in order to enter the neophyte must suffer resigned, stretched out on the floor face up, a series of blows by sticks on his belly in the midst of shouts, chants and blows by the members" (123). The rite continued with the implicit assumption that there occurred a religious act: "they make him drink the cock's blood, an animal to whom they render worship" (123). The last act of the initiation included the shedding of human blood. On command the neophyte was required to stab an innocent passerby: "they hand him a dagger so he can go out into the street *to try the iron*, which he does by beating and stabbing the passerby of his choice" (123–24, emphasis in the original).

These details about the supposedly secret rites of the *ñáñigo* appear almost verbatim in Bachiller y Morales, but his is a longer treatment of the subject. He portrays the *ñáñigos* as an example of "a species of flock . . . a mysterious society," composed of freed Blacks who were not members of a Catholic-related Black Cofradía (115). Originally, Blacks who had been restricted from taking into the streets their dances, or *tangos*, began "to evade the law [ . . . ] by covering their faces as the bozales were doing, and thus they passed for Congos, whose drums and tunes are most common among Black Cubans" (115). Within a period of time vaguely indicated as "with time" and "after the government of General Vives" (117), these masked Blacks eventually became known as "ñáñigos," and they were organized as a religious group: "they formed their rites and their ceremonies" (115). Although originally an all-Black institution, the *ñáñigos* at a later stage allowed "some White man to lead them" (115).

*Náñigos* were also considered criminal gangs. Previously, Bachiller y Morales had related them to the Black *curro* [thug]. From the Black thug, *ñáñigos* inherited brutal street behavior: "Also it was assured that one's level in his apprenticeship and his becoming an officer were determined not by courage but by cruelty" (116). Again, according to unconfirmed documentation, the *ñáñigo* was obliged by honor "to wound unknown persons for no reason other than to do them harm or to kill them, since it was indispensable to stab his fellow men in order to be considered good" (116).

Although acknowledging that his accounts were based on rumors, Bachiller y Morales continued to report on the alleged religious component of the *ñáñigo* initiation rites, including the mention of a rooster, as did de las Barras y Prado: "They say that upon entering the society they were swearing extermination of their enemies and they sanctified the oath with the sacrifice of a cock" (116).

Part of the *ñáñigo* folklore was the *diablitos*, figures that Bachiller y Morales leaves underdescribed. He makes a brief reference to them: "On Diablitos days, or when the tangos were out, they used to carry these plucked birds" (116). The lack of data on these presumably religious acts is even more evident in Bachiller y Morales's comment in passing about a police seizure of "books and signs written with blood, but it could not be justified whether all the Náñigos had the same, nor their true importance" (116).

Bachiller y Morales exhibited interest in documenting by visual corroboration the religious activities of the *ñáñigos*. He recorded having witnessed another "sinister sign of Black societies in Cuba," besides the parading of a "cock plucked or with feathers" (116). That terrible sign was that they "paraded an immense artificial snake: a boa constrictor that was being placed in the center of the patio of the Palace" (116). The reference to the patio, although not clear, may have referred to the Captain General's headquarters. The reason for the activity is also left unexplained, but it must have occurred in an approved public musical performance, as indicated by the preferred location where it took place.

As Bachiller y Morales described the performance, it is clear that it was part of his listing of barbaric ceremonies by Black Creoles. Once the boa was placed in the center of the patio of the Palace, Blacks of unspecified gender "were dancing around in circles with a song half-Spanish, half-African" (117). The simple poem of two lines: "'La culebra se murió/Sángala muleque . . .'" [The snake died/Sángala muleque . . . ] (117) received a rather simplistic interpretation, which ignored the potential ritual aspect of the untranslated line: "The Spanish part served for petition, satire, etc., and the droning of the intelligible part, a monotonous beat, was accompanied by rustic musical instruments" (117). The celebrations ended with "la fiesta de los diablitos Náñigos" [the feast of the little devils *náñigos*], details that Bachiller y Morales ignored, as did Fernández y Carrillo, who limited his description to praise of an engraving by the artist Víctor P. de Landaluze: "that only needs to speak or to move in order to be alive" (374).

As a whole, Costumbrista writers, historians, and eyewitnesses had little sympathy for Black activities, particularly those of a religious nature. For example, in his article "Rezagos" [Remnants], José Cárdenas y Rodríguez examined reasons for the backwardness of nineteenth-century upper-class male Cubans. In a portrait, he explored the childhood of the typical Cuban man, the proof of remnants, leftovers of a primitive raising and earliest education of most White Cuban children at the hands of Black nannies: "It happened that his parents abandoned him in his infancy to godmothers and wet-nurses, who nursed him with milk other than the milk provided by nature, and that instilled in him inclinations that should not be his" (187). Such an unnatural connection, represented in the child's consumption of Black maternal milk was, according to Cárdenas y Rodriguez, the beginning of a process in which Cuban children would adopt uncivilized Black traits: "Later they handed him over to stupid, mercenary servants and tutors, who entertained him with stories of the dead and of apparitions of saints, with the exploits of Pedro Urdemalas, with the witchcraft of Guinea, with the influence of the evil eye and with the pranks of the goblins" (187). The result of such upbringing, to Cardenas y Rodríguez's horror, was the current state of Cuban youth: "and all this rubbish made him credulous, superstitious and furthermore, extremely cowardly and subject to nightmares and convulsions" (187).

Whether because of the secrecy of the Black Creole religious groups such as the *ñáñigos*, or because Black belief systems were considered a backward example of the current state of development of Cuban culture struggling with technological advances available on the island because of international investors in the sugarcane market, few Costumbrista articles explored Black religious subjects as a central theme. Some of the Costumbrista writers, Francisco de Paula Gelabert (1834–1894) in particular, included such figures in their articles, but they were mere shadow characters. In "Niños precoces y desarrollados" [Children precocious and developed], Gangá Blacks persecute an innocent passerby while begging for tips from him: "some ten or twelve Black Gangás, who while playing gourds, and in their hellish singing, asked me for an aguinaldo" (99). In the "Vanidad y pobreza, todo en una pieza" [Vanity and poverty all in one piece], there were *ñáñigo* music players: "that were shaking with fury in the middle of the street, and with the Congos who were whirling with their extraordinary speed" (97).

The popular and public musical activities were limited, mainly by imposition of regulations pertaining to slaves' entertainment. This is the case in the Costumbrista article "Aguinaldos," by Juan Francisco Valerio (1829?-1878). He described adverse reactions to Blacks seeking *aguinaldos* "with decorum," "and we say with decorum, because they, if one wills, have a right to be granted on that only day of the year a small gratuity because of their condition and labor" (133). His negative view of this tradition was not, however, about Blacks asking for money, but about the many White men who took to the streets, begging for money that day: "more than two thousand men, dressed more or less decently, who manifest with such disgusting abuse their willingness to exchange their woolen frock coat for ñáñigo costumes and the Creole's stilts and dancing half an hour to obtain the tip properly given to poor slaves" (135).

The appearance on the streets of Havana of *diablitos*, or Iremes belonging to *ñáñigos* secret societies (Castellanos 4:199), was intended to be a sign of the Black *cabildos* daring to defy mainstream society, but their presence had little impact on Costumbrista literature. In a way, despite police control, the *diablito* had control of the Havana streets at least once a year. Francisco de Paula Gelabert in his article "Vanidad y pobreza, todo en una pieza" [Vanity and poverty, all in one piece] made a brief allusion to this colorful character: "seeing diablitos dance" (96). Those extravagant figures, disguised in a bizarre costume that inspired the name of a *diablito* [little devil], would be, however, an inspiration for artists such as Landaluze. They would not have much literary importance, remaining mainly as shadow characters.

Ultimately, Blacks associated with non-mainstream religious associations were not feared because their activities violated canonical law, but because their public demonstrations of Creole cult forms challenged civil laws promoting so-called civilized behavior. The *ñáñigo* was one such example. Daringly, like the Black *curros* before them, the *ñáñigos* resisted incorporation into the mainstream. That rejection was evident in their mysterious societies and in their brutal behavior on the streets, as proof of their open discontent and their challenges against civil laws.

# Conclusion

## Costumbrista Essays on Blacks: Nineteenth-Century Preconceived Notions of Civility

In the name of Almighty God, amen. May it be known that I Francisco de
Paula Matoso . . . believing as I firmly and truly believe in the mystery of the
most Holy Trinity, Father, Son and Holy Spirit, three persons truly distinct
and one true essence.

Quoted in Pedro Deschamps Chapeaux,
"Testamentaria de pardos y morenos libres en La Habana del Siglo XIX"

This overzealous declaration of Catholic devotion was from Francisco de Paula
Matoso, a freed Black and resident of the Havana Black neighborhood of Jesús
María, where he was born and where he had created a wealthy estate. Writing
his will, dated August 27, 1839, de Paula Matoso exhibited an exuberant expres-
sion of his professed affiliation with "our Holy Mother Catholic Church, the
Apostolic Roman Church, ruled and governed by the Holy Spirit, under whose
faith and belief I have lived and professed until death as Catholic and faithful
Christian" (104–5).

De Paula Matoso seemed to be putting the system through a test. As a mulato
fino, he expected the honors reserved at death for White gentlemen whom he so
closely imitated throughout his life. To him, the overtly Catholic faith expressed
in his will appeared to be the ticket for a White-like burial. Perhaps his extreme
Catholicism was intended to force the system to do just that—a reward for a
life subjugated to mainstream cultural values that heavily prescribed behavioral
patterns.

Of interest to scholars tracing the development of Black Creole religious
systems, de Paula Matoso's rather detailed statement of his blind faith in the te-
nets of the Roman Catholic Church reflect that institution's influence on slaves
and freed Blacks. In deviation from Father Nicolás Duque de Estrada's manual
of catechism for slaves, which offered a diluted version of official theological

teachings, de Paula Matoso's descriptions of his preferred types of devotion reveal a complex affiliation with certain designated spiritual elements.

One item in particular in de Paula Matoso's proclamation, his devotion to the Holy Virgin Mary, is, however, central in his discourse as a mulato fino. His complete faith in the powers of "Most Holy Mary, our Lady and Lady of all sinners" (104) echoed Father Duque de Estrada's emphasis on the Virgin Mary, but de Paula Matoso viewed her as "my lawyer . . . the very Sovereign Queen of the Angels, Mary Our Lady, in order that she may intercede with her precious Son, to pardon the gravity of my guilt and put my soul on the path to salvation" (105).

This concept of Mary as intercessor had parallels in Cuban slave traditions, particularly in rural settings, such as plantations. White women often served as "godmothers" to slaves whom they wanted to protect against the rage of overseers. The slave's first test to learn how to behave as a gentleman was his special treatment toward his savior White mistress. Mulatos finos would refine those flattering skills to perfection, always in their attempts to behave like the perfect "White" gentleman.

Mulatos finos were not, however, completely comfortable in their carefully disguised figures as gentlemen. In the case of de Paula Matoso, as visual proof of his Catholic devotion and love for Our Lady, he states in a final dispensation that he should be buried wearing "the habit of Our Lady of Mercy" (105). This display of devotion, although today it may seem lame, was for a mulato fino used to imitating fashions of the White gentleman, a considerable sacrifice. Of course, it could also have meant that de Paula Matoso on his deathbed had decided to reject those trappings of so-called White culture.

De Paula Matoso's example goes beyond a mere display of his gratitude for a life well lived or even an illustration of the impact of Roman Catholicism on the religious practices of Blacks. It also reveals the peculiar ways that freed Blacks found to personalize mainstream practices. The cult of the Virgin Mary stands out significantly because devotion to her among Blacks went beyond the Spanish Marianist tradition. Our Lady became much more powerful as an intermediary between slaves or free Blacks and the other Almighty, an abstract concept of God. There was here a strong suggestion of hidden reverence for a female orisha, syncretized by de Paula Matoso as his beloved Lady of Mercy.

For victims of slavery and of the many restrictions imposed upon freed Blacks, the Creole religious systems appeared to restore human significance to lives otherwise devoid of personality and considered worthwhile only in their capacity as workers (Moreno Fraginals, "Cultural Contributions" 19). There is here also the possibility that in the so-called syncretic process, in the words of

Cuban poet Nancy Morejón, were the origins of Cuban identity: "We were not assimilated, that is to say, our culture was not assimilated into the Spanish or the African; with a highly creative spirit, in a constant search for our national being, we were produced as a people of mixed blood, heir to and supporter of both components, without being any more Spanish, or African" (222).

The impersonal, detached approach of the White Costumbrista writers clearly ignored such a strong personality of Blacks, particularly of slaves on sugarcane plantations. Slaves working in sugarmills were kept anonymous, although they had simple names for identification purposes. They were considered part of the machinery of the sugarmill, which in the nineteenth century had developed highly specialized work tasks. Slaves were expected to have a certain productivity and durability. As long as their productive efforts were controlled and they were provided with "adequate maintenance . . . , the slaves themselves were transformed into machines" (Moreno Fraginals, "Cultural Contributions" 19).

With a handful of exceptions, rural slaves remained invisible, a mere shadow of the modern machinery that they operated. This romanticized view of slavery—also the official governmental policy—was present often in the popular art of the time.

The Costumbrista writer Suárez y Romero's essays daringly managed to illustrate snippets of the slaves' mistreatments on a sugarcane plantation in the province of Havana. In this stand he attempted to elude the censorship in place, one strong enough to silence successfully details around the operation of the mighty millionaire operations of the sugarmill.

More importantly, Suárez y Romero expressed his positive view that slave practices had an impact on a developing Cuban rural national identity throughout the nineteenth century. The rural plantation economy, the "sugarocracy," as Cuban scholar Antonio Benítez Rojo pointed out, produced distinctive "sociocultural surfaces" (39), which explain the regional cultural patterns observed throughout the Caribbean. This was despite stringent restrictions imposed upon Blacks' practice of their own cultural traditions. For example, numerous regulations limited slaves' forms of entertainment in musical activities, and drumming in particular.

The silence of Costumbrista writers in their documentation of Black cultural productions went beyond political restrictions. It was also self-imposed, as a result of their own biased views of Blacks. Costumbrista writer Félix Tanco Bosmeniel (1797–1871), writing to his mentor Domingo del Monte, commented on the racist view that he perceived in the literature written at time: "Let's abandon the ridiculous notion or the error of painting a chosen society: only the White society, isolated because Blacks stain and soil that society, and it is necessary to view it with the soot left by the friction of the two: that is to say, that it is necessary, indispensable, to see the *negritos*" (qtd. in González del Valle 152, my emphasis). Tanco Bosmeniel, in spite of his expressed sympathetic views toward Blacks, could not escape the rampant racist attitudes of the time. This was reflected in his last use of the word for Blacks: "negritos," which may stand as a derogatory label.

In spite of their inherent limits, today the study of Costumbrista writings and a plethora of historical accounts, theological texts, and slavery regulations produced throughout the nineteenth century goes beyond the traditional consideration of these texts as "narratives of supremacy and superiority" (Henry 163). That is not to say that slaves and freed Blacks were treated as equals to the dominant White society that determined conditions of slavery; however, as this book has shown in its portrayal of specific Black Creole figures, Blacks fought back against the system. Those struggles, as the Cuban anthropologist Fernando Ortiz stated in his transatlantic theoretical approach to Cuban traditions, should lead researchers not only to identify the African connections, but also to consider how they became adapted to life in Cuba (*Entre cubanos* 88).

Within limits Costumbrista writers often challenged preconceived notions of civility as determined by Spanish laws. They were self-declared designers of a developing Cuban national identity. The numerous discussions about the negative impact of urban Black Creole cultural traditions had roots in national campaigns to gain international recognition as a booming, industrialized country. Cuba remained a colony of a weakened European power, and political debates about that condition and the prospects of independence or of annexation to the United States of America appeared in literary and historical publications allowed on the island. Because of its economic importance and regardless of the political status discussed, slavery was at the center of these national discussions.

The presence of Black Creole cultural byproducts was often documented throughout Cuba's colonial period in a variety of texts. These Black activities were feared as causes of civil discontent and as indications that Blacks refused to conform to patterns of civility. For example, the well-organized Black *cabildos*, social associations that provided refuge for some of these new religious practices, served also as centers of political discontent, and as promoters of revolutionary activity.

One case illustrative of the *cabildo's* political functions is especially important. José Antonio Aponte was a freed Black and head of the *cabildo* Shangó Teddún, located in Havana. In January 1812, he led a slave rebellion. It failed, mainly because civil authorities were informed of the plan by Black informants (Deschamps Chapeaux, *El negro* 43). This well-organized political movement had Black allies in the nearby province of Camagüey. The authorities took note of the religious connections among the insurrectionists. According to reports, possessions found in the rebels' houses included the "white banner with the image of Nuestra Señora de los Remedios [Our lady of remedies]," which Aponte had decided to use to indicate that the uprising had taken place (Franco, *Las conspiraciones* 21). Other rebels were found with items associated with Creole Black religions. Among the freed Blacks, Clemente Chacón had documents that used Abakuá signs and Salvador Ternero produced unidentified African objects catalogued generically as "witchcraft" (*Las conspiraciones* 23, 24). Connections between Afro-Cuban practices and civil discontent were also evident throughout Esteban Montejo's memoirs, from his description of the secret "marks of saints" (32; trans. 36) in huts to his detailed narrations about the *brujos'* handling of supernatural powers to keep masters and cruel plantation overseers at bay and under control.

In spite of the individual Costumbrista writer's biases about Black Creole cultures, their essays exhibit numerous literary figures as examples of thriving urban Black traditions. Collectively, they represent distinctive phases of the incorporation of certain elements of African culture into mainstream Cuban identity: the house slave, the calesero [the coach driver], the medicine woman, the woman fruit vendor, the mulatos finos and mulatas finas, the *negro curro*, the *ñáñigo*. The formation of these figures was part of a gradual process, which reflected specific historic moments in Cuban slavery. They displayed preference for some cultural elements (food and music) and condemnation of others considered to be examples of African/Black uncivilized behavior (sexual and religious practices).

The rise and the decrease of Black literary types at specific historical times reflect struggles for a developing Cuban identity. Slaves and freed Blacks, restricted to a limited field of action (whether it was the sugarmill or the Black *extramuros* neighborhoods of Havana) presented Black Creole cultural traditions in their fights against a tight socioeconomic status quo. These creations had resonance among White spectators, as numerous eyewitnesses reported; among not well-disguised indications of displeasure, some White observers could not fail to recognize the ingenuity in most cases and in extreme cases the boldness of the Blacks in redefining Creole cultural practices within a slavery-based society.

Slaves, freed slaves, or Cuban criollo Blacks could not tell their stories, at least not within the literary format of a Costumbrista article. One major example of Costumbristas' prejudiced view in their treatment of Black cultural byproducts is their restricted documentation of Black Creole religions. Many

Costumbrista writers chose to ignore their existence mainly because they were proof of mainstream society's failure to force slaves into foreign cultural patterns of so-called civil behavior. Possible censorship of taboo religious subjects, particularly given the strength of the Catholic Church, may also explain their absence from Costumbrista essays.

That is why the testimony of Juan Francisco Manzano is central to the understanding of the development of a Black identity in Cuba as part of an emerging national consciousness. He was writing from a very peculiar perspective, that of a privileged mulato fino, who saw himself as equal to Cuban White gentlemen because of his proven rational, intellectual abilities. In his elaborate use of the Spanish language, in his writing of poetry, and in his drafting of an autobiography, Manzano set himself up as different from all Blacks (slaves or not) around him, dismissing them as insignificant.

While Manzano asserted in his autobiography that he developed into such a worthy mulato fino, a "White" individual because of his association with mainstream Cuban culture, the proud runaway slave Esteban Montejo preferred to remain wholly Black, untainted by such foreign cultural influences. In his *Biografía de un cimarrón*, the only text discussed that was not produced in the nineteenth century, Montejo provided data relevant to understanding this self-directing figure of the Cuban slavery system who stood in opposition to the accommodating mulato fino. Montejo's testimony often stressed that the rebellious runaway slave was the opposite of the mulato fino, whose suave behavior was often despised as effeminate. Another of Montejo's contributions was in-depth discussions of rural slaves' religious practices, particularly those in the booming sugarmills of the nineteenth century; they filled in obvious omissions from Costumbrista articles.

In their recording of Black customs, although mostly prejudiced, Costumbrista writers explored the earliest examples of concrete, emerging Cuban national customs with roots in the highly developed Cuban slave system. Their articles documented distinctive Black types that reflect, as the Cuban anthropologist Lydia Cabrera indicated, a folklore that would become representative of a developing Cuban identity: "Who in Cuba doesn't know that batúba is a food? That a ñámpe or a ñánkue is dead; ñampearse to die and ñampear to kill. A boyfriend will say to his fiancée that he will love her until ñánkue, until death" (*La sociedad secreta* 10).

The late Cuban poet Nicolás Guillén (1902–1989), considered to be the initiator of the Afro-Caribbean Black Poetry movement in the 1930s, often spoke about how mainstream Cubans incorporated Black culture, urban Black dancing styles in particular, as part of their national identity. Writing in 1941, and indirectly pointing out racist attitudes observed in large Cuban cities, particularly in Havana, he stated:

> Blacks are undeniably ardent and sensual. Their dances communicate that temperament. That means to say that in a country like Cuba, Blackwhite, crossbred, the dark influence is exceedingly clear, paradox intended. It is what is popular, indigenous, almost like the Indian in many other places of the Continent. When a conga line passes "sweeping," it drags along men and women of all colors, but its common denominator is the powerful influence of the African ancestor, inherited or acquired. In Cuba, therefore, Black men and women are not the only ones who shake their hips, but also White women and men. One could say, "Cuban, move your waist!" and that would never be a silly invitation. (22)

Guillén was mindful, however, that such traditional display of Cuban "ethnicity" tied to Black musical traditions may cloud a proper expression of a more rounded Afro-Cuban heritage: "Even so, Blacks are far from being all dance, nor has this constituted their total influence on the development of our sensibility" (22).

Ultimately, the importance of explorations by the Costumbrista writers and by other White eyewitnesses writing in the nineteenth century is the fact that, in spite of their prejudiced view of Black culture, they documented certain key Creole Black social types that had already become part of mainstream Cuban identity. Their limitations, including their biased views, as the Costumbrista writer Cirilo Villaverde indicated, were related to their perceived role as writers in a highly structured and moralized society: "[the writer] has brought forth the accursed tendency to see the weak side where the rest of the peoples see only the strong side; he who burns with lively desire to improve his species by raising its moral standards; where he finds mania, absurdity, laziness or extravagance, there he lashes his whip" (qtd. in Cárdenas y Rodríguez 8). They were not free from stereotypical views, not any more so than those presumably White writers that Guillén warned against. Their eyewitness documentation of the life of Cuban slaves and freed Blacks in the nineteenth century is today of invaluable importance because of their representation of the earliest Black literary figures, such as the male and the female mulatos finos, the female Black vendor, the snappy-dresser coach driver, and the colorful and dangerous Black thug. As illustrated in their counterparts in today's multiracial and multinational societies, these Black types reveal elements of the dynamics behind race relations and the impact of racial discrimination on behavioral patterns.

# Notes

## Chapter 1. Cuban Costumbrista Portraits of Slaves in Sugarmills

1. For a comprehensive list and descriptions of the Cuban publications published between 1781 and 1840, see Bachiller y Morales, *Apuntes* 207–66.

2. This book examines only the political mechanisms in colonial Cuba that prevented negative reports about slavery. There was also a strong ecclesiastical censorship that operated throughout the nineteenth century (Bachiller y Morales, *Apuntes* 187–205).

3. Other brutal types of punishment imposed upon slaves did not appear in any Costumbrista essays. Their absence was conspicuous in the few descriptions of rural slavery practices with field hands or with workers in sugarmills or coffee plantations.

4. Cuban scholar Elías Entralgo, speaking about the few instances that overseers became literary characters, attributed it to their small numbers in the Cuban countryside (*Períoca* 12).

5. For comprehensive studies on the development of the sugarcane plantation in Cuba, see Moreno Fraginals, *The Sugar Mill*; Marrero; Pérez de la Riva, *La habitación* and *El barracón*. Also see Pérez de la Riva, *El café*, for a study of the specific conditions of coffee plantations in Cuba.

6. The *ñáñigos* were members of a secret nineteenth-century religious order initially composed of only Black males in urban settings. For studies on the *ñáñigos*, see Lydia Cabrera's *La sociedad secreta Abakuá narrada por los viejos adeptos* [The secret Abakuá society as described by old followers] and *La lengua sagrada de los ñáñigos* [The secret language of the náñigos].

7. Founded in 1865–1866 by the Puerto Rican Julio Vizcarrondo (1829–1889), the Society published a newspaper, *El abolicionista español* [The Spanish abolitionist]. It tracked violations to international treaties banning slave trade, while avoiding discussions of the legality of slavery itself (Soler 270).

8. The list of international visitors who were attracted by the booming slave popular culture and went to Cuba is extensive. Prominent among them was the Swedish suffragist and novelist Fredrika Bremer (1801–1865). Her travelogue, *The Homes of the New World* (1853), depicted her 1851 three-month visit to Cuba, which included an extended stay at a sugarcane plantation in the province of Matanzas.

9. That *tertulia* included distinguished Costumbrista writers: Ramón de Palma y Romay (1812–1860), José Antonio Echeverría (1815–1885), Juan Francisco Manzano (1797?–1854), José Ramón Betancourt (1823–1890), Ramón Zambrana Valdés (1817–1866), José Silverio Jorrín (1816–1897), José Joaquín Govantes (?–1881), José Jacinto Milanés (1814–1863),

Francisco Ruiz (1797?–1857), Cirilo Villaverde (1812–1894), José María Cárdenas y Rodríguez (1812–1882), José Victoriano Betancourt (1813–1875), Plácido (1809–1894), Rafael Matamoros y Téllez (1813–1874), and Felipe Poey (1799–1891) (González del Valle 9; Mijans 145–46; Bueno, *Domingo del Monte* 10). The critic Francisco G. Del Valle in his introduction to the letters by the Costumbrista writer José Zacarías González del Valle broadened the del Monte group to include political activists José de la Luz y Caballero (1800–1862) and the historian José Saco (1797–1879) (9). Other writers associated with the del Monte group were Ramón Zambrano (1817–1866), Gaspar Betancourt y Cisneros (1803–1866), Félix Tanco y Bosmeniel (1797–1871), Manuel Costales y Govantes (1815–1866), Francisco de Frías y Jacott (1809–1877), and Ramón de Palma y Romay (1812–1860) (Fernández de Castro 37–42; Mitjans 145–46). Besides his association with Suárez y Romero, another notable contribution of del Monte was his promotion of works by the Black writers Plácido and Juan Francisco Manzano.

10. Other abolitionist texts given to Madden were: *Elegías cubanas* [Cuban elegies] by Matamoros y Tellez, and a poem by José Zacarías Tallet (1810–1893), the youngest writer of the del Monte group (González del Valle 11–12). I have found no source to explain why Madden eventually declined to publish *Francisco* in England.

11. For exhaustive research on the Spanish government's violations of the trade of slaves, which then included traders from Cuba, refer to Franco, *Comercio clandestino de esclavos*.

12. The "album" was a popular tradition in the Caribbean. Libia González described its strong hold among the upper-class members in Puerto Rico: "An 'album' was understood to be an offering or declaration of affection made public in a publication or magazine. The most common 'albums' were poems, biographical sketches or obituaries, that did not use visual images but that conveyed friendship or affection. The concept was used in the title of regional pamphlets and as art reviews with a limited circulation in the cities" (36).

13. A review of the sentimental literature of the "letters," often published in an album format, reflected the writer's preferences to explore various aspects of a developing Cuban culture. One example was *Aguinaldo Matanzero* [Gift from Matanzas] (1847), a collection of Costumbrista essays, coedited by José Victoriano Betancourt and Miguel Teuribe Tolón y de la Guardia (1820–1857), that brought together works by a number of writers in praise of traditions observed in the province of Matanzas. Perhaps because the collection was dedicated to women readers, the purpose was "to present to the modest eyes of our ladies a book whose pages offered to them the beautiful: the goodness of virtuous thoughts, of chaste images and of praiseworthy tendencies" (*Aguinaldo* n.p.). The traditions portrayed were rather sanitized, devoid of negative aspects, such as any references to slavery. This was in spite of the fact that Matanzas, like Havana, was home to important sugarcane plantations and, thus, like Havana, was a producer of Black traditions.

14. The issue of deforestation was covered by the press of the time. In an extensive article for Havana's publication *Diario de la Marina*, March 24, 1849, Miguel Rodríguez Ferrer addressed the unsupervised destruction of forests, which he blamed directly on sugarcane plantation owners' "poorly understood interest in the owners' speculation about the forests and woods that they posses" (732).

15. See, for example, Justo Germán Cantero's 1857 introduction to *Los ingenios: Colección de vistas de los principales ingenios de la Isla de Cuba* [Sugarmills: Collection of prints of the main sugarmills of the island of Cuba].

16. Rather than using *labrador* as a romantic term, Suárez y Romero may have been

using agricultural terminology of his time. Leví Marrero indicated that the *labrador* in the sixteenth century was the one "ordered to sow and to cultivate the cane fields" (309).

17. The *guajiro* culture was fundamentally an implant of agricultural traditions from the Canary Islands. Although *guajiros* eventually adapted some cultural practices from the local indigenous people and even from the Blacks, they remained associated with a White culture that would be praised as the heart of Cuban culture. *Guajiro* is a word whose origins are lost today, although the nineteenth-century Cuban scholar Antonio Bachiller y Morales attributed it to an indigenous language. This was his explanation for the negative reaction of Cuban peasants upon hearing that word: "Our farmers find the name repugnant. Our fathers would not want to see themselves compared with the wild Indians" (*Cuba* 109–10). J. M. de Andueza in his history book *Isla de Cuba* [Island of Cuba] (1841) had a positive image of the *guajiro*, whose poetic *décimas* he portrayed as a highly developed artistic medium of "the true expression of a melancholic heart" (10).

18. For an analysis of the impact of slave women workers, considerably fewer in number than their male counterparts, see Pérez de la Riva, "El índice de masculinidad."

19. The issue of whether or not there was an African-based Creole language in Cuba, as there was in other English- and French-speaking Caribbean islands, has not been fully studied. Cuban scholar Tomás Fernández Robaina denied the existence in Cuba of a "Creole language, Creole with words and syntax from African languages," but he asserted that certain African languages remained alive as "liturgical languages of ethnic groups that possessed the strongest cultures" (6). The scene described in the text, and others in which the narrator served as interpreter, seem to contradict Fernández Robaina's statement.

20. One major exception was Cirilo Villaverde's "Diario del Rancheador" [Diary of a slave hunter], a manuscript left unpublished, which was based on the memoirs of Francisco Estévez, a historic slave hunter.

## Chapter 2. Juan Francisco Manzano's *Autobiografía de un esclavo*

1. It is a historical fact that Cuban Blacks had already become known as accomplished poets. The most important poet was the freed Black known as Plácido, Gabriel de la Concepción Valdés (1809–1844). His reputation as a classical poet was well recognized in Cuba. One piece of evidence indicating that Blacks had ventured into poetry was an advertisement that appeared in the *Diario de la Habana* [Havana Daily], on December 19, 1833: "Poems of the Colored Laureano Pérez y Santa Cruz; are printed in Paris in 1832, and they are found for sale for the moderate price of two reales [ . . . ] we hope that this learned public will receive it with pleasure, for the harmony of its versification and raptures of the most ardent and lively imagination, as well as for being productions by the first individual of color that has dedicated himself to this enchanting art" (qtd. in Deschamps Chapeaux, *El negro* 18–19).

2. Manzano did not say whether the fact that his wife was a poet was an exception. Israel M. Moliner cited Juana Pastor, "teacher and poet," who wrote for the publication *El Criticón*. Her letter, "El gusto del día" [Today's fashion], which appeared in November 1804, spoke against Cuba's "fever for gold and the eagerness for luxury of Havana's society, as well as the scorn that they manifest for the fine arts" (201–2).

3. Madden's abolitionist zeal became well known and feared among Cuban slave traders and plantation owners. He was also responsible for the releases of African captives imported illegally by slave traders, one of whom, Pedro Blanco, was well known in Cuba

(Burton 33). In 1849, Madden published *The Island of Cuba: Its Resources, Progress and Prospects*, a compilation of documents on his involvement during the period of 1836–1839.

4. See Vera M. Kutzinski's discussion of this phenomenon in an advertisement depicting a Negro *bembón*, "a thick-lipped, broad-nosed black dandy whose presumably hilarious offense is to have taken the idea of whitening far too literally" (58).

5. For studies on urban Black artisan and musician communities, see Serviat 151–52; Deschamps Chapeaux and Pérez de la Riva *Contribución*.

6. For a study on how freed Blacks on a higher social level were often preferred as godparents, see Mellafe 137.

7. For restrictions on these Black schools, see Arredondo 48. Some of those teachers had an excellent reputation in Havana (Deschamps Chapeaux 121–32). Manzano's schooling there helped him to become educated: "knowledgeable in all that a woman could teach me about religion, I would recite not only the entire catechism by heart but also almost all of Fray Luis de Granada's sermons" (48; trans. 49).

8. The *Diccionario de la literatura cubana* [Dictionary of Cuban literature] points out the fact that Manzano wrote short stories "in which miraculous apparitions were mixed with African legend" (2:544). I have not been able to locate these stories.

9. In the articles "Laws for the Protection of Slaves in Cuba" and "Emancipation of Slaves in Cuba," in *Poems by a Slave in the Island of Cuba*, Madden discusses the legal recourses available to abused slaves in Cuba. He argues, however, that seldom did these options become a reality for slaves, even though many were badly abused. Many were killed by their masters, who often faced no major consequences.

10. An unsigned and undated cover of the original manuscript of Manzano's autobiography, housed at Havana's National Library, indicates, however, that Manzano set the purchase price at 850 "demanded by his mistress" (Manzano, *Obras* 3).

## Chapter 3. Urban Slaves and Freed Blacks

1. The term *pardos* in Cuba often referred to freed Blacks. According to historian Rafael L. López Valdés, during the medieval period in Spain it alluded to a plebeian, or a rural property owner, artisan, or merchant with enough funds to provide himself a horse, which enabled him to take part in military incursions into Arabic-dominated territories. In the Americas, the term became equated with mestizo or mulatto (30).

2. Although there is no indication that this bathing had a religious context, there is in today's Santería practices the observance of ritualistic baths prior to attendance at key ceremonies.

3. The mention of a Chinese man suggests that the piece was written after the arrival of thousands of Chinese workers, contracted to work on Cuban plantations as coolies, or *culíes*, as they were known in Cuba, after 1848 (Pérez de la Riva, "Los culíes" 115–62; Guanche, 72–87).

## Chapter 4. The Costumbristas' Views of Manly Black Males

1. The late Costumbrista Cuban writer Ildefonso Estrada y Zenea in *El quitrín* (1880) also dealt in detail with the history of the *quitrín* in its last years of popularity, including the drivers' abuses of pedestrians.

# Bibliography

Acosta, Mariano de, and Antonio Pérez de Guzmán. *Memoria sobre la Ciudad de San Felipe y Santiago*. Havana: Sociedad Patriótica de la Habana, 1830.

Allabar, Anton L. "Sugar and the Politics of Slavery in Mid-Nineteenth Century Cuba." In *Sugar, Slavery, and Society: Perspectives on the Caribbean, India, the Mascarenes, and the United States*, edited by Bernard Montt, 110–34. Gainesville: University Press of Florida, 2004.

Amador Gómez-Quintero, Raysa E., and Mireya Pérez Bustillo. *The Female Body: Perspectives of Latin American Artists*. Westport, Conn.: Greenwood Press, 2002.

Andueza, José María de. *Isla de Cuba pintoresca: Recuerdos apuntes, impresiones de dos épocas*. Madrid: Boix Editor, 1841.

Arenal, Concepción. "La esclavitud de los negros." *El cancionero del esclavo*. Madrid: Publicaciones Populares de la Sociedad Abolicionista Española, 1866.

Arnalte, Arturo. *Los últimos esclavos de Cuba. Los niños cautivos de la goleta Batans*. Madrid: Alianza Editorial, 2001.

Arrate, José Martín Félix de. *Llave del Nuevo Mundo, Antemural de las Indias Occidentales, La Habana Descripta: Noticias de su fundación, aumentos y estado*. Havana: Sociedad Amigos del País, 1830.

Arredondo, Alberto. *El negro en Cuba*. Havana: Editorial Alfa, 1939.

Ayala, Manuel Joseph de. *Diccionario de gobierno y legislación de Indias*. Edited by Milagros del Vas Mingo. Vol. 3. Madrid: Ediciones de Cultura Hispana, 1988.

Azorín. "Comento a Larra." In *Mariano José de Larra: Artículos de costumbres*, 9–13. Madrid: Espasa Calpe, 1969.

Bachiller y Morales, Antonio. *Apuntes para la historia de las letras y de la instrucción pública en la isla de Cuba*. Havana: Cultural, S.A., 1936.

———. *Cuba primitiva: Origen, lenguas, tradiciones e historia de los indios de las Antillas Mayores y las Lacayas*. Havana: Librería de Miguel de Villa, 1883.

———. *Los negros*. Barcelona: Gorgas, c. 1887.

Barnet, Miguel. *Biografía de un cimarrón*. Barcelona: Ediciones Ariel, 1968.

———. *Biography of a Runaway Slave*. Translated by W. Nick Hill. Willimantic, Conn.: Curbstone Press, 1994.

Barras y Prado, Antonio de las. *La Habana a mediados del siglo XIX. Memorias de Antonio de las Barras y Prado*. Edited by Antonio de las Barras de Aragón. Madrid: Imprenta de la Ciudad Lineal, 1925.

Barreda, Pedro. *The Black Protagonist in the Cuban Novel.* Translated by Page Bancroft. Amherst: University of Massachusetts Press, 1979.

Bastide, Roger. *African Civilizations in the New World.* Translated by Peter Green. New York: Harper and Row, 1971.

Bayle, Constantino. *Los cabildos seculares en la América española.* Madrid: Sapientia, S.A. de Ediciones, 1952.

Benítez Rojo, Antonio. *The Repeating Island: The Caribbean and the Postmodern Perspective.* Translated by James Maraniss. Durham: Duke University Press, 1992.

Betancourt, José Victoriano. *Artículos de costumbres.* Havana: Publicaciones del Ministerio de Educación Dirección de Cultura, 1941.

Betancourt, José Victoriano, and Miguel T. Tolón, eds. *Aguinaldo matanzero.* Matanzas: Imprenta de Gobierno y Marina, 1847.

Betancourt y Cisneros, Gaspar. *Escenas cotidianas.* Havana: Publicaciones del Ministerio de Educación, Dirección de Cultura, 1950.

Brathwaite, Edward Kamau. "The African Presence in Caribbean Literature." In *Slavery, Colonialism, and Racism,* edited by Sydney W. Mintz, 73–109. New York: W. W. Norton, 1974.

Bremer, Thomas. "The Slave Who Wrote Poetry: Comments on the Literary Works and the Autobiography of Juan Francisco Manzano." In *Slavery in the Americas,* edited by Wolfgang Binder, 487–501. Wurzburg: Koningshausen and Newmann, 1993.

Bueno, Salvador. *Bosquejo histórico de las letras cubanas.* Havana: Ministerio de Relaciones Exteriores, Departamento de Asuntos Culturales, 1960.

———. *Costumbristas cubanos del siglo XIX.* Caracas: Biblioteca Ayacucho, 1985.

———. *El negro en la novela hispanoamericana.* Havana: Letras Cubanas, 1986.

———. "Introduction." *Domingo del Monte.* Havana: Pablo de la Torriente, 2000.

Burton, Gera C. *Ambivalence and the Postcolonial Subject: The Strategic Alliance of Juan Francisco Manzano and Richard Robert Madden.* New York: Peter Lang, 2004.

Bush, Barbara. *Slave Women in Caribbean Society, 1650–1838.* London: Heinemann Publishers, 1990.

Cabrera, Lydia. *Anagó: Vocabulario lucumí (El yoruba que se habla en Cuba).* Miami: Ediciones Universal, 1970.

———. *Ayapa: Cuentos de Jicotea.* Miami: Universal, 1971.

———. *El monte: Igbo finda ewe orisha vititi nfinda (Notas sobre las religiones, la magia, las supersticiones y el folklore de los negros criollos y el pueblo de Cuba).* 6th ed. Miami: Colección del Chicherekú en el Exilio, 1986.

———. *Koeko Iyawó: Aprende novicia. Pequeño tratado de regla lucumí.* Miami: Colección del Chicherekú en el Exilio, 1980.

———. *La lengua sagrada de los ñáñigos.* Miami: Colección del Chicherekú en el Exilio, 1988.

———. *La sociedad secreta Abakuá narrada por viejos adeptos.* Havana: Ediciones C & R, 1958.

———. *Reglas de Congo: Palo Mayombe.* Miami: Colección del Chicherekú en el Exilio, 1979.

Cabrera Saqui, Mario. "Vida, pasión y gloria de Anselmo Suárez y Romero." In *Francisco (El ingenio o las delicias del campo),* 7–36. Havana: Publicaciones del Ministerio de Educación, 1947.

*El cancionero del esclavo*. Madrid: Publicaciones Populares de la Sociedad Abolicionista Española, 1866.

Caldera, Ermanno. "La vocación costumbrista de los románicos." In *Romanticismo 6: Actas del VI Congreso El Costumbrismo romántico*, 45–52. Roma: Bulzoni, 1996.

Cámara, Madeline. "La mulata, cuerpo-símbolo de la cultura cubana." *Monographic Review/Revista Monográfica* 15 (1999): 121–29.

Cáñizares, Raúl. *Walking with the Night: The Afro-Cuban World of Santería*. Rochester: Destiny Books, 1993.

Carbonell, Walterio. *Cómo surgió la cultura nacional*. Havana: Biblioteca Nacional José Martí, 1961.

Cantos Casenave, Marieta. "'Gitanofilia': De algunos rasgos costumbristas del 'género andaluz.'" In *Romanticismo 6: Actas del VI Congreso El Costumbrismo romántico*, 65–70. Roma: Bulzoni, 1996.

Cárdenas y Rodríguez, José. *Colección de artículos satíricos y de costumbres*. Prologue by Cirilo Villaverde. Havana: Consejo Nacional de Cultura, 1963.

Carpentier, Alejo. *La música en Cuba*. Havana: Letras Cubanas, 1979.

Castellanos, Jorge and Isabel. *Cultura Afrocubana: El negro en Cuba, 1492–1844*. Vols. 1 and 2. Miami: Ediciones Universal, 1988, 1990.

———. *Cultura Afrocubana: Letras, música, arte*. Vol. 4. Miami: Ediciones Universal, 1994.

Cepero Bonilla, Raúl. *Azúcar y abolición*. Havana: Instituto del Libro, 1971.

Concha, José de la. *Memorias sobre el estado político, gobierno y administración de la Isla de Cuba*. Madrid: Establecimiento Tipográfico de D. José Trujillo, 1853.

Correa Calderón, Evaristo. "Introducción al estudio del costumbrismo español." In *Costumbristas españoles*, vol. 1, xi–cxxx. Madrid: Aguilar, 1964.

*Costumbristas españoles*. Vol. 1. Madrid: Aguilar, 1964.

Craton, Michael. "Forms of Resistance to Slavery." In *The Slave Societies of the Caribbean*, vol. 3 of *General History of the Caribbean*, edited by Franklin W. Knight, 222–70. UNESCO, 1997.

Cros Sandoval, Mercedes. *Worldview, the Orichas, and Santería: Africa to Cuba and Beyond*. Gainesville: University Press of Florida, 2006.

Cruz, Manuel de la. "El guardiero." In *Obras de Manuel de la Cruz: Literatura cubana*, vol. 3, 111–33. Madrid: Editorial Saturnino Calleja, 1924.

———. *Obras de Manuel de la Cruz: Literatura cubana*. Vol. 3. Madrid: Editorial Saturnino Calleja, 1924.

Curmer, Louis, ed. *Les Français peints por eux-mêmes: Encyclopédie morale du dix-neuvième siècle*. 9 vols. Paris: L. Curmer, 1840–42.

Day Corbitt, Roberta. "A Survey of Cuban Costumbrismo." *Hispania* 33, no. 1 (February 1950): 41–45.

del Monte, Domingo. *Centón epistolario de Domingo del Monte*. Edited by Joaquín Llaverías y Martínez. Vol. 5, *1841–1843*. Havana: Academia de la Historia de Cuba, 1938.

———. *Domingo Del Monte*. Introduction by Salvador Bueno. Havana: Pablo de la Torriente, 2000.

———. *Ensayos críticos*. Edited by Salvador Bueno. Havana: Pedro de la Torriente, 2000.

———. *Escritos de Domingo del Monte*. Edited by José A. Fernández de Castro. Vol. 1. Havana: Cultural, 1929.

Deschamps Chapeaux, Pedro. *El negro en la economía habanera del siglo XIX*. Havana: Unión de Escritores y Artistas Cubanos, 1970.

———. "Las comadronas o parteras." In *Contribución a la historia de la gente de color*, edited by Pedro Deschamps Chapeaux and Juan Pérez de la Riva, 67–82. Havana: Editorial de Ciencias Sociales, 1963.

———. *Los cimarrones urbanos*. Havana: Editorial de Ciencias Sociales, 1983.

———. "Testamentaria de pardos y morenos libres en La Habana del Siglo XIX." *Contribución a la historia de la gente de color*, 97–110. Havana: Editorial de Ciencias Sociales, 1963.

Díaz, Fernando. "Introducción." *Francisco, el ingenio o las delicias del campo*, i–viii. Montevideo: Doble J., 2007.

Díaz Soler, Luis M. *Historia de la esclavitud negra en Puerto Rico*. Río Piedras: Editorial Universitaria, 1974.

*Diccionario de la literatura cubana*. Havana: Letras Cubanas, 1980.

Duke, Dawn. *Literary Passion, Ideological Commitment: Toward a Legacy of Afro-Cuban and Afro-Brazilian Women Writers*. Lewisburg, Pa.: Bucknell University Press, 2008.

Duque de Estrada, Nicolás. *Doctrina para negros: Explicación de la doctrina cristiana acomodada a la capacidad de los negros bozales*. Edited by Javier Laviña. Barcelona: Sendai Ediciones, 1989.

Ely, Roland T. *Cuando reinaba el azúcar*. Buenos Aires: Editorial Sudamericana, 1963.

Entralgo, Elías. *La liberación étnica cubana*. Havana, 1953.

———. *Períoca sociográfica de la cubanidad*. Havana: Edición Unión, 1996.

Escobar, José. "Costumbrismo: Estado de la cuestión." In *Romanticismo 6: Actas del VI Congreso El Costumbrismo romántico*, 117–26. Roma: Bulzoni, 1996.

Estorch, Miguel. *Apuntes para la historia sobre la administración del Marqués de la Pezuela en la Isla de Cuba*. Madrid: Imprenta de Manuel Galiano, 1856.

Estrada y Zenea, Ildefonso. *El quitrín: Costumbres cubanas y escenas de otros tiempos*. Havana: Imprenta La Industrial, 1880.

Feijóo, Samuel. *El negro en la literatura folklórica cubana*. Havana: Letras Cubanas, 1987.

———. *Mitología cubana*. Havana: Editorial Letras Cubanas, 1986.

Fernández Carrillo, Enrique. "El ñáñigo." Edited by Salvador Bueno. In *Costumbristas cubanos del siglo XIX*, 371–75. Caracas: Biblioteca Ayacucho, 1985.

Fernández de Castro, José Antonio. *Tema negro en las letras de Cuba*. Havana: Ediciones Mirador, 1943.

Fernández Robaina, Tomás. *El negro en Cuba (1902–1958): Apuntes para la historia de la lucha contra la discriminación racial*. Havana: Editorial de Ciencias Sociales, 1994.

Figarola-Caneda, Domingo, ed. *Centón Epistolario de Domingo del Monte*. Havana: Imprenta El Siglo XX, 1926. Vol. 3.

Franco, José Luciano. *Autobiografía, cartas y versos de Juan Francisco Manzano*. Havana: Municipio de La Habana Administración del Alcalde, 1937.

———. *Comercio clandestino de esclavos*. Havana: Editorial de Ciencias Sociales, 1980.

———. *La conspiración de Aponte*. Havana: Comisión Nacional de la Academia de Ciencias, 1963.

———. *La diáspora africana en el Nuevo Mundo*. Havana: Editorial de Ciencias Sociales, 1975.

———. *La presencia negra en el Nuevo Mundo*. Vol. 7. Havana: Cuadernos de la Revista de Casa de las Américas, 1968.

——. *Las conspiraciones de 1810 y 1812*. Havana: Editorial de Ciencias Sociales, 1977.

——. *Plácido: Una polémica que tiene cien años y otros ensayos*. Havana: Unión, 1964.

Fraunhar, Alison. "Mulata cubana: The Problematics of National Allegory." In *Latin American Cinema: Essays on Modernity, Gender and National Identity*, edited by Lisa Shaw and Stephanie Dennison, 160–79. North Carolina: McFarland, 2005. Friol, Roberto. *Suite para Juan Francisco Manzano*. Havana: Editorial Arte y Literatura, 1977.

Gallardo, Jorge Emilio. *Presencia africana en la cultura de América Latina: Vigencia de los cultos afroamericanos*. Buenos Aires: Fernando García Cambeiro, 1986.

Gelabert, Francisco de Paula. *Cuadros de costumbres cubanas*. Havana: Imprenta de la Botica de Santo Domingo, 1875.

Gómez del Valle y Ramírez, Francisco. *La Habana en 1841*. Havana: n.p., 1952.

González, Libia. "Feliciano Alonso's Álbum of Puerto Rico: Monument and Impressions of Memory." In *Álbum de Puerto Rico* by Feliciano Alonso, 33–48. Madrid: Ministerio de Educación y Ciencia and Consejo Superior de Investigaciones Científicas, 2007.

González, Michelle A. *Afro-Cuban Theology: Religion, Race, Culture, and Identity*. Gainesville: University Press of Florida, 2006.

González del Valle, José Zacarías. *La vida literaria en Cuba (1836–1840)*. Havana: Publicaciones de la Secretaría de la Educación, 1938.

González Echevarría, Roberto. Cuban Fiestas. New Haven: Yale University Press, 2010.

González-Wippler, Migene. *Santería: The Religion, A Legacy of Faith, Rites, and Magic*. New York: Harmony Books, 1989.

Guanche, Jesús. *Componentes étnicos de la nación cubana*. Havana: Unión, 1996.

Guerra y Sánchez, Ramiro. *La industria azucarera de Cuba*. Havana: Cultural, S.A., 1940.

——. *Sugar and Society in the Caribbean: An Economic History of Cuban Agricultura*. Foreword by Sydney W. Mintz. New Haven: Yale University Press, 1964.

Guerrero, Teodoro D. "La mujer de la Isla de Cuba." *Las mujeres españolas, portuguesas y americanas tales como son en el hogar doméstico, en los campos, en las ciudades, en el templo, en los espectáculos, en el taller y en los salones*, edited by Miguel Guijarro. Madrid: Imprenta y Librería de D. Miguel Guijarro, 1876.

Guillén, Nicolás. *Prosa de prisa*. Buenos Aires: Editorial Hernández, 1968.

Hall, Gwendolyn Midlo. *Slavery and African Ethnicities in the Americas: Restoring the Links*. Chapel Hill: University of North Carolina Press, 2005.

——. *Social Control in Slave Plantation Societies: A Comparison of St. Domingue and Cuba*. Baltimore, Md.: The Johns Hopkins Press, 1971.

Hazard, Samuel. *Cuba with Pen and Pencil*. Hartford, Conn.: Hartford Publishing Co., 1871.

Hernández Chiroldes, Alberto, ed. *Los cubanos pintados por sí mismos*. Miami: Editorial Cubana, 1992.

Heuman, Gad. "The Social Structure of the Slave Societies in the Caribbean." In *The Slave Societies of the Caribbean*, vol. 3 of *General History of the Caribbean*, edited by Franklin W. Knight, 138–68. New York: UNESCO, 1977.

hooks, bell. *We Real Cool: Black Men and Masculinity*. New York: Routledge, 2004.

Jackson, Richard L. *Black Writers in Latin America*. Albuquerque: University of New Mexico Press, 1979.

Kennedy, Randall. "Racial Passing." *Ohio State Law Journal* 62, no. 1145 (2001): 1–28.

Kirkpatrick, Susan. "The Ideology of Costumbrismo." *Ideologies and Literature* 2, no. 7 (1978): 28–44.

Knight, Franklin W. "Slave Society in Cuba." In *The African in Latin America*, edited by Ann M. Pescatello, 112–26. New York: Alfred A. Knopf, 1975.

———. *Slave Society in Cuba during the Nineteenth Century.* Madison: University of Madison Press, 1970.

Kutzinski, Vera M. *Sugar's Secrets: Race and Erotics of Cuban Nationalism.* Charlottesville: University Press of Virginia, 1993.

Labat, Jean Baptiste. *Nouveau Voyage aux Isles de l'Amerique.* Paris: Guillaume Cavalier, 1972.

Labra, Rafael M. *La brutalidad de los negros.* Havana: Imprenta de la Universidad de la Habana, 1961.

Lane, Jill. *Blackface Cuba, 1840–1895.* Philadelphia: University of Pennsylvania Press, 2005.

Laplante, Eduardo. *Los ingenios: Colección de vistas de los principales ingenios de azúcar de la Isla de Cuba.* Edited by Luis Miguel García Mora and Antonio Santamaría García. Madrid: Ministerio de Fomento, 2005.

La Rosa Corzo, Gabino. *Los cimarrones de Cuba.* Havana: Editorial de Ciencias Sociales, 1988.

———. *Los palenques del oriente de Cuba.* Havana: Editorial Academia, 1991.

Láscar, Amado. "A Slave Is a Dead Soul: Francisco Manzano." Editorial Poetas Antiimperialistas de América. http://amado-lascar.com/revista/poeta/ensayo/impresora_17.shtml.

Laviña, Javier, ed. *Doctrina para negros, Explicación de la doctrina cristiana acomodada a la capacidad de los negros.* Nicolás Duque de Estrada. Barcelona: Sendai Ediciones, 1989.

Leal, Rine. *La selva oscura.* Havana: Editorial Arte y Literatura, 1975.

León, Julio A. "Los cabildos afro-cubanos." *Caribe* 2, no. 2 (1977): 123–30.

Lezama Lima, José. "Conferencia sobre Manuel de Zequeira y Manuel Justo de Rubalcava." In *Fascinación de la memoria: Textos inéditos de José Lezama Lima*, edited by Iván González Cruz, 61–89. Havana: Letras Cubanas, 1993.

———. "D. Ventura Pascual Ferrer y 'El Regañón.'" In *La cantidad hechizada*, 57–82. Madrid: Ediciones Jucar, 1974.

———. *El Regañón y El Nuevo Regañón.* Havana: Comisión Nacional Cubana de la UNESCO, 1965.

———. "El romanticismo." In *Archivo de José Lezama Lima: Miscelánea*, edited by Iván González Cruz, 185–276. Madrid: Editorial Centro de Estudios Ramón Areces, 1990.

López Valdés, Rafael L. *Africanos de Cuba.* 2nd ed. San Juan, Puerto Rico: Centro de Estudios Avanzados de Puerto Rico y el Caribe, 2004.

———. *Pardos y morenos esclavos y libres en Cuba y sus instituciones en el Caribe hispano.* San Juan, Puerto Rico: Centro de Estudios Avanzados de Puerto Rico y el Caribe, 2007.

Losada, José Manuel. "Costumbrismo in Spanish Literature and Its European Analogues." In *Nonfictional Romantic Prose: Expanding Borders*, edited by Steven P. Sondrup, Virgil Nemoianu, and Gerald Gillespie, 333–46. Amsterdam: Benjamins, 2004.

Luis, William. *Literary Bondage: Slavery in Cuban Narrative.* Austin: University of Texas Press, 1990.

Madden, Richard R. *The Life and Poems of a Cuban Slave.* Edited by Edward J. Mullen. Hamden, Conn.: Archon Books, 1981.

Manzano, Juan Francisco. *Autobiografía de un esclavo/Autobiography of a Slave.* Introduction and modernized Spanish version by Ivan A. Schulman; translation by Evelyn Picon Garfield. Detroit: Wayne State University Press, 1996.

———."Juan Francisco Manzano: Autobiography of a Teen-Age Slave." In *The African in Latin America*, edited by Ann M. Pascatello, 127–36. New York: Alfred A. Knopf, 1975.

———. *Juan Francisco Manzano: Obras*. Havana: Instituto Cubano del Libro, 1972.

Marrero, Leví. *Cuba: Economía y Sociedad. Siglo XVI: La Economía*. Madrid: Playor, 1974.

Martínez Furé, Rogelio. *Diálogos imaginarios*. Havana: Cuadernos de Arte y Sociedad, 1979.

———. "Imaginary Dialogue on Folklore." In *AfroCuba: An Anthology of Cuban Writing on Race, Politics and Culture*, edited by Pedro Pérez Sarduy and Jean Stubbs, 109–116. Melbourne, Australia: Ocean Press, 1993.

Mellafe, Rolando. *Breve historia de la esclavitud negra en América Latina*. Mexico: Secretaria Educación Pública, 1973.

Mesonero Romanos, Ramón. "El autor de Bucólica." In *El costumbrismo románico*, edited by José Luis Verela, 71–73. Madrid: Colección Novelas y Cuentos, 1970.

Mitjans, Aurelio. *Historia de la literatura cubana*. Madrid: Editorial América, 1918.

Moliner, Israel M. "Juan Francisco Manzano, el poeta esclavo y su tiempo." In *Juan Francisco Manzano: Obras*, 199–231. Havana: Instituto Cubano del Libros, 1972.

Molloy, Sylvia. "From Serf to Self: The Autobiography of Juan Francisco Manzano." In *At Face Value: Autobiographical Writing in Spanish America*, 36–54. Cambridge, UK: Cambridge University Press, 1991.

Montesinos, José F. *Costumbrismo y novela: Ensayo sobre el redescubrimiento de la realidad española*. Madrid: Editorial Castalia, 1983.

Morejón, Nancy. "Nación y mestizaje." In *Afro-Cuba*, edited by Pedro Pérez Sarduy and Jean Stubbs, 217–27. Río Piedras: Editorial de la Universidad de Puerto Rico, 1998.

Moreno Fraginals, Manuel. "Aportes culturales y de culturación." In *Africa en América Latina*, edited by Manuel Moreno Fraginals, 13–33. Mexico: Siglo XXI, 1977.

———. "Cultural Contributions and Deculturation." In *Africa in Latin America*, edited by Manuel Moreno Fraginals and translated by Leonor Blum, 5–22. New York: Colmes and Meir Publishers, 1984.

———. *The Sugarmill: The Socioeconomic Complex of Sugar in Cuba (1760–1860)*. Translated by Cedric Belfrage. New York and London: Monthly Review Press, 1976.

Neal, Mark Anthony. *New Black Man*. New York: Routledge, 2005.

Neimark, Philip John. *The Way of the Orisa: Empowering Your Life Through the Ancient African Religion of Ifa*. New York: HarperCollins, 1993.

*Ofrenda al Bazar de la Casa de Beneficencia*. Havana: Imprenta del Tiempo, 1864.

Ortiz, Fernando. *Entre cubanos*. Havana: Editorial de Ciencias Sociales, 1987.

———. *Historia de una pelea cubana contra los demonios*. Havana: Editorial de Ciencias Sociales, 1975.

———. "Los cabildos afro-cubanos." *Revista Bimestre Cubana* 16, no. 1 (January-February, 1921): 5–39.

———. *Los negros brujos*. Havana: Editorial de Ciencias Sociales, 1995.

———. *Los negros curros*. Edited by Diana Iznaga. Havana: Editorial de Ciencias Sociales, 1986.

———. *Los negros esclavos*. Havana: Editorial de Ciencias Sociales, 1987.

———. *Nuevo Catauro de cubanismos*. Havana: Editorial de Ciencias Sociales, 1974.

————. *Orbita de Fernando Ortiz*. Havana: Instituto del Libro, 1973.

Paget, Henry. "The Caribbean Plantation: Its Contemporary Significance." In *Sugar, Slavery and Society: Perspectives on the Caribbean, India, the Mascarenes, and the United States*, edited by Bernard Moitt, 157–85. Gainesville: University Press of Florida, 2004.

Pascatello, Ann M. "Juan Francisco Manzano: Autobiography of a Teen-Age Slave." In *The African in Latin America*, 127–36. New York: Alfred A. Knopf, 1975.

Pérez de la Riva, Juan. "1860, Un diplomático inglés informa sobre la trata clandestina en Cuba." In *Contribuciones a la historia de la gente sin historia*, edited by Pedro Deschamps Chapeaux and Juan Pérez de la Riva, 251–82. Havana: Editorial de Ciencias Sociales, 1974.

————. *El barracón y otros ensayos*. Havana: Editorial de Ciencias Sociales, 1975.

————. *El café: Historia de su cultivo y explotación en Cuba*. Havana: Jesús Montero Editor, 1944.

————. "El índice de masculinidad." In *Para la historia de las gentes sin historia*, 120–24. Barcelona: Ariel, 1976.

————. *La habitación rural en Cuba*. Havana: Grupo Guamá, 1955.

————. "Los culíes chinos y los comienzos de la inmigración contratada en Cuba (1844–1847)." In *Contribuciones a la historia de la gente sin historia*, edited by Pedro Deschamps Chapeaux and Juan Pérez de la Riva, 115–62. Havana: Editorial de Ciencias Sociales, 1974.

————. *Para la historia de las gentes sin historia*. Barcelona: Editorial Ariel, 1976.

Perkinson, Jim. "The Body of White Space: Beyond Stiff Voices, Flaccid Feelings, and Silent Cells." In *Revealing Male Bodies*, edited by Nancy Tuana, William Cowling, Maurice Hamington, Grez Jonson, and Terrance MacMullan, 173–97. Bloomington: Indiana University Press, 1992.

Pezuela, Jacobo de la. *Ensayo histórico de la Isla de Cuba*. New York: Imprenta Española de R. Rafael, 1842.

Pfaff, Françoise. *Conversations with Maryse Condé*. Lincoln: University of Nebraska Press, 1996.

Pichardo Viñals, Hortensia, comp. *Documentos para la historia de Cuba*. Vol. 1. Havana: Editorial de Ciencias Sociales, 1977.

————. "Estudio preliminar." In *Descripción de la Isla de Cuba con algunas consideraciones sobre su población y comercio* by Nicolás Joseph de Ribera, 11–29. Havana: Instituto del Libro, 1973.

Pichardo y Tapia, Esteban. *Pichardo Novísimo o Diccionario provincial casi razonado de vozes y frases cubanas*. Havana: Editorial Selecta Librería, 1953.

Portuondo, José Antonio. *Bosquejo histórico de las letras cubanas*. Havana: Ministerio de Relaciones Exteriores, Departamento de Asuntos Culturales, 1960.

Pozzi, Gabriela. "Imágenes de la mujer en el costumbrismo." In *Romanticismo 6, Actas del VI Congreso (Nápoles, 27–30 de Marzo de 1996), El costumbrismo romántico*, 249–57. Roma: Bulzoni, 1996.

Ramos Santana, Alberto. "Las tabernas, escenarios costumbristas." In *Romanticismo 6, Actas del VI Congreso (Nápoles, 27–30 de Marzo de 1996), El costumbrismo romántico*, 259–63. Roma: Bulzoni, 1996.

Reff, Daniel T. "Making the Land Holy: The Mission Frontier in Early Medieval Europe and Colonial Mexico." In *The Spiritual Conversion of the Americas*, edited by James Muldoon, 17–35. Gainesville: University Press of Florida, 2004.

Ribera, Nicolás Joseph de. *Descripción de la Isla de Cuba, Con algunas consideraciones sobre su población y comercio*. Editor Hortensia Pichardo Viñals. Havana: Instituto del Libro, 1973.

Riverend Brusone, Julio J. Le. *La Habana (Biografía de una provincia)*. Havana: Imprenta Siglo XX, 1960.

Rodríguez Ferrer, Miguel. *Naturaleza y civilización de la grandiosa isla de Cuba o estudios variados y científicos, al alcance de todos, otros históricos, estadísticos y políticos*. Vol. 1. Madrid: Imprenta Dr. J. Noguera, 1876.

Roig de Leuchsenring, Emilio. *Actas capitulares del Ayuntamiento de La Habana*. Vols. 1 and 2. Havana: Municipio de La Habana, 1937, 1939.

———. *El sesquicentenario del Papel Periódico de la Havana, primera de las publicaciones literarias de Cuba*. Havana: Molina y Compañía, 1941.

———. Los escritores: *La literatura costumbrista cubana de los siglos XVIII y XIX*. Vol. 26. Havana: Oficina del Historiador de la Ciudad de La Habana, 1962.

———. *Los periódicos: El Papel Periódico de la Havana*. Vol. 24. Havana: Oficina del Historiador de la Ciudad de La Habana, 1962.

———. *Los periódicos: Los continuadores del El Papel Periódico*. Vol. 24. Havana: Oficina del Historiador de la Ciudad de la Habana, 1962.

Romero Tobar, Leonardo. *Panorama crítico del romanticismo español*. Madrid: Editorial Castalia, 1994.

Rout, Leslie B. *The African Experience in Spanish America*. London: Cambridge University Press, 1976.

Sáenz, José Manuel. "Las comparsas: Su trayectoria histórica." *Actas del Folklore* 1, no. 4 (April 1961): 21–25.

Sale, Kirkpatrick. *The Conquest of Paradise: Christopher Columbus and the Columbian Legacy*. New York: Knopf, 1990.

Santovenia, Emeterio S. *José Victoriano Betancourt: Estudio Biográfico*. Havana: Editorial La Universal, 1912.

Serra, Otto Mayer. *Panorama de la música hispanoamericana*. Mexico City: Colegio de Mexico, 1944.

Serviat, Pedro. *El problema negro en Cuba y su solución definitiva*. Havana: Editora Política, 1986.

Suárez-Murias, Marguerite C. "Cuba Painted by Cubans: The Nineteenth Century Journalistic Essay." *Review of Inter-American Bibliography* 30, no. 4 (1980): 375–86.

Suárez y Romero, Anselmo. *Colección de artículos*. La Habana: Consejo Nacional de Cultura, 1963.

———. "El cementerio del ingenio." In *Ofrenda al Bazar de la Real Casa de Beneficencia*, 13–29. Havana: Imprenta del Tiempo, 1864.

Sweeney, Fionnghuala. "Atlantic Countercultures and the Networked Text: Juan Francisco Manzano, R. R. Madden and the Cuban Slave Narrative." *Forum of Modern Language Studies* 40, no. 4 (2004): 401–14.

Torre, José María de la. *Lo que fuimos y lo que somos o La Habana antigua y moderna*. Havana: Imprenta de Spencer, 1857.

Ucelay Da Cal, Margarita. *Los españoles pintados por sí mismos (1843–1844): Estudio de un género costumbrista.* Mexico: El Colegio de México, 1951.

Urfé, Odilio. "Music and Dance in Cuba." In *Africa in Latin America,* edited by Manuel Moreno Fraginals and translated by Leonor Blum, 170–188. New York: Colmes and Meier, 1977.

Valerio, Juan Francisco. *Cuadros sociales. Colección notablemente corregida y aumentada de artículos satíricos de costumbres.* Havana: Viuda de Soler y Compañía, Editores, 1876.

Varela, José Luis. "Introducción." In *El costumbrismo románico,* 7–15. Madrid: Colección Novelas y Cuentos, 1970.

Villaverde, Cirilo. "Diario del Rancheador." Edited by Roberto Friol. *Revista de la Biblioteca Nacional José Martí* 15 (January–April 1973): 49–148.

Wedel, Johan. *Santeria Healing: A Journey into the Afro-Cuban World of Divinities, Spirits, and Sorcery.* Contemporary Cuba series. Gainesville: University Press of Florida, 2004.

Williams, Lorna Valerie. "Juan Francisco Manzano's Autobiografía." In *The Representation of Slavery in Cuban Fiction,* 21–31. Columbia: University of Missouri Press, 1994.

Willis, Susan. "Crushed Geraniums: Juan Francisco Manzano and the Language of Slavery." In *The Slave's Narrative,* edited by Charles T. Davis and Henry Louis Gates Jr., 199–224. Oxford: Oxford University Press, 1985.

Zanetti, Oscar, and Alejandro García. *Sugar and Railroads: A Cuban History, 1837–1959.* Translated by Franklin W. Knight and Mary Todd. Chapel Hill: University of North Carolina Press, 1987.

Závala, Silvio A. *Las instituciones jurídicas en la conquista de América.* 3rd ed. Mexico: Editorial Porrúa, 1988.

# Index

Rafael Ocasio, Charles A. Dana Professor of Spanish, teaches Latin American literature and Spanish-language courses at Agnes Scott College. A specialist in revolutionary and counterrevolutionary Cuban literature, he is the author of two books on the Cuban dissident writer Reinaldo Arenas: *Cuba's Political and Sexual Outlaw* and *A Gay Cuban Activist in Exile*. Ocasio is currently working on *Franz Boas in Puerto Rico: Retention and Reinvention of Puerto Rican Folklore*, an edited, critical anthology of oral folklore documented by that reputable anthropologist in Puerto Rico in 1915.